A new economic policy for Britain

Essays on the development of industry

edited by
Keith Cowling *and* Roger Sugden

Manchester University Press
Manchester and New York
Distributed exclusively in the USA and Canada by St. Martin's Press

Published by Manchester University Press
Oxford Road, Manchester M13 9PL, UK
and Room 400, 175 Fifth Avenue
New York, NY 10010, USA

Distributed exclusively in the USA and Canada
by St. Martin's Press, Inc.,
175 Fifth Avenue, New York, NY 10010, USA

British Library cataloguing in publication data
A new economic policy for Britain: essays on the development
    of industry
    1. Great Britain. Industrial development
    I. Cowling, Keith   II. Sugden, Roger, *1958–*
    338.0941

Library of Congress cataloging in publication data

A New economic policy for Britain: essays on the development of
    industry/edited by Keith Cowling and Roger Sugden.
    p. cm.
    ISBN 0–7190–3270–9. – ISBN 0–7190–3271–7 (pbk)
    1. Industry and state–Great Britain. 2. Great Britain–Economic policy–1945–
    3. Socialism–Great Britain. 4. Labour Party (Great Britain) I. Cowling,
    Keith. II. Sugden, Roger.
    HD3616.G73N48   1990
    338.941–dc20   90–5573

ISBN 0 7190 3270 9 *hardback*
     0 7190 3271 7 *paperback*

Typeset in Great Britain
by Megaron, Cardiff, Wales
Printed in Great Britain
by Biddles Ltd, Guildford and King's Lynn

Contents

Preface

This book has grown out of recent work by the Industrial Strategy Group. The Group comprises academics and researchers who first came together in 1986 to discuss Britain's economic and industrial future. It has worked alongside John Smith MP and Bryan Gould MP – when each was Principal Opposition Spokesman for Trade and Industry – and its members made detailed submissions to the Labour Party's recent Policy Review process. Following this, in 1989 the Group published an assessment of Labour's policies under the title 'Beyond the Review. Perspectives on Labour's Economic and Industrial Strategy'. That work formed the starting point for the collection of essays in this volume.

The broad aim of the volume is to contribute to debates that the Policy Review has fed or initiated, and to stimulate anybody interested in economic policy in general or industrial policy in particular. The idea is to present readable, non-technical yet fully supported analyses of the sort of economic and industrial policies which the Group believes Britain (and similarly placed countries) needs if its industry is to thrive and prosper in the 1990s. More specifically, to provide a significant contribution to the debate on the future economic and industrial policies to be adopted by the Left.

Keith Cowling
University of Warwick
Coventry, England
Roger Sugden
University of Edinburgh
Edinburgh, Scotland
24 November 1989

Bryan Gould MP

Introduction

Most observers agreed that, viewed as a technical exercise, the 1987 general election campaign was won by Labour. Although the centre parties were pushed into a decisive third place, the Party, however, failed to make much dent in the Conservative vote. The only possible conclusion the Party could draw was that there was something wrong with the message we were trying to put across.

The 1987 conference therefore agreed to establish a thorough-going review of the whole of Labour's policy platform. Although we should remain true to Labour's democratic socialist aims and values, there was a wide consensus that the policies needed modernizing. Labour had to stop promising a better yesterday, and grapple with the rapidly changing world of the 1990s.

In some ways it was a brave decision. To some extent Labour had lost its nerve in the face of the Thatcherite onslaught. Too many had begun to believe that perhaps the new Right was now the dominant ideology, and were afraid that socialism had lost its relevance. How much easier then to stay on the secure ground of previous policies.

But it was the right decision. Although the first stage of the Policy Review, presented to the 1988 Labour Party conference left much to be desired, primarily because the harsh timetable meant that we had to start drawing the reports up almost before we began any thinking, it quickly became apparent that there was a wealth of new thinking on the Left across the whole field of policy.

This was particularly true in the field of economic and industrial policy, the group that I was charged with co-chairing with John Evans MP. Other issues may come and go, but in almost every election I have been involved with it is economic issues and perceived economic competence that have been most important at the end of the day. That is why I was pleased to make early contact with the Industrial Strategy Group – whose members have contributed the essays in this volume – and find some ready-made new approaches to a socialist economic strategy for the 1990s. Members of the group played a vital role in advising the Policy Review Group, and gave up many hours to present papers, attend meetings and talk through sticky issues with us. They have performed a great service to the Labour Party, and I am particularly pleased to welcome this volume of essays, although I should say that they should not be taken as a statement of Labour Party policy, nor of my views.

The final report of the Policy Review, 'Meet the Challenge, Make the Change', presented to the 1989 Party conference, was a triumphant vindication of the decisions taken in the dark days immediately after Labour's general election defeat. Its publication, in the run up to the Euro-elections, proved a turning point in the Party's fortunes. At the time of writing Labour has enjoyed the kind of consistent opinion poll lead secured by oppositions who go on to win subsequent elections, while an increasingly accident prone government lurches from blunder to blunder, and from one piece of bad economic news to another.

The starting point for the Policy Review on economic policy was the conviction that we could not go on as we are. Our long-standing and cumulative failures can no longer be concealed by the fortuitous bonus of North Sea oil. Our £120 billion worth of North Sea wealth and nearly £80 billion worth of government revenues have been and gone and have left us worse prepared for the more competitive world of the 1990s than we were at the beginning of the 1980s.

We face the single European market with a record trade deficit, the highest interest rates and inflation rate in the advanced industrial world and an industrial economy which is ill-equipped, badly trained and under-invested. If we are to survive – let alone prosper – we have to tackle the long-standing and deep-seated mistakes in policy which have helped to create the endemic weakness of the British economy.

To do this, we have to understand how and why those mistakes have arisen. The Thatcher government has applied policies which have exacerbated those mistakes and magnified the damage they do, but the mistakes lie deep in our economic history.

The present government is totally committed to a 'free market' ideology which dictates that government has little or no role to play in trying to strengthen our industrial performance. This is in marked contrast with the experience of more successful rival economies where the great advantages of government/industry co-operation are clearly perceived.

We have turned our backs on these advantages, not just because of the obsessive ideology of the present government but because we have for a long time misread our own economic history. We continually hark back to the period in the mid 19th century when we were the world industrial leader. We remind ourselves that this leadership was achieved at a time of *laissez faire* policies. We conclude, as a result, that if we wish to regain industrial leadership we should again revert to the operations of an unfettered free market.

What we overlook is that the market may have been appropriate to the circumstances of an industrial pioneer. We faced no direct competition. There were no signposted routes to follow. We had little option but to proceed piecemeal and experimentally, with the market deciding which initiatives succeeded and which failed.

Other countries, which had to make up an industrial and technological gap, understood that the market could not be relied on to achieve that faster and more directed advance. They developed what Marquand calls the notion of a developmental state which, in addition to its regulatory role, worked positively with industry to direct resources and investment into the most promising and technologically important areas. It is this concept which has benefited them so greatly. It is this concept which we, even today, still dismiss as being dangerously corporatist or Marxist.

We suffer from a related error which is even more deeply embedded in our national economic history. As the world's most powerful imperial economy, we developed valuable assets all round the world. This not only required a military capability to protect them, but it also gave rise to an economic policy which placed great importance on maintaining the value of those assets. We grew accustomed to living off the income produced by the assets rather than having to earn our living by making and selling goods and services. We developed the City of London as a great international financial centre in which those assets could be traded.

The result has been a constant bias in British economic policy for well over a century. That bias has always favoured the interests of asset holders as opposed to wealth creators. It has always led to policies of financial orthodoxy. It was Winston Churchill who said in 1925 as Chancellor of the Exchequer, 'I would rather see industry more content and finance less proud.'

We see the same bias today in the constant recourse to high

interest rates and the overvaluation of the currency – policies which are very much in the interests of asset holders (at least in the short term) but which do great damage to our competitive position and industrial base.

It is mistakes such as these which have created the damaging and debilitating disease of short-termism which is increasingly recognized as the British sickness. It is short-termism which leads to under-investment. Little wonder that we spend less on research and development than any other advanced industrial country, when such expenditure is regarded as a drain on short-term resources rather than an investment in long-term strength.

It is short-termism which leads to an untrained and unskilled workforce for exactly the same reason. It is short-termism and an exaggerated faith in the short-term operations of the private market which lead to a crumbling infrastructure and cuts in spending on basic science. It is short-termism which produces a frenetic rate of takeover activity – the mark of an economy which does not think of the future or of investing in improved capacity but naturally turns to the short cut routes to increased market share of acquisition and the elimination of competitors.

It is short-termism which produces the constant recourse to deflation, high interest rates and overvaluation. It is short-termism, in short, which means we are woefully ill-prepared as an economy for the more competitive and technologically advanced world which now confronts us.

It is these weaknesses in the British economy which the Policy Review is intended to address. There are no magic solutions on offer – indeed one of the greatest distractions in British economic policy-making has been the search for the short-term fix, rather than making the tough decisions needed to remedy deep-seated weaknesses.

The essays in this book all deal in their various ways with this central problem of the British economy. In Chapter 1, Keith Cowling, a valued co-opted member of the Policy Review Group, spells out the need for a strategic approach that gives a new priority to wealth creation in economic policy making.

As Henry Neuburger and Malcolm Sawyer recognize in Chapter 6, we have to remedy the mistakes in macro-economic policy which have continually prejudiced the interests of our productive base. We need an economic climate in which it makes sense for investors – whether public or private – to invest capital in new productive capacity.

We not only have to encourage new investment but ensure that it takes place. This means supplementing the current sources and mechanisms of investment, in particular in those areas such as venture capital for small businesses, which existing institutions overlook, and which are looked at in more detail in the chapter by Richard Minns and Mary Rogers.

We have to recognize the crucial role of new technology and new skills for the competitive success of advanced economies. This means working with industry to ensure that training and research and development get done. It means taking the lead where necessary – as with British Technology Enterprise – to make sure that we make a nationally co-ordinated effort to make progress at the leading edge of technology, as recognized by Paul Geroski and Nigel Stanley in their chapters. It means providing the right framework of ownership, accountability and public investment to allow us to push forward crucially important advances – such as the broad band cable network – which the market cannot properly achieve.

It means, in other words, the government taking responsibility for making good the deficiencies of the short-term market and playing its proper role in advancing the national interest. Government alone can provide the longer term perspective, the organizing and co-ordinating capacity and in some cases the resources to ensure that we make the essential provision for success – topics taken up in the chapters by Michael Waterson and many others of the contributors.

A major priority for the next Labour government must be to restore regional balance to the country. It cannot be right that when an over-heating South East is threatened with cooling down, the rest of the country faces the deep freeze. The need to devolve power away from Westminster and Whitehall to the nations and regions of Britain is one of the most exciting and radical measures in the Policy Review, as Peter Totterdill recognizes in Chapter 8.

This is not of course the whole truth. There are other major aspects of our economic future which the Policy Review addresses and which are touched on in these pages – the control of inflation, our role in the European Community, the democratization of business enterprises (see Chapter 5 for example) amongst others. But it is an important part of the truth and one which is dangerously ignored by current economic and industrial policy. We can afford to ignore it no longer.

1 *Keith Cowling*

The strategic approach to economic and industrial policy

The debate about economic policy in Britain is usually sharply confined within a range defined by the Classical and Keynesian approaches to the macro-economy. The central debate is in turn confined to the question of appropriate monetary, fiscal and exchange rate policies, with an occasional breakaway movement concerned with the question of incomes policy. But, despite attempts by some monetarists to set medium-term targets for monetary growth, these policies essentially relate to the short-term performance of the economy and are essentially tactical in character. The question of whether or not a deeper, more long-term, industrial strategy should be the focus for debate is largely unaddressed. Implicitly or explicitly, both Classical and Keynesian views leave the long-term evolution of the economy to market processes,[1] although some commentators, particularly those of Keynesian views, do offer, almost as a postscript, the suggestion that an industrial strategy is highly desirable without either offering a coherent argument to support their position or developing the essence of such a strategy. With a few notable exceptions this is true of both Britain and the United States. When the debate does break out into the unfamiliar territory of industrial strategy it is usually guided not by economists but, more likely, by political scientists or those coming from business or industry.[2] It's not that industrial policy is ignored in Britain and the United States. Obviously a form of industrial policy is operated in both countries and this form is, in turn, evaluated by the economics profession. It is more a matter that industrial policy is not seen to be pivotal in these economies and it is therefore not developed in a systematic or coherent fashion as a centrepiece of a government's approach to economic policy-making.

Within the other advanced market economies, things are rather different in the rest of Europe and very different in Japan and on the Pacific Rim.

This book seeks to redress the balance in Britain and brings industrial strategy to centre stage, where, it is argued, it belongs. In doing this we are following immediately at the heels of the recent policy review conducted by the Labour Party.[3] Within that review there is a clear recognition that whilst appropriate monetary, fiscal and exchange rate policies can contribute much towards enhancing the performance of the British economy, nevertheless such policies only deal with the symptoms of deeper problems. The main bulk of that review focuses on supply-side strategies, which are seen to be necessary to resolve these deeper problems, and so does this book. This particular chapter offers some explanation of the essential requirement for such a supply-side strategy and offers a way forward which builds on the Japanese experience, but which identifies a distinctively British approach to the problems of the British economy. Other chapters pursue aspects of this in greater detail. Complementary macro-economic policies receive detailed attention in Chapter 6.

The present context

In recent years there has been much talk of the strength of the British economy, although an increasing number of commentators now seem to be becoming increasingly nervous about this, with the current account of the balance of payments in substantial deficit and inflation causing concern. The central element of that strength to which people refer is the substantial rate of growth in manufacturing productivity since the early eighties, and the questions that arise are, what were the sources of this improved performance and can it be sustained under existing policies?[4]

It can be argued that monetary and fiscal policy in the early years of the Thatcher government provided an environment conducive to raising the short-term productivity of labour whilst holding down real wages and, at the same time, to raising the supply of small-scale entrepreneurs (largely by displacing them from their former paid employment)[5] and thereby increasing the proportion of work done in open competitive markets – supporting the growth of a dual economy. Large-scale unemployment was seen as a necessary

instrument, alongside legislation aimed at weakening the unions,
for securing a significant change in the balance of power between
unions and management, and unemployment was the consequence
of the restrictionist monetary and fiscal policy of the early eighties.
The fear of unemployment allowed management to begin to exert
greater control over the work process, as well as damping down
union wage expectations and the militancy with which they were
pursued (which does not, of course, imply that there is no other
way).[6] At the same time an increasing supply of potential, small-
scale entrepreneurs was created which also contributed to the same
ends by offering an alternative source of inputs for the large
corporations.

There is no question but that the pace of work in British industry
has substantially increased in recent years and that this has made an
important contribution to productivity growth.[7] There is also no
question but that this is basically a one-off increase. It is of the
nature of human endeavour that its intensity cannot be increased
without limit, nor without real cost. Whereas the productiveness of
labour can be increased by equipping it with better tools and
machines, by education and training, and, as we have seen
historically, without any discernible slackening in its rate of
growth,[8] simply creating conditions in which people have to work
progressively harder must quickly encounter diminishing returns.
Perhaps British industry needed this transformation in the intensity
of work, and is better for it, but we cannot presume that this will
provide a ready source of future gains in productivity.[9] That will
only be provided by a fundamental change in the way, for instance,
we approach industrial investment, research and development,
education and training. Britain's performance in these activities is
inferior to that of its major rivals, and the degree of inferiority has
got worse. For example, real investment per employee in manufacturing in the period 1979–83 in Britain had declined to 96% of its
level in the previous five-year period, whereas for Japan it had risen
by 44% and for West Germany by 19%. Despite some recovery
since 1983, gross investment in manufacturing increased by only
0.6% throughout the period 1979–88, whilst for industry and
agriculture as a whole gross investment actually fell by 8.4%.

Thus the fundamentals of the British economy are not right. Its
recent rate of growth has been internationally respectable because
of the slackening of fiscal and monetary policy over the past few

years.[10] But if we look at the record since 1979 it is not impressive. For the period through to the end of 1988 the growth of Gross Domestic Product has averaged only 2.1%, with the inflation rate averaging over 8% and the unemployment rate about the highest among the major industrial countries. We cannot expect a better performance in the near future under present policies because the present government is neglecting the real base of industrial dynamism; indeed that very neglect has now led to the present deflationary policies which will undoubtedly hold back the growth of the economy. It is clear that the economy does not have the capacity to grow at more than a modest pace without generating substantial balance of payments problems. Its much vaunted strength is increasingly seen to be an illusion.

Why we need an industrial strategy

As we have already indicated, mainstream economics does not identify a central role for a coherent industrial strategy within economic policy-making. Cases are made for intervention, but these are seen as responses to imperfections in the market rather than systemic deficiencies. Here we set out the case for a strategy of intervention on the grounds of major systemic deficiencies within the market. This does not deny the crucial importance of the market operating within that overall strategy and indeed we start out by identifying and briefly explaining the market imperative, the current movement in both East and West, towards the extension of the dimensions of the market. We then turn to the planning imperative, putting the case for intervention in a modern context. This will identify an essential requirement that the state take an active developmental role in the economy, as well as regulating the forces of the market. It will be concluded that Britain needs an industrial strategy and it needs it on the grounds of long-term, dynamic efficiency.

The market imperative[11]

It may be argued that in a relatively static world comprehensive centralized planning is both feasible and efficient, although this must be a matter of considerable doubt. A decentralized and devolved system of power must generally be preferred to one which places it exclusively at the centre, not simply on the grounds of democracy but also on the grounds of efficiency, since the appropriate weights to be used to measure inputs and outputs are given by the democratic process. (We shall return to this matter in Chapter 5.) Democracy and efficiency are mutually supportive, and it is wrong to pose them as if to be traded off in seeking an optimum. Indeed efficiency has no meaning outside of democracy. In an economic system where decision-making is in a few hands we need always to ask when questions of efficiency are raised – efficiency for whom? Only economic democracy can begin to guarantee that economic systems generate efficient outcomes.

However the static case is of limited relevance. We live in a world characterized by great turbulence and uncertainty. In such a world it is impossible to conceive how a detailed, comprehensive, centralized planning system could cope, no matter the level of development of the underlying technology of planning. This point need not be belaboured. By their comments and their actions almost everybody who has been thinking about these matters has reached similar conclusions. Thus the role of the market is being extended in the centrally planned economies.

But a related movement has been under way in the capitalist economies. Privatization, deregulation, liberalization, are the orders of the day. Partly, of course, this has reflected the emerging dominance of right-wing ideology: but, in this area, it has an objective base. There has been widespread concern, in some cases disillusion, with the performance of the state sector of industry, and indeed with the provision of public services. The remedy proposed and implemented by the right has been the extension of market forces into almost every area of production: by the privatization of public assets, the deregulation of state controlled activities, and the entry of private enterprise into the provision of public services.

A further, and particularly interesting, illustration of this tendency can be observed in the long-term evolution of industrial policy in Japan, as the earlier mode of state control gave way to the present mode of co-operation between the state and private enterprise. The state in Japan has substantially withdrawn from an operational role within the economy, but has retained a strategic involvement in the market.

We can conclude that markets have advanced, are advancing; the state as comprehensive, central planner and as owner of productive assets is in retreat. We have seen a broad measure of consensus emerge in recent history in both East and West. But does this mean there is no role for planning by public agencies? Is everything to be left to the market and to private enterprise? We shall argue that countries in both East and West, with some notable exceptions, are in danger of throwing the baby out with the bathwater. We need to establish a much sharper focus on the nature of planning and its complementary existence with the market. This will allow us to identify an essential role for democratic, public agencies in guiding the long-term evolution of industry and the economy.

The planning imperative

Within the capitalist economies there has, since the beginning, been a clear recognition that situations can arise where the public interest may be served by the supercession of the market by the collective actions of citizens, acting via the government or via other institutions.[12] Traditionally these concerns have centred on monopoly power, externalities (like pollution or congestion), the provision of public goods (in the narrow, technical, sense as in the case of defence, where my consumption does not interfere with yours) and the distribution of income and wealth. Arguably, these issues could be resolved within the regulatory activity of the state (e.g. by taxing polluters), or, in the case of public goods, by public provision (e.g. as in the case of defence). Market failure in these traditional senses need not require that a coherent system of economic planning be imposed on the private sector of the economy.

This is not entirely clear. Some would argue that the evolution of the monopoly or oligopoly phase of capitalism poses such systemic threats to both micro-economic and macro-economic efficiency, and to equity, and indeed democracy itself, as to require a coherent system of overall and continuing control which is much in excess of, and of a different nature to, any system of regulatory activity which is currently manifest. We would tend to this position, but it is arguable so long as one restricts the basis of intervention to the rather narrowly interpreted, traditional, arguments. Instead of developing the case at this point, we wish to extend the terrain over which the argument will be fought. Just as there are systemic arguments for relying on market forces to play a centrally important role in modern economies, there are parallel arguments for imposing on these market forces a coherent, national (and community) economic strategy, within which they are allowed to operate. At the present time there would seem to be three fundamental reasons: transnationalism, short-termism and centripetalism, all interrelated and all related to an underlying concentration of power, and therefore decision-making, in modern economies.

Transnationalism[13]

The growth in dominance of the transnational corporation poses a significant threat for any national market economy. The global perspective and ambitions of the major industrial and financial corporations may cut across the interests of any particular nation state, or any particular community. The fundamental issue relates to the asymmetry of power between corporation and community, which derives from the transnationality of the corporation – and the international perspective and flexibility which that implies – compared with the locational rigidity of a specific, local, regional or national community. To achieve its own objectives the transnational can switch investment and production, or threaten to do so, whenever conditions in any one country or region appear disadvantageous, for example because wage costs or profit taxes are too high.

Thus any nation can be de-industrialized by the actions of transnational corporations – and the implication is that only when wage costs are cut, or profit taxes reduced, will capital return. Thus, to protect itself, any community has to intervene in the strategy-making of the transnationals – or accept their dominance in its own affairs. To do so is to admit that a nation, or community, has no real autonomy.

But can a nation effectively control these powerful international organizations? There are obvious difficulties, the very basis of their power, but there is also an obvious source of leverage. Whilst the transnational will wish to produce at locations of minimum cost (for example, where wage costs and profit taxes are low) it requires access to markets in order to sell its product. National communities can deny, or threaten to deny, access to national markets. Thus, access may be tied to production within that nation.[14] This implies a willingness to intervene in international trade – a movement away from free trade towards 'managed trade'. But this is not a new concept. We only have free trade at the moment in the sense of a general freedom from state intervention.[15] Trade is managed by the transnationals: most trade is intra-firm and is therefore directly controlled by these corporations, and much of the rest is indirectly controlled by them via sub-contracting, licensing and franchising arrangements. It has been estimated that the transnationals account for 70–80% of world trade outside the centrally-planned economies.[16] This control gives power to these organizations which can be used to secure their own objectives at the expense of communities which have no say in such decisions.

This is a perfectly general phenomenon. That is, without intervention, we are involved in a negative-sum game – national communities in general can suffer from the unrestricted activities of the transnationals. Any community considering a tax or wage-increase will be faced with the possibility that capital will migrate in response. The general, system effect is that wage and profit taxes will be held down against the wishes of each national community.[17]

Thus we have a basis for recommending international regulations on the transnationals: but it is also a basis for establishing a role for national economic planning. We need a framework of strategic planning within which to approach and position the transnationals. We need to approach them within the context of such a strategy, otherwise their strategy will inevitably become the national strategy and this may have little correspondence to what is best for the nation.

Short-termism

The second and related basis for requiring national economic planning is the systemic short-termism of the market.[18] In this context it is often argued that the financial institutions, and this is especially true in the UK, adopt a peculiarly short-term perspective with regard to investment. In Britain this is undoubtedly linked to the historical role of the banks in financing trade and funding bond issues – as opposed to being directly involved in industry via equity or long-term loans. (The situation in Germany and Japan has been different, with the banks being more closely tied to industry.) What this generally means is that incremental change can be handled quite well by market institutions, but more fundamental changes, involving quantum leaps in product, process or structure will not be handled so well.[19]

However, in a direct sense, the financial institutions themselves can only impose their short-term perspectives on industry via those firms otherwise incapable of raising finance internally. Thus new and small firms (especially in Britain) may be severely constrained in their investment ambitions by the short-term perspective of the British financial institutions, since it is these firms which will find it difficult to fund their own growth. In contrast the established, bigger corporations will generate substantial internal funds, will also be able to raise new equity on the stockmarket, will have considerable leverage over the financial institutions, and can go abroad, where necessary. Thus larger, better-established firms will retain a significant autonomy. However, an active market for corporate control – that is, an active market in the control of existing corporations via takeover/ acquisition – could overturn all of that.

Such a market allows the short-term perspective of the financial institutions to impinge much more decisively on the perspective of industry, which must, of necessity, take the long view in terms of its own industrial logic. That is, to secure the firm's long-term future, action must be taken today which will often reduce short-term profitability. For example, research and development need give no immediate payout, but not to do it may leave the firm in a vulnerable position in the long term. Falling behind rivals may threaten survival. But, with an active market for corporate control, most firms will fall victim of the short-term perspective, given that to ignore it may lead to an unwelcome takeover bid.

Recent developments in the financial markets have dramatically increased the likelihood of such bids. Wall Street, immediately prior to the Boesky scandal, provided the most vivid example of this phenomenon, with the so-called triple alliance of corporate raiders, junk bond dealers (merchant banks selling-off high yielding bonds created to finance takeovers) and arbitrageurs (people taking positions in companies they predict will be targets for corporate raiders), but the situation in London is very similar, and indeed closely connected.

This sort of financial environment is hardly conducive to the rational planning of the long-term future of the industrial base. Short-term decision making is crowding out long-term issues, and leaving industry weaker in the long term. No one is planning for the future in such market environments. Thus, within our market economy, we need to establish mechanisms and institutions to do this.

Centripetalism

Centripetalism, the third reason we have advanced for requiring that a coherent national economic planning system is an essential element of any efficient economic system, relates to the tendency for higher level activities and occupations to gravitate to the centre – to be lost to the regions; to be lost to the periphery. This is really a generalization of the issue of transnationalism, and indeed is one of its systemic features. At one and the same time the major corporations are internationalizing production and drawing the control of the use of an ever-increasing share of the world's economic resources into the ambit of the key cities of the world, like London.[20]

This sort of transformation has led to the loss of a substantial degree of local, regional, and national autonomy. Strategic decisions with major implications for many local, regional and national communities are being made outside those communities. The same centralizing forces imply a siphoning-off of resources to the centre, which reduces the capacity of the periphery to sustain its own economic, political and cultural development on which future self-determination is based. The almost inevitable outcome is the outmigration of the educated, leading to further decline in the cultural development of the community. Centripetal economic tendencies become centripetal political and cultural tendencies and the community enters a vicious circle of relative decline. It is also the case that such communities cannot easily break out of these processes of cumulative causation by supply-side adjustments, like investing in education, so long as the demand side remains outside their control. Increasing educational investment will only effect-ively contribute to the resurgence of the community if parallel action is taken to secure some strategic control of the demand for educated personnel.

Thus we have identified three central tendencies within modern market economies; transnationalism, short-termism and centri-petalism, which taken together point to the requirement for national/community economic planning in order to achieve efficiency in the allocation and utilization of national/community economic resources. However, in an earlier section, we have stated that, again under modern economic conditions, and perhaps more generally, comprehensive centralized planning is both infeasible and undesirable. Thus we can conclude that although we see planning as essential for efficiency, the nature of planning is all important. We therefore turn to examine a system which appears to have been used with enormous success – the Japanese model.

The nature of an industrial strategy for Britain

The Japanese model

We can identify two roles for the state in a market economy: a regulatory one and a developmental one. The regulatory role is a traditional focus of state intervention in economies like the US and Britain, with the state acting to remove market imperfections, acting as an adjunct to the market, working at the edges of the market system. In contrast, in its developmental role the state acts to shape the industrial landscape, taking a leading role in the industrial economy – a proactive rather than reactive role, with the market continuing to play a substantial, indeed crucial, part, but working within the long-term parameters set by government, at various levels, e.g. local, regional and national.

Within the US and UK the state has adopted such a role from time to time, and indeed Japan based its policy on the 19th century success of US developmental policy, but this has not persisted in any systematic form.[21] Europe and the US have not seen the fundamental intervention in the market economy as has typified the Japanese economy. Y Ojimi (former Vice Minister, MITI) has remarked about the US and Europe: 'industrial policy (meaning developmental policy) has amounted to a collection of measures that are an exception to the rule, and of but a fragmentary or transitional nature', OECD (1972).[22]

Japan is the most important case of the state taking on a central developmental role in the economy without directly owning most of the productive assets.[23] There are other cases of market economies where the state has a developmental role within that part of the economy which it directly owns and controls, but where otherwise it does not systematically seek such a role. Perhaps the UK, pre-Thatcherite, most of West Europe, and India would fall in this category. Generally it does not appear that such activities have been used as a basis of a coherent national economic planning system.

Within Japan, although various departments and agencies of the state are involved in industrial strategy, MITI – the Ministry of

International Trade and Industry – has a central and dominant role (see Chalmers Johnson, 1982).[24] What is the nature of such planning?

MITI targets certain key sectors of the economy, chosen after wide-ranging consultation and discussion throughout industry, and works to ensure, by a variety of interventions, both carrots and sticks, that those sectors grow rapidly and efficiently. One key factor at the time of rapid development in the 1950s and early 1960s was to protect domestic industry until it was fully internationally competitive. At the same time a substantial degree of domestic rivalry has evolved in most industries selected for this treatment. MITI relies heavily on market forces to support its own measures, and is undoubtedly helped in this by the long-term perspectives of the typical Japanese industrial firm, untrammelled by the threat of an active market for corporate control and supported by the long-term commitment of Japanese financial capital.

In contrast to French planning (except for a very brief period after the Socialists entered government in 1981), Japanese planning is active rather than passive, but selective rather than comprehensive. The keys to success in both approaches have been wide consultation, serious effort to reach agreement on the form of intervention and no day-to-day interference in operational decision-making (see Paul Hare, 1981).[25] Thus planning has been strategic, but wherever possible based on some notion of consensus.

The Japanese saw early on that static comparative advantage was not an adequate basis for national economic development. After World War II that would have left them as producers of rice, cheap toys and simple textiles. To break out into other areas of economic activity required that the state should be directly involved in the economic system. The market could not be relied on. Within the market there are vicious and virtuous circles of cumulative causation – once you get behind the pack the market will normally ensure that you get pushed further and further behind. The market had to be managed and directed – a national economic strategy had to be imposed, but leaving the market to do what it is good at doing: looking after all the myriad, incremental changes which are required within the broad strategy, and, of course, running those sectors which don't require strategic intervention. A well-developed international trading system removes any requirement that national planners need be involved in the detailed input

projections for a whole range of industries, which has often been
seen as a central requirement in national planning. Attempting to be
comprehensive is generally a diversion from attending to the crucial
matter of the strategic planning of key industries and providing the
necessary infrastructure for a dynamic industrial base.

Adapting the Japanese approach

We have quite deliberately chosen not to go into the detail of
Japanese planning, its various instruments, institutions and
mechanisms. These are a product of its own history and culture and
it would generally be wrong to consider that they could, or indeed
should, be transplanted to countries characterized by quite different
historical and cultural circumstances.[26] What it is important to learn
from the Japanese case is the approach to the problem. To begin to
be as successful with our economies as the Japanese have been with
theirs will require the same degree of commitment by the government to economic development as has been the case with Japan. At
the same time we have to learn the other lesson of the Japanese
experience; that the role of the state at the national level[27] should be
limited to the strategic oversight of development, rather than
getting involved with the operational detail, and also that strategic
oversight is only essential in the case of a limited array of key
industries, many sectors being left to market processes without
strategic guidance. The role of the state has to be seen as catalytic,
proactive rather than reactive, bringing guidance where the market
offers little. Policy in most Western countries tends to be *ad hoc* and
reactive, because of suspicion of state planning. The message of the
Japanese experience is that, properly organized, planning and the
market are complements rather than substitutes. Each has to be
allocated its appropriate role.

The success of the Japanese economy is obvious. But how much
of this success has been due to planning? In everything we have said
we have assumed that that success has been related to a substantial
degree to the developmental role of the Japanese state. And yet the
question has no answer in the sense of ascribing a certain fraction of
the Japanese growth rate to the presence of Japanese industrial
policy, with its related institutions. What we believe can be said is
that their industrial policy, operated mainly by MITI, was a
necessary, but obviously not sufficient condition for Japanese
economic success.[28] It could not have been achieved without MITI,

and despite our earlier assertion about Japanese institutions not being easily transplanted, we believe that something akin to MITI will have to be constructed in any country seeking a successful, proactive developmental role for the government. This institution would have to incorporate a small, entrepreneurial team dedicated to thinking strategically about the economy, and with the independent capability of implementing the strategy which evolves from the process of wide consultation with industry. Such an institution would have to provide continuity, consistency and commitment to the processes of economic development. In the case of Britain this implies a move from the sort of *ad hoc* intervention of the past toward a coherent strategic policy, with a proactive stance replacing a reactive one.

Strategic industries: issues of selection

Initially it is important to differentiate between industries which are strategically important in the functioning of a dynamic economy but which may, to all intents and purposes, at a particular stage of development, be left to their own devices, and those which are strategically important but require significant intervention by the state if their strategic role is to be fully developed. The dividing line between these two sets of industries will be partly determined by the history of the economy, its current stage of development and its independent future prospects, but will also be determined by the capacity and competence of the state to undertake a developmental role across a range of industries.[29] Some would argue that the inefficiencies of the market system are so pervasive that comprehensive intervention is justified, although we have argued against this. However, even if this were true, it is unlikely that significant intervention across the board would be warranted given the limited capacity and competence of state institutions. As well as avoiding detailed intervention by the state in the operation of industry, as opposed to imposing some degree of strategic control, we should also be careful to limit strategic intervention to those parts of the economy where intervention is going to have its most significant potential impact on the dynamism of the economy as a whole. Initially we will need to give priority to those industries, both old and new, which appear viable and indeed strategically important in a long-term perspective, but which are vulnerable in the short or medium term without significant intervention. Such industries have to be provided with the resources and commitment to allow them to grow and mature, so that in the longer term the degree of intervention can be progressively reduced and the focus switched to other industries which have emerged as new priorities. The infant industry argument for intervention has a significance in advanced industrial countries as well as developing countries, and has a particular significance in the case of manufacturing in Britain following its dramatic loss of competitiveness in the early eighties which in turn led to enormous gaps in the network of manufacturing processes.

It is clear that the sort of intervention described above is both a difficult and a dangerous project. It is difficult to identify certain areas of economic activity on which resources should be concentrated, and, as a result, tend to neglect others; and it is also potentially dangerous to protect certain areas of economic activity from the discipline of international competition. Nevertheless we have to face up to the consequences of selective intervention, and we need to remind ourselves that it is not necessarily the case that free trade imposes a beneficial discipline in a world of dominant, transnational corporations. In such a world the solution may be efficient from the viewpoint of the transnational but may cut across the interests of nation states in general.

The process of selection of sectors and enterprises for government attention and support is often described as 'picking winners'. Those dubious about the whole process, that is most members of the economics orthodoxy, will then express their, perhaps well-founded, doubts about the superiority of civil servants compared with private entrepreneurs in this process. We believe it is wrong to pose the matter in this way. The central issue is the 'creation of winners' as a result of the continuing and careful nurturing of strategic industries and enterprises. Government will never be able to claim any special ability not held by private entrepreneurs, although it may act to redirect the talents of the most able to real industrial issues rather than allowing their waste in the process of shuffling paper assets around within the City. The essential difference between the public and private selection process lies in the difference of perspective – in the ultimate objectives of such a process – rather than wholly in the efficiency with which any specific objective is pursued. The aim of government in the area of economic policy is to create a dynamic and productive national economy and private decision-making may not be consistent with this.

It is important to distinguish various categories of strategic industries, some of which are straightforwardly susceptible to economic analysis, others requiring a much wider-ranging consultation of expert scientific and industrial opinion. The first case in point is that of Extant Industries which are seen as vital components in the evolution of a self-sustaining, dynamic economy but which are threatened by the processes of the capitalist, market system. In these cases the application of economic analysis is relatively straightforward. We can assess the potential importance of the industry by modelling the consequences for the economy as a whole of its demise. Which consequences are we specifically interested in? Ultimately the impact on the sustainable rate of growth of the economy, and its constituent regional parts, is likely to be the central issue. The demise of a specific industry will impact on this directly, as a component of such growth, and indirectly via the diffusion of the impact of such demise on other industries and sectors, and in turn such direct and indirect effects may raise balance of payments issues which feed back on the sustainability of such growth. Conceptually and technically it is quite possible to develop a programme of industrial modelling which would allow us to identify key industries, in this category, whose demise would have substantial, long-term effects on the growth of the national economy, and/or its distribution across regions. The criteria are obviously dynamic and forward-looking and focus on the nation's ability to maximize the welfare of its population, assuming that we are adequately measuring the real costs of resource use and leisure foregone.

New Industries raise more difficult issues. Economic analysis offers no straightforward way of calibrating for their precise potential effects. Their very newness means that we cannot build models representing our experience of the national economy with these industries as constituent parts. Thus we cannot easily assess the impact of not having them. We may be able to examine the experience offered by similar industries producing similar products, or by different countries which have been earlier innovators, but they will undoubtedly raise serious problems of interpretation and extrapolation. In other cases the new industries may be so different from our collective experience that it will be even more difficult to assess their impact on the economy as a whole. In this case it will be absolutely necessary to conduct wide-ranging consultation within science, technology and industry in order to try and establish the broad parameters of such potentially new industries.

New Processes raise similar issues but we need to examine them at two levels: their production (as a New Industry) and their adoption (by Extant and New Industries). This implies wide-ranging consultation within science and technology and industry concerning production, plus consultation among potential users of the new process. Similarly the economic analysis of new processes would proceed at each of the two levels once the essential parameters had been identified in the process of consultation.

In many cases we will effectively be dealing with networks of firms spanning several industries and, rather than attempting to measure the impact of adding or removing a single industry to or from the national economy, we shall be considering adding or removing a set of interrelated industries. This may not be simply a more realistic description of alternative scenarios, it may be also more manageable as a piece of economic analysis given that the impact of adding or removing a major chunk of the economy may be more easily assessed than adding or removing smaller constituent parts. Problems of data and statistical inference are likely to loom larger in the latter case.

We conclude that the question of the selection of strategic industries is not a case of anyone's guess. It is quite possible to break down the general question into more manageable parts. In some cases the selection process can be quite straightforwardly guided by economic analysis and industrial modelling (e.g. steel). In other cases we need to tap scientific and industrial experience and opinion before proceeding to such analysis and modelling (e.g. biotechnology). The central conclusion is that the selection of strategic industries is a question which we should approach as a matter of rigorous, economic investigation, whilst recognising the limits of such enquiry.

An institutional structure

This last section is intended to outline a network of institutions appropriate to the formulation and implementation of an interventionist industrial strategy. It is not intended to go into detail on the functions, structure and operation of specific institutions – that comes later in the book after we have decided at this point how they might fit together as a coherent whole. The suggestions made here follow from the earlier analysis and prescriptions. The section starts by emphasizing the irrelevance of institutional change without the necessary commitment to fundamental industrial change; sets out the central core of strategic planning, before getting into sectoral and regional policy; turns to participation and accountability and ends on suggestions for institutions to control transnational and monopoly power.

Commitment and institutions
Whilst institutions with a strategic planning role are a necessary part of any attempt to introduce a long-term perspective to economic policy-making in this country, the institutions themselves are derivative from a prior commitment to such fundamental change in policy. They therefore represent a commitment to replace the short-term perspective of the traditional Treasury view, and that of the financial institutions, with one much more favourable to industry and production. Coupled with this has to be a commitment to intervene decisively in the strategies of the transnationals and to act to secure a democratic structure of intervention and development. Without such commitments, no matter what the new structure of institutions, such policy will founder on short-term expedients, the conservatism of the Civil Service, the power of the transnationals or the resistance of the people.

Of central importance is the establishment of the case for decisive intervention in industry to secure a long-term reversal in its relative (or absolute) decline. Institutions can formalize the commitment to such policies, and their structure, procedures and personnel can act to ensure that such commitments cannot easily be reversed, but they are simply ratifying some position already established. The history of planning in Britain shows how fragile was the commitment, despite the creation of many new institutions. The lack of teeth of the Department of Economic Affairs was obvious, and could be said to be due to the Treasury view predominating. And yet, more recently, we have seen how the Treasury view is a malleable thing. With clear goals, and a determination to pursue them, institutions with teeth should be forthcoming, despite the conservatism of the Treasury and the Civil Service in general.

The central core

At the centre, as the Labour Party's Policy Review recognizes, we will need a revamped and reorganized Department of Trade and Industry (DTI), of at least equal status with the Treasury – a powerhouse dedicated to raising the quantity and quality of investment in British industry. Economic policy will be built around the twin pillars of Treasury and Industry; the former with a relatively short-term demand perspective, the latter with a longer-term supply perspective. The new DTI should be organized around the requirements of a Strategic Planning Agency, with a long-term commitment of substantial funds, and the powers to intervene decisively in crucial sectors of the economy in terms of the provision of finance, new product and process initiatives, and the ability to bargain with the transnationals over the location of production and investment and the degree of foreign sourcing.

Given that industrial strategy should not be concerned with detailed operational decision-making in industry, but with strategic interventions in key sectors, the core planning staff should consist of a small, entrepreneurial team rather than a vast bureaucracy. The team should be recruited partly from within the Civil Service, but also from NEDO, business and the academic world: a new look DTI would need some new look civil servants.[30] Its function would be to map out the broad process of industrial strategy and co-ordinate the strategies being developed at sectoral level and by other departments such as Energy and Transport. The aim would not be to create a static blueprint for intervention, but rather to isolate a sequence of interventions which could be flexibly adapted to changing conditions; retaining coherence without attempting to be comprehensive. Our resources are too limited for such ambitions.

Also at the core should be two new institutions: a National Investment Bank aimed at raising additional funds for long-term investment in the British economy from pension funds and the money market, and a State Holding Company which would act to stimulate industrial development by equity involvement in existing companies or by taking a leading role in the creation of new companies. To successfully fulfil its function the Investment Bank needs to be kept quite separate from the Strategic Planning Agency – but should be informed by its work, whereas the State Holding Company should act more as an extension of the agency doing exactly those things which existing, Whitehall-based, public institutions fail to do, whilst standing as a formally distinct entity.

Sectoral policy
Whilst having a strong core, planning should be neither comprehensive nor centralized. A loose and transparent hierarchy linking the Strategic Planning Agency of the DTI with other government departments involved in industrial investment (e.g. Energy and Transport), and with Sectoral Agencies (also part of the DTI) and Regional and Local Enterprise Boards, would decentralize much of the work of the department. The Strategic Planning Agency would remain as the central co-ordinating structure, but it would lie at the apex of an information structure, not a command structure. Plan formulation and implementation would be decentralized to a considerable degree via our sectoral policy and via the relatively autonomous Enterprise Boards. We need to get away from Whitehall for the detailed development of our industrial strategy for the interrelated reasons of efficiency and democracy. Sectoral Agencies should be part of the DTI, but normally housed in the regions, close to the industries with whose future they will be so intimately concerned. Variety and flexibility should be the essence of the planning structure, with different Sectoral Agencies being allowed considerable autonomy in determining their own mode of operation, and adjusting it as experience accumulates. Our objective will be a dynamic industrial economy rather than sticking to a set of rigid rules imposed by a central bureaucracy. There should be no immediate attempt to cover all sectors, nor all regions of the economy. We must avoid squandering people and resources over a whole range of activities where potential gains are of dubious significance.

The areas of activity should reflect the priorities established at the centre and within the regions. The process could be started off by the Strategic Planning Agency (SPA) within the DTI identifying sectors in which strategic intervention is desirable as a matter of urgency. This process of identification would clearly involve the widest possible consultation within industry and with professional opinion. The SPA would then set up the appropriate Sectoral Agencies (SAs) and determine their initial budget. This would be added to after the SAs reported back with their initial plans. In the meantime the SPA would be negotiating with other ministries to set up their own sectoral long-term planning agencies, e.g. for energy and transport, which could also be decentralized. The number of sectoral planning agencies would tend to grow over time as the SPA identified additional key industries in which strategic intervention was seen as desirable, but, as already argued, the SPA should not regard its task as one of achieving a comprehensive coverage. Increasingly the SPA's work would switch from the creation of a system of SAs, to the monitoring and co-ordination of that system. Increasingly it would determine the pattern of intervention by redirecting capital flows between existing Sectoral Agencies, both directly and indirectly via its influence on the National Investment Bank and the State Holding Company. Sectoral Agencies when no longer relevant to overall strategic aims would be wound up.

In addition to the Strategic Agencies, the DTI should create agencies covering New Technology (including research and development, and the innovation and diffusion of the results of such activity) and Technical Education and Training. In the case of technology the agency would be concerned with a fundamental reorganization of government funded R & D. The present budget allocates most resources to Military/Aerospace R & D which has had a very limited pay-off. This money has to be reallocated to research on manufacturing production and new product development over a broad range of industries. In the case of those industries targeted for selective intervention, the question of technology will be fused with the general strategy of investment in those industries; in other cases consultation on the appropriate role for public R & D will emerge from industry-level consultations. Collaborative projects between industry and the universities could be encouraged and funded, and these would supply exciting and challenging jobs for scientists and engineers released from military/aerospace/ nuclear projects.

The agency for Technical Education and Training would be concerned with co-ordinating the activities of the Department of Education and Science with the needs identified by the Strategic Planning Agency, but would also take overall responsibility for training, where no such responsibility currently exists. The Training Commission (former MSC) plays a central role, but its perspective and achievements are essentially negative (see Coventry Ecstra, 1986).[31] The new agency would develop a programme of training based on the requirements of the industrial strategy formulated within the DTI. It would probably prove most efficient to work through the Training Commission to achieve such objectives.

Regional policy
The formulation and implementation of sectoral planning by Sectoral Agencies within the regions would allow concrete linkages between industrial and regional policy. The Sectoral Agencies would be responsible for the strategic planning in their specific industries wherever they may be located within the UK, but the location of the agency at the heart of the sector in question will inevitably mean that that agency will also perform a key role in the industrial regeneration of that region. For example, consider the auto industry, Birmingham and the West Midlands. A Sectoral Agency for autos would develop and implement a strategy for that sector, whether or not located in the West Midlands, but inevitably such policy would have a potentially dramatic impact on the West Midlands regional economy. The act of putting the strategic decision-making machinery within the region most affected would also make it more accessible to the regional planners. Such juxtapositions would aid the development of both regional and industrial strategies.

We can help to revive the regions by moving to such a polycentric system of industrial intervention, and in return our industrial ambitions will be built on firmer foundations – industrial strategy will be based on a fuller knowledge of the resources and needs of the regions which provide the locations for such strategy. However, to make real progress on the regional problem will require deep penetration of our industrial problem. Investment and talent gravitates to the South-East, and our traditional industrial regions are left denuded. To reverse this tendency we have to be quite radical. We believe a policy aimed at countering the attraction of London by a massive programme aimed at regenerating the key regional cities is needed – changing the underlying cultural and economic dynamic so that talented people are no longer automatically drawn to London. The renaissance of a decentralized, regionally-based, financial structure should be a crucial component of such a programme. This implies broad-based investment in these cities to achieve a cultural renaissance – not just directly funding industrial investment, although this is also vital. These cities would then become the catalysts of dynamic city regions.

All this implies a new set of institutions – building on the experiences of the Scottish and Welsh Development Agencies – but redirected to fit in with the new strategic aims of government. Such agencies would be located in cities like Birmingham, Manchester and Newcastle and would liaise closely with local and regional government, Enterprise Boards and the relevant Sectoral Agencies, in formulating and implementing strategic, broad-based, plans for the region (see Chapter 8).

At this point many readers may be wondering about the proliferation of agencies which are being proposed. Indeed the author feels more than a twinge of embarrassment in this regard! However it is nevertheless true that countries, like Japan, and regions, like Emilia-Romagna in Italy or Baden Württemberg in West Germany, with successful industrial strategies do have a similar series of agencies. The fundamental point is that the nature of such agencies is catalytic and entrepreneurial rather than being negative and bureaucratic as many similar British institutions have been in the past. We need a series of agencies but we have to be careful of their nature.

Participation and accountability

No broad consensus for economic planning exists in Britain – it has to be created – and it can only be created by involving people in the process itself. To be successful our planning must be democratic. Our institutional structure must allow for participation at all levels. At the sectoral level we will need teams of professionals working on sectoral strategies. Their work must be infused by the participation of management and unions at two levels. First in the development of Corporate Plans by firms within the sector, which will form a potentially important input into the evolution of a sectoral strategy. (Such participation will be a requirement for government support.) And second, by the interaction of Sectoral Agencies with Sectoral Councils made up of management and worker representatives from the industries in question, together with appropriate DTI membership. The idea would be that the professional team of the agency would, after some preliminary discussion with the council, put up a tentative, fairly broad-based, strategic plan for the sector for comment and approval. The agency would then be responsible for the detailed implementation of the plan, with further monitoring of progress by the council.

A similar arrangement should prevail at the central core. Interaction between the DTI and the National Economic Development Council (NEDC) would lead to the implementation of the plan by the Strategic Planning Agency working through its sectoral branches, again with the NEDC monitoring its progress.

The above suggestions assume a tripartite structure in the specific councils (sectoral and national), much as we have seen with the NEDC. However, we should consider the feasibility of more democratic structures as are now contemplated in the Health Service, i.e. directly elected membership of Sectoral Councils and the NEDC. Creating a representative economic democracy, alongside our existing political democracy, complementing participative structures within the enterprise, should form an important part of our detailed policy-making. To back up the growth of participative structures we should also be considering detailed arrangements for collective share ownership by workers in the companies for which they work (see Chapter 5).

Transnational and monopoly power

As mentioned earlier, a successful industrial strategy requires wide consultation with the firm affected, a serious effort to reach agreement on intervention and no day-to-day interference with their operation. However, we should recognize that some important strategic issues are not capable of being resolved by agreement, and therefore, at the limit, the government must be prepared to follow its strategy if necessary without agreement, not by the use of arbitrary power, but based on a wider democratic consensus which may be at odds with the ambitions of a particular firm. The global strategies of the transnationals and the attempted accretions of monopoly power by the major corporations are likely to be cases in point.

Control over the transnationals will be difficult to establish because of the broad political questions it raises and, more specifically, because of Britain's membership of the EEC. We will need to monitor exactly what the transnationals are doing. We have at the moment no accurate record of their global activities. This information could be collated by a Transnationals Unit within the DTI (see Chapter 7). This would provide the basis on which the DTI and its Sectoral Agencies would enter discussions with the transnationals about their role within the government's strategic plans.

Leverage over the transnationals could also be gained by providing public support for attempts by unions to set up a transnational organization of their own (see Coventry Ecstra, 1986). The restoration of many of the provisions eliminated from the EEC (Vredling) proposed Directive on Consultation of Employees of Transnational Undertakings, and its adoption and vigorous enforcement in the UK, would also help trade union attempts at stopping the haemorrhage of British jobs. More generally we should work within the EEC to establish effective controls over the transnationals operating within the Community (see Chapter 7 for further analysis).

As with all other elements of policy-making it is necessary to show how our Monopoly and Merger Policy proposals can be linked-in to our general industrial strategy. What we need to do is identify the complementarities or inconsistencies which may exist between our broader industrial strategies and our policies on merger and monopoly, and thereby identify an appropriate interlocking institutional structure which will both exploit the former and minimize the latter.

The inconsistencies would appear minimal. A stringent anti-merger policy coupled with the tight regulation of monopoly power will also service our strategic ambitions for industrial dynamism, and in turn our willingness to create new firms and encourage new entry via, for example, the activities of British Technology Enterprise, will serve to moderate the monopoly powers of extant corporations. However, there will undoubtedly be cases where, either we see merger as contributing to our industrial strategy, or alternatively where, to get the compliance we seek, we are willing to give up something on the merger front. In terms of our network of institutions, this suggests that those engaged in operating our merger and monopoly policy should be infused with the thinking and objectives of our industrial strategy. This could be achieved by appropriate cross membership between the Strategic Planning Agency and the monopolies and mergers group within the DTI, together with a similar arrangement linking the NEDC with the Monopolies Commission, which itself will require an expansion in membership and changes in its present membership to cope with its new responsibilities. For further details, see Chapter 4.

Concluding remarks

This chapter has sought to establish a case for industrial intervention based on the inefficiencies of the market system; described the form an industrial strategy should take; explained the issues surrounding the selection of strategic industries and finally made suggestions for a network of institutions appropriate to the detailed formulation and implementation of an interventionist industrial strategy. The key point is that the paper identifies the need for a strong developmental role for the state to raise the momentum of industrial change and to ensure that such change fully reflects the broader national interest. We have ended up by specifying a range of appropriate institutions, but it is the strategic approach rather than the precise set of institutions which is the essence of this chapter – the institutions themselves are derivative from that approach. We will need to identify strategic industries which require nurturing in order to achieve a more dynamic industrial economy. This is essentially a matter of creating winners, rather than picking them. There will be no vast bureaucratic machinery: the approach will be entrepreneurial. The regional dimension of the strategy could be achieved via regional and local enterprise boards working alongside regional development agencies. At this level one crucial link to be established involves the pension funds, as an enormously important source of investment finance, and the enterprise boards as democratically accountable institutions concerned with long-term industrial investment. Establishing successful links could revolutionise the British industrial economy of the 1990s. These matters are pursued in Chapters 3 and 8.

We have said very little about changing the nature of the enterprises with which the strategy has to deal. One of the reasons that the Japanese industrial strategy has been so successful is that Japanese industry and finance has tended to take the long view. It is of great importance that we should construct a new companies act which will serve to encourage British companies to take the long view by opening them up to a broader representation of interests (e.g. workers and the community) via the diffusion of information and power, and couple this with measures aimed at encouraging the long-term commitment of finance to Britain's industrial regeneration and the formation of new private, regionally-based, institutions to channel British savings into real industrial investment in Britain. By these means we would be able to bend the private enterprise system toward a greater complementarity with the aims and methods of the public industrial strategy we plan to inaugurate and thereby significantly enhance its prospects for success. We offer some initial analysis on these questions in Chapters 3, 5 and 8.

Lastly, the issues and opportunities offered by Europe. We have tried to develop an approach which has a basic validity at all levels of policy-making – local, regional, national, supranational. Linkages between the various levels pose real difficulties but we have tried to begin to examine the issues in the chapters that follow. They pervade all areas – science and technology, finance, merger and monopoly, economic democracy, macro-policy, the transnationals and the public utilities. In all these areas of policy-making in Britain EC policy looms large, but, equally, developing the European dimension of our approach offers a framework for the long-term evolution of a strategy for European industry and the European economy.

Notes

1 Keynes did, of course, advocate 'a somewhat comprehensive socialization of investment', John Maynard Keynes, 1936, *The General Theory of Employment, Interest and Money*, New York, Harcourt Brace, but this was directed at the short-term aim of restoring full employment rather than the long-term aim of altering the direction and pace of development.

2 Witness the debate on industrial policy in the United States in the early eighties, R. Norton, 1986, 'Industrial Policy and American Renewal', *Journal of Economic Literature*, 24, 1–40.

3 Labour Party, 1989, *Meet the Challenge, Make the Change — A New Agenda for Britain. Final Report of Labour's Policy Review*, London, Labour Party.

4 There is some controversy about whether this improved performance is more apparent than real. Certainly it is apparent if we consider the period starting in the deep slump of 1981, but it is real if we measure the change peak to peak, from 1979 to 1988. Output per employee in manufacturing went up by an average of 4.9% p.a. over that period, whereas over the period 1973 to 1979 it rose by 1.1% p.a. The data strongly suggest a real improvement.

5 This is not to deny that for many this can, ultimately, be a liberating experience.

6 Whilst research has revealed a positive relationship between productivity growth and the level of unemployment in Britain and the United States, the same author has demonstrated a negative relationship in the case of Sweden and West Germany (see T. Weisskopf, 1987, 'The Effect of Unemployment on Labour Productivity: An International Comparative Analysis', *International Review of Applied Economics*, 1, 127–51). The inference is that there is no necessary inconsistency between sustained high levels of employment and high rates of productivity growth – it depends on how the employment relation is organized.

7   Living in Coventry over the period allowed fairly direct observations of this phenomenon. This is supported by numerous plant-level reports in the *Financial Times* over the early eighties.

8   Productivity growth rates generally, within advanced industrial countries, have not shown any tendency to fall off in the twentieth century – rather the reverse. The post-World War II period has been characterized by productivity growth rates generally exceeding any previous recorded levels (see A. Maddison, 1987, 'Growth and Slowdown in Advanced Capitalist Economies', *Journal of Economic Literature*, 24, 649–98). The only exception to this general rule appears to be the United States over the period since 1973.

9   Indeed, exactly the reverse could prove to be the case as a result of the long-term legacy of resentment following from the initial imposition of a higher pace of work.

10   The recent rate of growth is also unsustainable, witness the build-up of the enormous trade deficit since 1987 and government projections for lower future growth.

11   This will be dealt with quite briefly because it appears generally less controversial than the other matters which are raised.

12   We do not consider Keynesian intervention to secure full employment in the same light. We regard such demand-side intervention as enhancing the market system, or indeed saving it, rather than superceding it. We do not deny its fundamental importance, but it is not an issue we address directly at this point.

13   For a fuller development of the argument see Keith Cowling and Roger Sugden, 1987, *Transnational Monopoly Capitalism*, Brighton, Wheatsheaf.

14   Membership of the EC raises additional difficulties, but also additional opportunities, and indeed dramatically raises the central issue of the dimensions of 'community'.

15   We are referring here to the general relaxation of trade barriers within the capitalist system over the post-World War II period. We are well aware of the many impediments to trade that continue to exist.

16   F. Clairmonte and J. Cavanagh, 1981, *The World in their Web*, London, Zed.

17   This does not, of course, mean that wages or taxes are the sole determinants of industrial location: general social and economic infrastructure and access to markets will also figure prominently in such decisions. The point is that the transnational organization of production implies great flexibility in moving to locations of lowest cost whatever the degree of skill of the relevant labour force and given that access to markets is secure and will ultimately serve to determine that level of cost.

18   Related within the context of any one nation given the transnational stance of the major firms operating within that nation. Their strategy will inevitably be more short-termist within that nation because they have only a limited commitment to it in the long term, at least as a location for production.

19   It is also the case that many possible alternatives to the market would fail to adequately handle these matters. Our interest in the Japanese model (see later) was triggered partly by the apparent success that has been achieved in the case of Japan in making exactly these quantum industrial leaps.

20   The present major imbalance in the development of London and the South compared with the rest of the country is a reflection of these forces.

21   The pressure for government to maintain such a role in the economy is likely to be less marked when that economy has established a world lead. The pressure to adopt such a role will be more intense when such a lead is lost, or being lost, or where the country in question has been late to industrialize.

22 OECD, 1972, *The Industrial Policy of Japan*, Paris.

23 It is interesting to note that the other dramatically successful economies of the Pacific Rim – South Korea, Taiwan, Singapore and Hong Kong – have organized themselves in rather similar fashion.

24 Chalmers Johnson, 1982, *MITI and the Japanese Miracle: The Growth of Industrial Policy 1925–75*, Stanford, Stanford University Press.

25 Paul Hare, 1985, *Planning the British Economy*, London, Macmillan.

26 It is important to recognize that what is being proposed is not the Japanization of the British economy. The question of the organization of work is not being addressed here. We are simply focusing on the relevance of the approach by the state to the question of industrial strategy.

27 Of course where there is a close, local link between the state and industry, for example where the state acts as a venture capitalist within the context of a local or regional enterprise board, then it would be completely appropriate to develop a richer and deeper relationship with the enterprises in question (see Chapter 3).

28 Chalmers Johnson (1982) offers persuasive support for this view.

29 This issue looms large for any future government contemplating a significant and coherent developmental role in the economy. Early priority will need to be given to the question of the organization of decision-making and the identification of personnel to accomplish the various tasks. It is clear that the present Civil Service will need substantial reconstruction, retraining and re-staffing to successfully adapt to its new role.

30 Suitably trained people are obviously going to be in short supply and it will be important to develop plans for appropriate training facilities in readiness for a change in government. Nevertheless in the short-term it will be largely a matter of adapting people to a new role, and learning by doing will inevitably form an important element of such adaptation.

31 Coventry Ecstra, 1986, *Sectoral Industrial Planning: The Case of the Car Industry*, Coventry.

Encouraging investment in science and technology

Introduction

Industrial policy under Mrs Thatcher's Tory government has been surprisingly consistent in its failure to address the real problems facing UK manufacturing industry, largely (but not entirely) because successive ministers at the DTI have managed to avoid thinking seriously about science and technology policy for a decade. As the trade balance shows, a consequence of this neglect has been a steady decline in UK competitiveness. Mrs Thatcher's too numerous Industry Ministers have not, of course, been totally inactive. They have reoriented the DTI's portfolio of activities on several occasions to reflect different views about how it should be positioned *vis-à-vis* industry, and have delivered numerous moral lectures reflecting these views to managers from a wide variety of public platforms. However, underlying these repositioning exercises and public pronouncements has been an unyielding policy stance designed to disengage the government from the problems of industry. Possibly the most positive industrial policies that have been pursued by the government are those which have encouraged the formation of small firms, those that have facilitated the establishment of assembly plants in the UK by foreign-based multinationals and those which have tried to alert UK managers to the looming menace of 1992. None of them have done much to stimulate industrial innovation.

The recent report of the Labour Party's Policy Review Group on the Productive and Competitive Economy, 'Competing for Prosperity',[1] makes a refreshing change from the mind-numbing adulation of *laissez-faire* that passes for serious policy thinking amongst Tory ministers. Arguing that the UK's performance in research and development is distressingly poor by international standards, the report contains a clear recognition of the need to encourage R & D and stimulate both the generation and the diffusion of innovation. The report seeks to outline the basis of a Medium-Term Industrial Strategy that will expand the role and responsibilities of the DTI, mandating it to adopt a 'pro-active role providing continuity, consistency and commitment to the process of economic development'. Its goal will be to raise both the quantity and quality of investment in British industry, and that means encouraging investment in science and technology (amongst other things).

More substantively, the report contains a list of at least four types of policy that a future Labour government is likely to use in trying to encourage investment in science and technology. First, the existing hodgepodge of *ad hoc* arrangements supporting R & D will be rationalized, criteria for support will be made both more clear and more strictly defined, and bureaucratic decision-making procedures will be made more straightforward and less time consuming. This will involve, *inter alia*, introducing a system of automatic grants and the use of tax incentives to stimulate R & D. Second, attempts will be made to change private sector attitudes towards R & D. These will, it is hoped, be affected by the Party's clear commitment to manufacturing industry, and its unwillingness to share the common Tory view that specializing in low tech service sectors is an acceptable answer to Britain's current economic woes. More concretely, the report argues that there is a need for reforms in the accounting treatment of R & D and in the market for corporate control, reforms designed to prevent the City from imposing its (alleged) preoccupation with short-term cash flows on decision makers in industry. Third, the report proposes the creation of a new institution – the British Technology Enterprise – to play a role in financing new innovative activity, and encouraging the development of new high tech sectors. Among other things, it is hoped that the BTE will develop a set of 'alternative' commercial criteria which will enable it to compensate for what are seen as the short term, risk averse, hands-off lending policies of the City. Fourth and finally, the report advocates supporting (at least) two large scale infrastructure projects that, it is hoped, will provide major benefits to the community at large while, at the same time, encouraging the development of technologies in areas where the UK might legitimately aspire to developing a competitive advantage in world markets. The two broad areas of the infrastructure targeted for action are the environment, and the development and installation of a national broad band fibre optic cable network.

The report seems to be a logical starting point for any discussion of alternative economic and industrial policy strategies for the UK. It is a serious and fairly well balanced attempt to develop an alternative to Tory policies, and the polls (currently) indicate that it is an alternative that has an increasingly real chance of being implemented. Our goal is to examine the three substantive proposals contained in the report – the proposal to use automatic grants and tax incentives to stimulate R & D, the proposed creation of the BTE, and the planned implementation of big projects – on the basis of what is known about the success of similar policies implemented on other occasions in other countries. In fact, the evidence that is available does not give unambiguous support to all of the proposals in the report. Automatic grants and tax incentives, in particular, are likely to prove to be extremely cost ineffective. However, the BTE and the use of procurement policy to stimulate innovation are both extremely promising initiatives that can yield substantial pay-offs if managed properly. We shall consider each in turn.

Supply-side policies

Supply-side economics has been in vogue ever since right wing politicians first discovered that tax cuts for the rich could be passed off to the general public as being necessary to increase incentives, and, therefore, as being necessary to stimulate productivity growth. Although it is conceivable that modest gains can be realized in this fashion, concentrating on the supply-side to help rejuvenate a stagnant economy involves examining a much wider range of policies than cuts in income tax, or, indeed, than in just using the tax system to affect various types of economic behaviour. Any kind of thoroughgoing supply-side policy must go much deeper than this and address the problem of whether an adequate infrastructure exists to support an improvement in economic performance. This means that supply-side policies must, sooner or later, examine the institutions that mould economic behaviour. The first of the two supply-side proposals discussed in the report – the use of automatic grants and tax incentives to stimulate R & D – is very much a traditional type of supply-side policy. The second proposal – to create a British Technology Enterprise – is a more fundamental supply-side initiative that addresses the institutional arrangements for providing financial support for R & D activities in the UK.

The proposed use of automatic grants and tax incentives to subsidize R & D is, quite simply, a bad idea. At best, they reward expenditure on inputs into the R & D process and, at worse, they reward creative accounting practices that shift expenditures from one poorly defined accounting category to another in search of tax efficiency. In neither case do they reward what is of importance, namely, the production and use of new products and processes. They create almost no incentives whatsoever for firms to efficiently transform expenditures on inputs into new products and processes that create value for users. Furthermore, like other kinds of subsidies and grants, R & D subsidies can create a client constituency of firms who are particularly adept at filling in forms and lobbying MPs, civil servants, ministers and so on, firms whose income ultimately depends on their political skills, not on their research skills. In short, R & D subsidies are an unattractive policy option because they often have a tendency to affect behaviour in ways that can be inimical to innovation.

Automatic grants and tax incentives that subsidize R & D have a second major failing as a method of stimulating the development of science and technology, and that is that they are a poorly targeted method of support. Any type of industrial policy that is not custom made for a carefully selected set of firms runs the risk of not meeting the needs of those to whom it is addressed, and of wasting resources on those who do not require support. Generalized non-discretionary support schemes (such as those typically implemented through the tax system) are administratively convenient, but that is almost their sole virtue. Rather like other subsidies that are implemented through the tax system, automatic grants and R & D subsidies are awarded on the basis of eligibility rather than need. Some firms receive assistance that they don't need, while others in need don't receive enough assistance. What is worse, such grants and R & D tax incentives often effectively act as a hidden subsidy that benefits large firms at the expense of small and medium sized firms. The problem here is that grants and tax incentives tend to flow mainly towards large firms since they are, effectively, the only firms that maintain formally organized R & D labs and, therefore, are the only firms that report R & D expenditures in their accounts. This would, of course, be perfectly reasonable if it were true that such firms accounted for the lion's share of major innovations. Unhappily, this is not the case, and, in fact, the evidence suggests that research activities conducted in formal R & D labs are by no means the only or the most important source of useful innovative output. Indeed, R & D expenditures are rather poorly correlated with research output like innovations (or patents), not least because innovative small and medium sized firms draw on a much wider range of sources of new ideas than large firms which rely on formal R & D programmes.[2]

Third and finally, it often turns out that, in practice, automatic grants and R & D tax incentives concentrate on stimulating the generation of new innovations without paying much attention to the problem of ensuring that what is produced is as widely used as possible. Indeed, a country like the UK will only ever produce a small percentage of the total world stock of new inventions and innovations, and it is, as a consequence, more sensible to focus science and technology policy on encouraging industry to use what is available, adapting it as quickly and as efficiently as possible, than on generating new inventions and innovations. One consequence of the almost total neglect of users that is implicit in the use of grants and tax incentives for R & D is that there is a tendency for the public sector to end up financing 'second best' projects. Projects with a clear commercial potential based on a set of clearly expressed user needs often attract some private sector support, leaving their more risky and more speculatively conceived projects to the public sector. While many of these do respond to real, if inchoately expressed, needs, some are just plain poorly conceived (particularly, it often seems, those that drape themselves in the flag of national prestige). Such projects also frequently seem to be inordinately technically sophisticated, and public sector evaluation procedures often give heavy weight to 'big science' without seriously considering the commercial prospects of the project. Although this is certainly not true of all projects financed by grants and subsidies, it is nevertheless true that there is often a reason why some projects have been reduced to seeking public funding, and why more careful, more discretionary policies ought to be used to evaluate them.

The bottom line, then, is that automatic grants and tax subsidies on R & D are not likely to be a particularly efficient or cost effective way to stimulate industrial innovation. This conclusion is clearly consistent with the data that we have on the success of these programmes. Studies of the effect of such policies in Sweden, Canada and the US suggest that they are extremely expensive, costing between £2.50–£3.30 in lost revenue for each additional £ of R & D generated. Further, the rate of return on such publicly funded projects is often rather low, and is typically much lower than that on privately financed R & D. Finally, comparative studies of clusters of major post-war innovations suggest that the effects of subsidies in their development has generally been 'small' or 'negligible'. Procurement policies, it turns out, have proved to be a far more effective way to stimulate industrial innovation, and have been responsible for a wide range of new products and processes introduced in numerous sectors.[3] In short, it is hard to believe that more effective supply-side policies cannot be devised.

The basic thinking behind automatic grants and tax incentives for R & D is that the major constraints on industrial innovation are supply-side constraints, and arise almost entirely from the problem of financing risky, speculative research projects. There is a lot to be said for this view, and there is no doubt that the issue ought to be addressed by policy makers. What is needed is some method of providing long-term financial support that is more selective than grants and subsidies, involves a more careful monitoring of efficiency and less undermining of incentives, and adopts a more commercial or user-based orientation in evaluating requests for support. However, it is hard to believe that finance is the only supply-side constraint that inhibits innovation. Small firms or firms in a state of crisis often need a package of finance and management skills, or a partner that is willing to shoulder some of the risk and bear some of the burden of setting up operations in new high tech sectors (more generally, see the essay by Richard Minns and Mary Rogers in this volume). What is needed to support this kind of venture, then, is a package of financial and managerial support. This is, more or less, the thinking behind the proposed creation of a British Technology Enterprise.

Creating a supporting institution like the BTE is not the radical proposal that it may seem to be at first sight, not least because the new institution is likely to be able to build upon the not inconsiderable successes enjoyed by the National Enterprise Board introduced during the last Labour government. It is worth recalling just what these successes were. The NEB was launched in the 1975 Industry Act, and was given a broad mandate to help rejuvenate British industry. In the words of Eric Heffer, the NEB was expected to: '. . . influence major companies in every manufacturing sector through competitive stimuli by giving a lead on investment, would reorganise the industrial structure in each major sector in line with longer term public need rather than short term market considerations, reduce private monopoly power by inserting public enterprise competition, and create a more evenly balanced regional location of industry'.[4] To this end it was given a set of commercial criteria determining its rules of operation and an initial war chest of £200m. In the event, it developed an interest in computers and electronics, taking substantial shareholdings in Ferranti and ICL, and creating new firms in semi-conductors (INMOS), office equipment (NEXOS), and computer software (INSAC). However, its operations were almost totally dominated right from the start by the need to care for the lame ducks foisted on it, Rolls Royce, British Leyland, Alfred Herbert and Cambridge Instruments. Of the £780m received by the Board from the public coffers by March 1979, about £570m went to BL and £95m to RR. These two companies accounted for about 90% of the value of the NEB's shareholdings, its turnover, its profits and the total value of loans made by it. The total expenditure made by the Board in all its other roles was a mere £17m in 1976, £12m in 1977, and £49m in 1978.

Although the performance of the NEB is rather difficult to assess because it was saddled with a number of lame ducks and was not allowed a free hand in dealing with them, there are obviously lessons for managing the BTE to be learned from the experience of the NEB. Judged on strictly commercial criteria, the NEB was at least a modest commercial success. It failed to reach its (rather arbitrarily set) performance targets of 15–20% return on capital, realizing a return on capital of 11.8%, 11.4%, 11.3% and 4.8% (excluding BL and RR) between 1976 and 1979. The performance shortfall before 1979, however, can hardly be deemed to have been serious. More encouragingly, the investments it made in Ferranti proved to be extremely profitable, and its positive interventions in the area of micro-electronics (and, in 1980, in biotechnology) met with considerable success, leading to the creation of a domestic chip producer, INMOS, that insured a viable UK presence in that market. NEXOS, the office machinery venture, grew fairly rapidly, concentrating mainly on marketing the products of UK companies, a venture from which it achieved at least a modest degree of success. INSAC, the software company, was the least successful of the three ventures initiated by the NEB, and was later reorganized. Not surprisingly, the performance of the NEB in caring for its lame ducks was distinctly mixed. Some success can be claimed for the work done with Ferranti and ICL, but Alfred Herbert and Cambridge Instruments failed to revive despite the NEB's ministrations, and parts of both were eventually sold off despite large expenditures of public money that were never recovered.

The moral seems to be fairly clear. There is scope for a positive, proactive investment institution financed and managed by the public sector, and there is no reason to think that the package of finance and management skills that it could offer cannot yield a respectable rate of return whilst, at the same time, stimulating the growth of new high technology firms across a range of sectors. The experience of the NEB shows, however, that the laudable goals of such an institution are easily subverted by the claims of short-term political expediency. Well established mature industries (particularly those located in marginal constituencies) have far deeper political roots to call upon in crisis than new, yet-to-be-established growth sectors do, and this means that political policy-making – uncritical and myopic as it frequently is – will always be biased towards supporting sunset rather than sunrise sectors. If the BTE is to be successful, this tendency to react to what is (or what was) rather than to what might be must be resisted. If it can be resisted – and the report is clear in insisting that BTE should not be saddled with lame ducks – then there is no reason why the BTE cannot play a valuable role in stimulating industrial innovativeness.

Demand-side policies

There is very little point in pursuing a policy which eases supply constraints if there is no demand for what is produced. Indeed, in an activity as risky and speculative as R & D, firms will always be reluctant to put resources into developing a new product or process unless they feel sure that an adequate market for the product or process will come into being if they succeed. Rather than 'pushing' investment in science and technology with grants, tax subsidies and other terms of assistance, it may be far more sensible to try to 'pull' out such investment by stimulating demand. Of the several ways in which this might be done, one of the most potent is through procurement policy. Innovation occurs when firms push back technological frontiers to meet user needs, and government procurement decisions which express a demand for products and processes beyond current capabilities are likely to stimulate the development of those capabilities. The public sector is an enormously large consumer of goods and services, and, like any other consumer, it has needs and is capable of looking after its own self interest. Further, public purchasing is highly concentrated in a number of high tech sunrise industries, and, because quality is often more important than price in government contracts, it often provides an early testing round for new products, giving firms an opportunity to experiment with different product variants free from short-term commercial pressures. Since public sector procurement decisions flow from the needs of government as a consumer, using procurement policies to stimulate innovation has the considerable further advantage of not requiring civil servants to second guess private sector needs or demand.

One of the most celebrated examples of the success of procurement policy is the US semi-conductor industry. Although the original invention of the transistor occurred in the private sector, subsequent innovations (such as the silicon transistor and the integrated circuit) emerged at the prompting of the US military. Regardless of what one thinks about the desirability of military spending on strictly national security grounds, the important point for science and technology policy is that the military's needs are clear and the market created by defence purchasing is large. This kind of user demand has had an important effect on the evolution of technology in the semi-conductor industry, encouraging the development of small components and transistors with low power consumption, low failure rates and an ability to operate in diverse conditions. Of particular importance to the development of this technology was the military's willingness to pay and its insistence on very high quality standards, since this enabled manufacturers to learn about new products and unfamiliar production processes at government expense in a way that simply would not have been possible had short run commercial decision making been applied to product choice and development. Many of the early products produced in this sector were initially so expensive to make that they would have failed to attract enough private sector users to initiate a thorough enough learning process to reduce costs. Military demand for various products enabled firms to get far enough down the learning curve to create a lucrative private sector market.

Military demand also led to a limited number of spillovers to the civilian sector, generating civilian products and processes that might not otherwise have appeared (or appeared as quickly). One important factor stimulating the diffusion of new technology in this (and other sectors) was the implementation of a 'second sourcing' policy in purchasing by the Pentagon. This helped to diffuse knowledge of advanced technology by facilitating the entry of new firms to the market. Procurement contracts provided both the cash and the access to knowledge needed to encourage the entry of new competitors who, in turn, pioneered the development and diffusion of a range of products designed for a wide variety of civilian uses. One of the most interesting features of this particular industry has been the rapid diffusion of the basic technology, and the early US dominance in this sector was largely due to entry by new spin-off firms continually challenging market leaders. This mobility of firms within the sector was a direct consequence of procurement policies, designed, in part, to maintain competitive pressures on market leaders. Market leaders in this sector were not those firms lucky (or adept) enough to be chosen by civil servants to be national champions; rather, they emerged as a consequence of a competitive process whose vitality was, in part, sustained by a judiciously managed procurement programme.

It is important not to think that military spending is necessarily a good way to stimulate industrial innovation; nor is it wise to equate public procurement policy with defence spending. The positive effects that defence spending can have on innovation often appear only early on in the industry life cycle, and this was (and is) particularly true in the case of semi-conductors. By the late 1960s and early 1970s the flow of spillovers from military to civilian users began to reverse, and firms began to initiate advances in circuit density that were aimed primarily (if not entirely) at the civilian market. Further, a number of military backed projects have proved to be expensive failures, leading firms into what turned out to be technological cul-de-sacs that did not generate anything useful for either the public or the private sector. By the 1970s, the civilian market was far larger than the military market, and it has since proved to be more than capable of sustaining its own momentum. The initial congruence of military and civilian needs that grew up largely as a consequence of the inchoate nature of the latter disappeared as the commercial market developed. From that point on, public support was as often a hindrance as a help to innovation: 'Indeed, most spillovers today probably flow in the reverse direction. Recent advances in circuit density and the associated improvement in memory and microprocessor capacity have been aimed first at civilian applications . . . the circuits now purchased by the military are several years behind the best practice technology in terms of line width and circuit function destiny.'[5]

The power of procurement policy arises from the fact that it provides a powerful channel through which at least certain types of users can express their needs to innovators. Further, procurement contracts are often large enough to guarantee that a sufficiently large market for the innovation exists to make it worth pursuing. There is, of course, no reason why one need rely on military expenditures to have this effect. Japan, for example, has successfully nurtured a computer industry using both protectionism and, more interestingly, certain types of promotion policies, including financial assistance, the sponsorship of co-operative R & D projects, and a quasi-governmental computer rental company called the Japanese Electronic Computer Company (JECC). The JECC acted as a sort of centralized buying agency that helped to develop the domestic market for computers by making them available to as wide a range of users as possible. Basically, it bought computers from the member firms that owned it, and then rented them to the public at rather low fees. Rental contracts at low rates not only created a wide pool of users but more importantly, enabled users to upgrade the quality of their machines as fast as domestic firms could introduce innovations. This, of course, created incentives for firms to continually improve their products. It is important to emphasize that the demand for computers expressed to computer producers through the JECC did not involve the JECC in second guessing private sector needs. The JECC only bought computers that users wished to rent; it acted as a focal point for demand rather than as a source of demand itself. This arbitrage function effectively expanded the domestic market for computers, providing a channel through which user needs could be communicated to the producers of computers, and it enabled support to be provided to firms in the computer industry that was tied to user demands for their products. As the domestic market developed, the JECC gradually disengaged, and the share of the domestic market served by computers rented through the JECC declined from 65% in the 1960s to about 11% in the early 1980s.[6]

Procurement policy is not, of course, likely to be very successful if it is poorly implemented. One rather typical failure of many procurement programmes is poor targeting. 'Buy British' purchasing strategies that are not focused on high tech products, that treat foreign multinationals who operate in the UK as if they were indigenous producers, or that encourage UK firms to reinvent the wheel when licensing technology developed abroad is cheaper are not likely to provide very much stimulation to the UK's scientific and technological base. The UK government has, for example, tried to use the oil discoveries of the late 1960s to assist companies in the UK offshore supplies industry to rejuvenate themselves, directing a 70% share of total expenditure on offshore petroleum exploration and development towards them. The policy has not, however, had much impact on the technological capabilities of indigenous firms as most of the expenditure has been channelled to areas where their pre-existing capabilities were strong. High technology specialist equipment has often been imported or bought from subsidiaries of foreign firms who were treated as if they were British, and the competitive position of indigenous firms has not been appreciably strengthened.

There is also nothing to be gained by trying to push firms faster than they are capable of moving. Firms that have consistently lagged behind the expanding frontier of technological advance are unlikely to be able to make up lost ground quickly no matter how big the procurement policy pull is. Strategies that encourage them to move towards the frontier (e.g. through licensing technologies developed elsewhere) must be successfully implemented before they can be expected to push back the frontier. The development of System X by the UK telecommunications industry, for example, went wrong in part because a decision was taken not to buy the necessary technology from abroad (where it was available), but, rather, to encourage UK firms to start almost from scratch. Licensing was acknowledged at the time to be a quicker and a cheaper way to update UK telecommunications services, but it was dismissed in the hope that a more ambitious policy might be used as a lever to stimulate a rather sleepy and unprogressive domestic supply industry. Users of phones in the UK will be paying the price of this poorly judged decision for quite some time to come. Licensing is, of course, a strategy that Japan has repeatedly utilized to enable it to catch up with, and then leap past international rivals in telecommunications and elsewhere.[7]

The kinds of procurement policies typically used throughout Europe have also often been a major disappointment because they have relied on the use of national champions or protected national suppliers. This strategy is usually justified on the grounds that large-scale highly integrated projects are an efficient way to generate new technologies, and is frequently buttressed by quite spurious claims about the need to maintain national security. However, the success enjoyed by both the US semi-conductor industry and collaborative programmes like Airbus suggests that large-scale research programmes can be successfully managed without relying on a protected national supplier. The problem with national champions is that protected markets have a way of eroding incentives to operate efficiently. Lacking any kind of yardstick competition to establish acceptable performance standards, public authorities have no substantive basis upon which to evaluate their performance and, naturally, the protected firms themselves have little incentive to perform existing activities to high standards since their market is assured come what may. The problem of ensuring an adequate performance by client contractors is a well known problem in the UK defence sector, and one that the MOD is slowly attempting to rectify.

Even less satisfactory have been the feeble attempts of defence contractors to apply the technology developed for the MOD to civilian uses. Spillovers from the UK defence sector to the civilian sector have been virtually non-existent. Most UK defence contractors are highly specialized in defence work and their subsidiaries are generally autonomously managed, paying little or no attention to exploring the possibilities of multilateral technology transfers between divisions, or in developing civilian spin-off products. It has been argued that the decentralization of operating divisions within these firms inhibits spillovers, and that gearing their corporate strategies to the demands of defence procurement (i.e. customer initiated and engineering led projects that lack strong cost controls) has robbed them of not only the incentive, but also the ability to seek out and respond to the needs of private sector firms. 'Thus defence companies in particular (and protected telecommunications suppliers to some extent as well) have tended to become trapped in a cycle of increasing dependence on these protected sectors and increasingly distinctive management structures and styles. The overwhelming evidence is that few companies world wide with significant involvement in the defence industry have been able to foster the kind of skills required to compete equally well in commercial business. Despite statements of intent to diversify, most foreign as well as UK defence orientated companies have become steadily more dependent on defence sales through time.'[8]

In short, there is no reason to think that carefully designed procurement programmes cannot be used to provide a major stimulus encouraging UK firms to invest in science and technology. Provided that clear signals about user needs are given, that a judicious mix of licensing and support for basic research is chosen and, perhaps above all, providing that the client industry is kept in a reasonably competitive state, then demand can be expected to pull domestic supplier industries up to and then beyond current technological frontiers.[9]

Creating a demand for innovations means, of course, expressing real user needs to those responsible for developing the innovation. The virtues of procurement policy are not only that it is an effective way to express needs to suppliers, but, perhaps more importantly, that it enables policy makers to express needs that markets either could not or would not be able to express. A prime example of needs that markets have difficulty in expressing are those associated with public goods that benefit all consumers in ways that are not appropriable by putative producers. As a consequence, assessing the true demand by consumers for such goods is complicated by the tendency of consumers to free ride, understating the intensity of their demand in an attempt to avoid contributing a share of the costs that reflects their need for, or likely usage of, the good. The general presumption of most economists is that such goods will be under-provided by markets. Although this does not, of course, mean that public sector decision-making will necessarily improve on the private sector provision of such goods, this is a possibility that cannot be dismissed out of hand. A classic example of a public good is, of course, a clean and healthy environment. Markets will never provide support for an adequate amount of research on energy conservation, hazardous waste, acid rain, the greenhouse effect, and so on (see Chapter 9). Properly directed spending on protecting the environment will not only provide residents of the UK with a more enjoyable place to live, it will also provide British industry with the technological know-how that it can apply throughout an increasingly green conscious world.

A second example of needs that markets will not generally express in their fullest intensity are those that give rise to externalities – that is, goods that provide knock-on benefits or spillovers well beyond their initial sphere of application. The problem is, again, that social and private rates of return diverge because private decision makers cannot appropriate all of the benefits that they create (or do not internalize all of the costs they generate for others). Although public sector agents may not be able to fully implement the appropriate remedies to restore private sector incentives, there is no doubt that they ought to be able to ameliorate egregious market failures of this type. Investments in infrastructure that give rise to positive externalities are a classic illustration of the kind of market failure that government activity ought to be able to rectify and the development of a national fibre optic cable network is an example of an investment project that is valuable both for the services that it provides to users, as well as for the considerable benefits that suppliers of the network will enjoy (see the essay by Nigel Stanley in this volume). Like the environmental 'big project' proposed in the report of the Policy Review Group, a project that supports the installation of a fibre optic cable network (or, if we have to wait that long, its technological successor) promises considerable potential benefits not only because it is an example of the kind of demand-pull policies that have worked well elsewhere, but also it is a strategically shrewd choice of a sector where major investments in science and technology could yield big dividends to consumers.

One final word is in order. However carefully they are designed, large public procurement projects tend, nevertheless, to make many public and private sector agents uneasy, and with good reason. As System X, Nimrod and other ill-fated public procurement ventures have amply demonstrated, Britain's lack of managerial talent is not confined to the private sector. An outdated, Victorian conception of excellence, a clubby but thoroughgoing resistance to scrutiny by outsiders, and unnecessary restrictions on recruitment into senior positions have made the UK Civil Service a rather uncertain instrument to use in managing all but the most routine tasks. Just as a vigorous and competitive private sector requires a supporting infrastructure, so a vigorous and proactive public sector also requires an infrastructure, albeit of a slightly different sort. Given that procurement policy is an efficient way to stimulate industrial innovation, it follows that a necessary concomitant of any activist policy to encourage investment in science and technology is that of investing in public sector human capital. Good ideas are all well and good, but without good hands they remain no more than just good ideas. Investment in management training and development by the private sector must be matched by no less active an investment strategy to develop managerial skills in the public sector. The two investment strategies are necessary complements – and not necessarily substitutes – because in the area of science and technology policy, public policy and business policy must work together if the UK is to regain its place in world markets.

Conclusion

As numerous right wing think tanks have repeatedly demonstrated, very little imagination is required to express a generalized scepticism about any kind of positive policy proposal, and no intelligence whatsoever is needed to turn vague scepticism into arguments for *laissez-faire*. Unfortunately, the half dozen or so senior ministers that Mrs Thatcher has saddled the DTI with over the past decade have turned in performances that also conform to this precept. The report of the Labour Party's Policy Review Group, 'Competing for Prosperity', is extremely welcome, not least because it provides a real alternative to the policy of disengagement that many Tories seem to regard as a creative piece of industrial policy-making. Although some of the proposals contained in the report are not very promising, others are likely to bring substantial benefits to industry if properly implemented. The evidence suggests that genuine supply-side initiatives like the BTE can effectively stimulate the growth of new innovative firms in high tech, sunrise sectors, and that a judicious administration of and investment in public procurement programmes can provide both necessary consumption goods for the public and a chance for supplier industries to catch up with and then leap ahead of international rivals.

Notes

1 See Labour Party, 1989, *Meet the Challenge, Make the Change – A New Agenda for Britain. Final Report of Labour's Policy Review for the 1990s*, Labour Party, London.

2 Keith Pavitt and his colleagues in SPRU at the University of Sussex have traced the origins of more than 4000 major commercial innovations introduced in the UK between 1945 and 1983. Firms smaller than 1,000 employees (in the UK) accounted for nearly 43% of the total number of innovations. In 1975, firms with over 10,000 employees accounted for over 80% of R & D spending, but only 47% of innovations introduced. By contrast, 112 small firms of less than 100 employees produced 12% of the total number of innovations, but did no R & D. See K. Pavitt, *et al*, 1987, 'The Size Distribution of Innovating Firms in the UK: 1945–83, *Journal of Industrial Economics*, vol. 35, pp. 297–316, and references cited therein.

3 See P. Stoneman, 1987, *The Economic Analysis of Technology Policy*, Oxford University Press, Oxford, Chapter 15, and R. Rothwell and W. Zegveld, 1981, *Industrial Innovation and Public Policy*, Frances Pinter Ltd., London, Chapter 6.

4 Cited in D. Coates, 1980, *Labour in Power? A Study of the Labour Government 1974–79*, Longman, London, pp. 90. For further discussion of the NEB, see W. Grant, 1982, *The Political Economy of Industrial Policy*, Butterworths, London, and J. Cubbin and P. Geroski, 'Industrial Policy and the 1974–1979 Labour Government', mimeo, London Business School.

5 See R. Levin, 1982, 'The Semi-Conductor Industry' in R. Nelson (ed.), *Government and Technical Progress*, Pergamon Press, Oxford, pp. 66; other useful discussions of semi-conductors can be found in J. Tilton, 1971, *International Diffusion of Technology: The Case of Semi-Conductors*, Brookings Institution, Washington, and E. Braun and S. MacDonald, *Revolution in Miniature*, 2nd ed., Cambridge University Press, Cambridge.

6 See M. Anchordoghy, 1988, 'Mastering the Market: Japanese Government Targeting of the Computer Industry', *International Organisation*, vol. 42, pp. 509–543. For an account of the considerable role played by conventional procurement policies (not all of which were initiated by the Pentagon) in stimulating the development of the US computer industry, see B. Katz and A. Phillips, 1982, 'The Computer Industry' in R. Nelson (ed.), *Government and Technical Progress*, Pergamon Press, Oxford.

7 On the policy towards the UK offshore supplies industry, see R. Rothwell and W. Zegveld, 1988, *Reindustrialisation and Technology*, Longman, London, pp. 124–6. On System X, see P. Grindley, 'System X: The Failure of Procurement', mimeo, Centre for Business Strategy, London Business School. Grindley suggests that there were about £5b hidden costs associated with this domestic procurement policy, doubling the apparent cost of the system.

8 See McKinsey & Co., 1988, *Strengthening Competitiveness in UK Electronics*, NEDO, London, pp. 75. Further discussion of these issues can be found in the Maddock Report, *Civil Exploitation of Defence Technology*, NEDO, London, 1983.

9   For a further development of this analysis, see P. Geroski, 'Procurement Policy as a Tool of Industrial Policy', forthcoming *International Review of Applied Economics*.

The state as public entrepreneur

Introduction

For some years economic policy in Britain has been infected by polarized extremes; state versus industry; public versus private; subsidy versus profit. There is a clear need for all of these dimensions: the state demonstrably cannot do everything, and the private sector represents partial interests. The question for us now is how we can develop a new concept of public enterprise for investment in industry. We do not just mean the provision of 'soft' finance by the state; we mean a much more sophisticated inter-weaving of practices and policies from both the public and private sectors to promote economic growth and opportunities for all. The aim of this chapter is to explain our approach to the local state's role in industrial investment, a role which was characterized as 'devel-opmental' in Chapter 1. In contrast to the role at national level, we believe that the local state *should* get involved in operational detail in the market place as an entrepreneur, identifying underprovision by the private sector and providing services on a business-like basis.

It is also important to tackle the centralist approach to economic policy in Britain of both the public and private sectors in order to redress regional imbalances in economic opportunities and prosperity. As suggested in the Policy Review of the Labour Party in 1989,[1] a devolved network of investment boards, regional investment banks – co-ordinated by a British Investment Bank – along with a regional focus for pension funds, provides a positive framework for national economic growth. It is not only superior to the top-down approach advocated and practised by governments in the past, but is also superior to the present London-centred system resulting from the concentration of private sector investment and location decisions. Our comments are about developing more precisely the role of the public sector at regional level within this overall economic strategy. Our experience is drawn from our work at Greater London Enterprise, where a public sector development agency, created by London local authorities, has successfully worked with the private sector. Our experience indicates ways in which the public and private sectors could work together more effectively within a different national economic framework. We also look at other examples.

Political opinion is probably in broad agreement that public investment does not just mean providing finance. The chapter by Peter Totterdill provides a useful summary of the major arguments for a comprehensive infrastructure, although we would be more cautious about the ability of the British state to engage successfully in 'sector strategies' beyond certain limits, particularly at a regional level. This chapter develops the integrated approach which combines finance with a wide range of other services to strengthen economic growth in specific companies and projects based on local sector research and specific sector skills. It is also designed to ensure that in the development of economic potential all social groups benefit from these resources.

But it is not only what is provided that matters; the way that this is done is equally important. Other proposals for the role of the public sector contain very little about method, often characterizing the state as some '*deus* (or *dea!*) *ex machina*' crafting its own superior logic of sectoral intervention on to a desolate map of private sector chaos.

In contrast we argue that to be effective in meeting social and economic goals, public investment agencies should operate as players within the mixed economy. They should also deploy the business methods developed by the most successful companies in the private sector, but in the context of a planned approach based on social goals. A common response from the Left to these ideas is that they represent no more than an attempt to beat the enemy at its own game – 'trying to be better capitalists than capitalists'. This is not our goal.

What we are describing is more complex – entrepreneurship in the public interest. It requires ingenuity to devise new operations and services in response to unmet and changing needs, and creativity to develop the right tools for the job, but seldom are the various business methods available appropriate for the job. They can be useful means, but they have been developed to fit specific narrow sectional interests. To fit broader economic aims they must be remodelled – as tools appropriate to the social management of investment. Addressing the inadequacies of the market and re-modelling business methods often reveals the inefficiencies of capital. Far from assuming that markets (and capitalists) are perfect, we think it is often not very difficult to be better than many capitalists and that public agencies should strive to be more efficient than their private counterparts.

Market versus the plan

The dogmatic orthodox Marxist and traditional Labour view that the market is bad and the public sector good must be firmly rejected. The experiences both of Western European social democracies – where the market has met many consumer and social needs successfully – and of the Eastern European socialist economies – where the public sector has manifestly failed to meet social need – demonstrate the redundancy of traditional leftist thinking on this subject.

We should accept that a growing involvement of the private sector in the public sphere need not necessarily threaten the achievement of democratic socialist policies. A number of Western European social democracies – Sweden and Austria in particular – furnish us with useful practical and successful experiences in this respect. Therefore when it comes to deciding whether the public or private sector is best placed to provide a product or a service neither one nor the other should be selected on the grounds of ideological principle.

The public sector should intervene and regulate on the basis that it represents non-sectional interests. It is not accountable to one group of private shareholders or consumers as opposed to another. But this does not mean it is 'neutral'. Far from it. The state should act to stimulate growth and to bring greater equity in the distribution of economic opportunities and benefits, not through personal tax incentives unrelated to investment but by clearly promoting productive investment and high quality employment As such it can promote different coalitions of interests. Once a government's direction becomes distorted by a specific sectional interest, be it trade unions under a Labour government or a local authority, or a particular business lobby under a Conservative government, or perhaps other more corrupt influences, then it is recognized as being partial, and its legitimacy can break down.

The private sector operates on behalf of sectional interests, but this does not mean that planning is the prerogative of the public sector. Although planning techniques are most closely associated with the public sector, private enterprises rely on business plans to chart their progress in meeting investment, production and marketing goals, to demonstrate the implications of different courses of action and to provide targets. Many companies – both large and small – would welcome the opportunity to collaborate with regional and national plans if it could be shown that they would benefit from the outcome of this longer-term approach. They recognize that their long-term prospects depend on the development of a sound social and economic infrastructure – ranging from the availability of skilled labour, adequate social facilities, transport and social and political stability.

What the market does not do

Markets do meet many consumer and social needs and have the capacity to be responsive to changing needs. However there are very obvious inadequacies to market-based provision, often based on short-term requirements of shareholders, where public agencies which can perceive the long-term public interest or economic interest are required. The British experience in the 1980s amply demonstrates the nature of these shortcomings.

In the UK, the markets supplying investment capital, investment in research and development, business training and elements of physical intrastructure do not fully meet the wide-ranging needs of businesses. Nor do they by any means identify the potentially profitable opportunities which exist in meeting some of these needs. It is the conventional wisdom in the City that smaller venture capital investments, for example, are more risky and time consuming, and they therefore cannot be accommodated within 'normal' commercial parameters.[2] It is interesting that the powerful market trend towards large, highly leveraged (indebted) management buyouts which dominated unquoted investment from the mid

1980s, was seriously threatened in 1989 as a result of rising interest rates.[3] There are also those companies which have growth potential which are not necessarily 'in the market' seeking finance. These have to be sought out and developed. This means that promoting growth also involves generating investment opportunities, and often being prepared to invest smaller sums than 'the market'. From our experience at GLE this is apparent even in London where there is a need for greater economic growth in many areas. This demonstrates a need for an active economic agent to work hard at generating profitable investment opportunities working closely with the London Boroughs. The conventional approach also means that a number of promising investment proposals are overlooked, especially those presented by companies headed by ethnic minorities, women and people with disabilities or businesses targeting specific social markets unfamiliar to conventional investors.

Another example is technology. Britain's record in funding technological development is depressing. An OECD report in 1989 suggested that Britain was the only Western industrial economy in which the percentage of national income devoted to research and development actually declined during the first half of the 1980s, against a background of strong growth in expenditure elsewhere.[4] But, as we have suggested earlier, both with venture capital in general and technology in particular, making finance available is not enough; developing companies also often need day-to-day advice and help in marketing, accountancy, product development and training where they lack experience and expertise.[5] This type of 'hands-on' service is very different from the market's version in the UK which is often limited to putting a director on the board and quite different from providing the range of back-up services which we will describe below.

Nor does the market unaided encourage a fair distribution of economic opportunities. Current education and training policies underutilize the skills of a number of disadvantaged social groups, especially those with a background of deprivation and hardship, particularly in certain regions of the UK such as the inner cities and Northern Ireland. Ethnic minorities, women and people with disabilities are other obvious examples of groups which suffer additional inequity in terms of job opportunities. The Conservative government's version of supply-side economic policy for most of the 1980s has meant that these concerns are seen as irrelevant or peripheral to the direct role of central and local government and instead responsibility and funding has been shifted to charity and 'corporate giving' along with exhortations for a greater voluntary role for the 'active citizen'.

It is economically inefficient to underutilize 'human capital' in this fashion. Britain fares particularly badly in its development of skills relative to its European partners. Research conducted in France and West Germany by the National Institute for Economic and Social Research shows that the level of technical qualifications of crafts employees is far superior to the standards achieved in the UK.[6] One recent report on training in the retail industry stated that the UK was creating 'a certificated semi-literate underclass'.[7]

In order to address these problems the traditional role of the public sector has been to provide subsidized finance in order to promote economic welfare and to promote new initiatives. In other words, a way of generalizing or socializing the cost of growth, or the cost of longer-term investment expenditure, is traditionally for the state to provide incentives to encourage investment in the private sector in the form of subsidies through cheap loans, tax breaks, capital grants and so on. Under different regimes these may be granted to individual firms in a fairly *ad hoc* manner or through sector priorities or regional policy. The question arises as to whether this subsidizing role is acceptable in all its variants and whether the state should be much more of an entrepreneur in its own right, making profits and adding commercial as well as social value. This raises the issue about what the investment is trying to achieve, and how its success or failure should be measured.

Redefining the public sector's role

During the post-war economic consensus in the UK – and indeed in all industrialized capitalist countries – the state's role in the economy was many-sided. Through a combination of macro-economic fiscal and monetary policies and longer-term social and economic policy (including regional policy), governments worked to promote economic development, often compensating directly for the imperfections of private sector provision. Intervention involved governments mainly in providing goods and services in areas where it was generally agreed to be uneconomic or unprofitable for the private sector to do so, as well as monitoring the standards and quality of private sector output.

The economic decline produced over the last ten years[8] indicates quite clearly the need for state intervention in the economy – both to catalyse economic development and to provide economic and social infrastructure. However the problem with previous Labour government policies, for example, has been the style and substance of public sector involvement. Too often central direction or nationalization has been the panacea intended to compensate for market failings, involving perhaps an arrogance of judgement. Central direction or public ownership may be required in certain areas but the public sector does not necessarily have all the answers. Of course the private sector has major failings, but frequently the public sector has been out of step with the best and most dynamic elements of the private. The internal management of public sector organization has frequently been inflexible and unresponsive.

The 1989 Policy Review of the Labour Party placed an emphasis on decentralization but this only goes part of the way in correcting the centralized 'bureaucratism' associated with much public sector provision. Our concern is to redefine the forms and scope of public sector and public agency involvement in the economy. Generally speaking we want to develop a strategy in which the state and its agents pursue social and broad economic goals in as efficient and creative a way as the best private sector companies seek increased profits. We want to see the emergence of the state as a 'public entrepreneur'.

Public and/or private

Like the best capitalists, public agencies supplying services for industrial growth need to be flexible, dynamic and targeted. There is also a strong case for public organizations working in partnership with the private sector in joint ventures structurally linking both the public interest and commercial dimensions to meet combined social and efficiency objectives.

But in the first instance it is often up to the public sector first to identify needs which are inadequately met by the private sector and then to establish services as necessary on social or broader economic grounds. Although there may be an upside profit potential in the longer term, the downside front-end investment in a new untested area will probably not be attractive to private capital bound by short-term financial imperatives.

In some cases, once established, there is a justification for retaining services wholly in the public sector, where they require major subsidy or where competition could be detrimental or non-existent. But we should not be religious on this count[9] and there may well be a case for incentivizing private organizations to take over delivery of the goods altogether, since these unmet needs can also mean potential opportunities for the market.

Another alternative is for the private sector to take an interest as a partner in a public/private joint venture either as manager or investor in the operation. Clearly this participation will depend on the return potential.

An interesting example of public and private collaboration is Initiatives SA, (ISA), a company created by Barcelona City Hall to act as a launch-pad for new businesses with a public dimension. The ISA board combines local government, the trade unions and the private sector. The company backs businesses in a range of industries – new technology and communications, industrial waste processing, traffic systems, leisure and tourism, urban development and financial services. Sometimes ISA sets up these businesses, whereas others have already been established by private capital. In both situations ISA takes a minority stake in each company for a limited period of three to six years.

In either scenario, under private or joint public/private control, it will probably be necessary to develop specific monitoring mechanisms to ensure that the social elements are maintained and, if necessary, to subsidize their continuity. But having played a creative part as an entrepreneurial initiator, the public sector can turn its resources and social creativity to developing new projects. In this way the public sector plays a more actively interventionist role than the more conventional catalyst, enabler or broker. The public sector maximizes its effectiveness by acting initially as entrepreneur and later manager or monitor. It participates as an active player in the market-place, taking profits generated from its investments whilst adhering to a planned approach based on long-term socially defined goals benefiting broad economic interests.

Public business

Having mentioned public sector subsidies, we should clarify what we do or do not mean by this. First we do not go along with assumptions that the greater the subsidy the greater the public benefit. There are plenty of examples which demonstrate that throwing money at problems does not necessarily resolve them and in some instances can make matters worse. We believe there is no case for subsidy, if with effective management and an innovative approach to generating income, a service can be self-financing. In fact the onus should be on all organizations to justify their claim for state support on the basis of a long-term plan demonstrating how within their objectives, they could use their assets and skills to increase their revenue. Obviously in some cases which are essentially non-viable, dedicating scarce skills to raising funds or making money is an unacceptable diversion (though there is often room for the more efficient management of resources). But where there is a clear case for subsidy – for non-viable services or in developing self-financing initiatives – then this should be tightly targeted with performance against targets regularly measured. As Paul Geroski argues in his chapter on investment in science and technology, the emphasis should be on output, otherwise public funds are likely to be wasted and can easily conceal inefficiencies.

Where public agencies, with their specific developmental role, are players in the market-place, this requires an ability to operate within the competitive arena and its profit imperative. For this reason we advocate that the public agencies taking an active role in economic and business development should themselves operate on a business-like basis, sharing in profits resulting from their investments. But this does not mean maximizing profit for its own sake. Unlike the private sector, this means that generating returns or profits as part of the social agenda is not an end in itself. Instead it means that the state must fulfil the aim of launching and managing new initiatives which meet social goals as effectively as the private sector pursues profit.

In Sweden the government is taking ideas of this sort very seriously, with the creation of a new high level unit in the Civil Department charged with improving public sector efficiency through combining the best of the public and private sector methods. This involves the introduction of new management systems, decentralization, introducing new financial controls, strengthening relations with the private sector and adopting the company model for more local authority operations. And Greater London Enterprise was recently visited by the entire staff of its Stockholm counterpart, keen to explore a new, more commercial approach to the management of regional investment.

Organizationally this course involves taking the tools of business, its methods and systems and adapting these to serve different ends. For instance, marketing investment services to different consumers such as women and ethnic minorities; incorporating the social interests of the community, consumers and producers in the appraisal of investment opportunities. In management it means combining social and commercial objectives in setting targets and considerable internal flexibility with negotiated bonuses and rewards given to staff on the basis of merit in return for performance against these targets.

A critical question in the implementation of this concept of the entrepreneural public/private hybrid, is personnel. Without commercially oriented people with a social or interventionist outlook, such plans remain on the drawing board. Their detailed development relies on advisers and civil servants with experience in the market-place. Making them happen depends on managers prepared to combine and balance developmental goals with business operations as well as being able to devise a developmental framework for profitable investment which is sensitive to local needs. Although personnel with commercial and industrial experience are vital to the success of enterprise boards, it is important to recognize that these skills have to be redirected to serve broader economic ends; otherwise by default profit maximization assumes priority, with the social and developmental goals relegated to bolt-on philanthropic options possible only when and if profits achieve certain levels. It is a new public sector entrepreneurial culture which has to be developed and we still have a long way to progress before we succeed in this.

Greater London Enterprise

The best way to explain how public entrepreneurship might work is to give a practical example, using an enterprise board – Greater London Enterprise (GLE) which was taken over by London Boroughs upon the demise of the GLC in 1986. GLE is concerned with seeking out opportunities for strengthening the economic potential of the businesses and people of London. The main objective is to tackle the problems of companies denied the facilities necessary to realize their growth potential – usually smaller businesses – while ensuring these opportunities are open to all social groups. These facilities include risk finance, premises, training and technological development. In doing this the organization addresses underprovision in the market and develops new operations. Some of these services GLE will retain under its control, some will be established as joint ventures and others, once established, should be floated off to operate under private control.

In operational terms the organization's goal is to combine certain business methods with the best of appropriate public sector practices with maximum effect.

GLE has four major areas of activity reflecting the economic needs of the region. These activities are funded by GLE's own resources and by raising external funds for management.

(1) *Technology and innovation*
Promotion of technical development and innovation by
(a) managing collaborative European programmes of work in areas such as computer systems and training technology;
(b) funding new ideas and embryonic technology to develop product prototypes and business strategies;
(c) investment in technical development of products to bring them to the market place.

(2) *Corporate investment*
Provision of risk capital for trading companies by
(a) active development of new opportunities to invest in companies wishing to expand;
(b) investment of venture and development capital with extensive back-up services to strengthen management, financial systems, marketing and to promote training and good employment practices;
(c) business incentive schemes through joint public/private sponsorship of low interest loans for ethnic minority enterprises and businesses run by women, people with disabilities and the long-term unemployed.

(3) *Skill development and training*
Supplying training courses and development programmes
(a) for companies and public bodies requiring business develop-
    ment training;
(b) by a Training Charter whereby the training needs of each
    employee in a company receiving GLE development capital can
    be addressed.

(4) *Workspace*
Investment in industrial and commercial property
(a) industrial estates and premises to provide premises for
    businesses;
(b) managed business centres with central services for small
    companies;
(c) development of new business units for sale; larger-scale
    developments through the GLE-Rosehaugh joint venture.

In each area GLE's work entails identifying the shortcomings
and gaps in the market, then spotting and developing opportunities
as they arise where the required services can be supplied within the
resource and return constraints which apply in each area. Although
the social agenda is paramount, this is essentially an entrepreneurial
role similar to private enterprise, requiring market investigation of
niche areas, business plans and tight targets.

In a few areas where the income generated is such that continued
subsidy is necessary, then these initiatives will remain under GLE's
umbrella, drawing in the maximum levels of public and private
sponsorship. Most operations however, are already, or will be
profitable by late 1991. Here GLE is an active player in the market-
place providing specialist services. In some areas there is a case for
GLE to retain a controlling interest where operations are beyond
the initial risk stage and fully established, to ensure that their social
orientation is maintained. In others once their profit potential is
demonstrated, there is no reason why they should not be privately
managed with the public sector retaining a monitoring role to
ensure that the original concept is maintained. In addition public
and private joint venture structures are either already established or
under discussion. These add expertise and bring access to new
opportunities to expand services and markets. Where we are selling
an interest, the cash from the new joint venture partner provides the

necessary resource to start new projects. The common factor in all these operations is that GLE has taken the initiative and initial risk in its role as public entrepreneur.

GLE is now organized as a corporate group, with some ten subsidiary companies established with working capital from the initial funding largely provided by the GLC. The enterprise board now receives no public funding and to maintain its developmental and investment role it must grow, making an overall profit as a group and expanding its underlying asset base. Each company must generate income compatible with its specific framework of long-term, social objectives and reduce its costs to the minimum. This is quite different from the conventional approach of maximizing profit as the primary goal, but it does require the same skills and experience to be brought to the task within a structure of management systems and targets reflecting GLE's social goals.

Obviously the operations of the organization reflect the current political and economic climate. Enterprise boards could certainly expand their range and the extent of activities as part of a comprehensive plan and a public infrastructure for developing the economy. With additional public resources, they could without doubt increase their effectiveness, but we do not believe there is necessarily any automatic correlation between state subsidy and output.

The government's abolition of the GLC and metropolitan county councils and its constraints on public expenditure at local level have forced enterprise boards to re-examine new ways of financing investment, generating income and cutting costs. Most boards now raise the main part of their funds for venture capital investment from pension funds and the private sector. They do not have the same restrictions placed on borrowings as are imposed on local authorities and raise further funds for property investment secured against their industrial property portfolios. Along with rental income, fee income for services such as fund-management has become increasingly important in providing a revenue stream to sustain their operations. At GLE operating costs need to be continually examined within the context of the longer-term more hands-on approach.

Having tackled the very difficult job of transforming an organization which consumed some £20 million a year of public funds with no serious prospects of a financial return on investment, to one

which has already began to operate on a financially effective basis,
we can see no virtue in putting the clock back. Quite the reverse.
Whether we are appraising prospective investments or managing
our own affairs, we should consistently apply standards and criteria
of financial and management efficiency.

That is not to say that we would turn our back on additional
funds. Currently our chief source of income for non-viable
programmes such as investment in start-up enterprises and some
employment-related training, comes as a cross-subsidy from profits
made elsewhere in the Group. But an absence of large profits
certainly limits the scope and effectiveness in these areas and in our
view the benefits justify increased public funding specifically
targeted for these purposes. But using public grant aid to compensate for poor investment decisions, inefficient management or a
lack of inventiveness in seeking out income-generating opportunities, is no longer acceptable.

Correspondingly, the Conservative government's inducements
to appeal to the largesse of large corporations is also a doubtful
strategy. GLE has done well in attracting such income (especially
given its political roots). But dependency on favours hardly
amounts to a policy and there are understandable limitations on the
possibilities of private enterprise agreeing to grant aid where there
is little benefit to be had other than some possible kudos. There is
certainly no prospect of planning sensibly on this basis. We should
not be wasting considerable time and resources in the long queue,
waiting cap in hand for favours and often very limited funds. By
contrast, our approach at GLE is to work with the private sector as
partners in enterprise, benefiting from their funds and expertise
within a business relationship.

Synergy

Venture capital investment in enterprises is designed to make a
profit through the long-term increase in the worth or value of the
company, rather than in short-term interest or dividend payments.
We can add commercial as well as social value to a company by not
only providing the right kind of long-term equity finance, but also
by providing a range of additional resources. These might include
training, or personnel services, company secretarial or legal
support, help on production layout and management, technical

support, advice or practical help with property or new premises. Companies are charged a fee for the tailor-made range of services which help all-round development of the investment, enhance the quality of employment, and represent a real 'hands-on' assistance for the investor. This income also adds to the viability of the venture capital operation.

As an illustration of this, an extreme version of the approach is provided by an investment in a company which manufactures Indian snacks and chilled foods. The company had inadequate food storage and preparation processes, health and safety procedures were poor, and turnover was struggling. What the company did have was a dedicated workforce and potentially excellent products based on unique recipes.

GLE invested in the company and committed a lot of time and effort. The enterprise board's involvement led to drastic improvements to premises layout to comply with the conditions of supply to major retailers, along with health and safety training courses and high level safety measures. An individual training programme was designed for each employee. Where there was a language difficulty courses were translated into the appropriate language, and where there was literacy difficulty the courses were put onto cassette. After the development work was completed the company became an accredited supplier to major high street retailers like Marks and Spencer. In doing so it made the leap from cottage industry to factory production.

In the course of the public sector work the company received a National Training Award. This is not to say that the company had no difficulty subsequently and in fact a major share of the investment was sold on to a larger manufacturer so that the enterprise board retained a smaller part of a national producer. It is, however, an interesting example showing how commercial and social value can be created at the local level by a public agency developing and participating in a wealth-creating opportunity which improves the quality of its employment in a key sector for ethnic minorities. Although not every investment involves such an array of back-up services, it is an example which demonstrates how finance can be only a part of investment necessary for success.

We believe therefore that the market inadequacies of training, finance, research and development, and property, have important overlaps. A company needs finance and premises; it requires support on technical layout, or patents. All this is especially the case at the small to medium sized company level where the company neither has the expertise, nor can it possibly afford to deal with all these issues. It also cannot necessarily secure the best investment solution if the different resources are not co-ordinated. This makes a regional infrastructure so important.

Regional investment

It is therefore very important that proposals such as those put forward by the Labour Party contain an organizational coherence; that, for example, a low interest loan scheme is also related to the work of regional enterprise boards, and that the proposed British Technology Enterprise has regional interests. We would suggest that this is accomplished through the regional banks being joint ventures between a British Investment Bank and regional enterprise boards; similarly that British Technology Enterprise be a shareholder in regional enterprise boards, either through joint subsidiaries, or in the boards themselves. This would help link the different facets of investment together, and also provide a solid regional dimension to investment.

We do also feel that cheap loans or grants as a generic policy measure in themselves are inadequate. This theme is also developed in the chapter on regional renaissance and industrial regeneration. Their justification rests on some of the traditional arguments about the role of the state – that it is a subsidizer and that the benefit of the subsidy is socialized through the greater economic benefit bestowed upon, and created by the subsidized company. This approach is not all that convincing when sectional interests – private managers and shareholders – are often the main beneficiaries from subsidies. We believe that the public sector should directly benefit too. Therefore a low interest loan, or low coupon preference shares, should be exercised in conjunction with a profit participation by the public sector either from the start of an investment or in the future by way of options. Hence the importance of introducing the approach of regional enterprise boards into the investment infrastructure.

Regional investment of the kind we describe is not aimed at promoting one area against another. Investment activity is designed to add to the sum total of investment capital, training, workspace and services available. Some analyses of regional investment appear to assume that there is a fixed amount of opportunities, and to invest in one area is to deprive another. Our approach does not assume such a zero-sum game.

We see enterprise boards as wealth creators, adding to the market by dealing with supply-side underprovision. They must make a net addition to value and wealth. Their investment must add to product ranges, must create better quality output and employment, must provide finance, services and opportunities where none properly existed, must support technical innovation where the market is deficient. The result has to be a better productive and competitive base for the UK economy. The stronger base is needed in order to expand the tax base for improving social services and the quality of life, as well as providing managers and employees with fulfilling and high quality jobs and wealth creating opportunities.

We can prioritize certain sectors with growth potential at the regional, and even national, level, but this means tackling clear supply-side underprovision. We believe that there are capital needs in certain areas of the electronics industry and in the media industry. We manage specific funds to address these needs. We manage European programmes designed to promote new forms of computer aided systems for the machine tool industry. Britain is appallingly weak in these high value added sectors, particularly in engineering and electronics.[10] Our work is targeted at investment and specific programmes geared to a particular product or company within commercial parameters. However, we believe that the potential role of the state in sector strategies must not be exaggerated. What we believe does work is the creation of opportunities by identifying the needs of sectors, or of different types of company, and by targeting investment funds, services and training on a commercial basis to those sector and company needs.

Finally, it is essential to continually relate the needs of the market to the needs of local areas. Technology programmes we manage for the EC must not only add value for a sector, they must also bring opportunities for the region. As well as being commercially viable, investment, training and technical development must add to the opportunities for local economic development. The private sector can ignore all this. The state as public entrepreneur cannot.

Conclusion

Our argument is that successful industrial investment implies an interventionist approach. Commercial value and social value are essentially linked and economic growth needs an integrated range of resources combining finance with training, technological and other services vital to economic development.

An essential feature of investment must be the creation of high quality employment. Strategies should ensure that all sections of the community benefit from these facilities particularly through targeted marketing of services and in carefully designed training programmes.

We believe that in key policy areas and in investment agencies themselves investment should operate on a business-like basis generating financial returns within the context of a socially defined agenda. The public and private sectors should co-operate in a range of different arrangements, each contributing what it does best and both participating in the financial returns.

In this relationship the public sector should play an entrepreneurial role, identifying the social needs and inadequacies of the market and developing new operations, but not necessarily controlling or owning these. Where public agencies participate in the market they should benefit financially but their primary role is not to maximize profit.

These parameters must be part of a more meaningful role for the public sector in its policies for investment in industry.

Notes

1　Labour Party, 1989 *Meet the Challenge, Make the Change – A New Agenda for Britain. Final Report of Labour's Policy Review for the 1990s*, London, Labour Party.

2　On the statistics relating to the size of venture capital investments see British Venture Capital Association, *Report on Investment Activity 1988* and also on attitudes 'Why "venture" is not so capital', *Financial Times* 3 November 1987.

3　'Caution takes hold in the LBO market', *Financial Times* 9 October 1989.

4　OECD Science and Technology Indicators Report No. 3 – R & D, Production and Diffusion of Technology, OECD, Paris, 1989.

5　For an interesting summary of the comprehensive support for smaller technical ventures in France, Germany and Spain see 'A route to realising innovative potential' *Financial Times*, 7 November 1989.

6　H. Steedman, 1988, 'Vocational Training in France and Britain', *National Institute Economic Review*; S. J. Prais and K. Wagner, 1988,

'Productivity and Management; the Training of Foremen in Britain and Germany,' ibid; H. Steedman and K. Wagner, 1989, 'Productivity, Machinery and Skills; Clothing Manufacture in Britain and Germany,' ibid.

7 S. J. Prais and V. Jarvis, 1989, 'Two Nations of Shopkeepers', *National Institute Economic Review.*

8 See for example, K. Coutts and W. Godley, 'The British Economy under Mrs. Thatcher', *Political Quarterly*, August 1989. Also by the close of 1989 interest rate policy was causing a significant increase in business failures: 'Business failures increase', *Financial Times*, 27 October 1989.

9 See also the approach in Chapter 9.

10 See, for example, D. G. Mayes 'Does Manufacturing Matter?' NIESR November 1987, and House of Lords, *Report from the Select Committee on Overseas Trade*, HMSO, 1985.

Merger and monopoly policy

This chapter seeks to map out a merger and monopoly policy within the broader context of a national industrial strategy. The organizing principle for such a strategy will be social efficiency which is facilitated by the extension of democracy into the economy. The case will be made for a stringent policy over merger, coupled with an attempt to roll back the implications of recent merger waves by either divestiture or more stringent controls on the giant corporations so created. Possible complementarities and inconsistencies with a broader industrial strategy aimed at the creation of a modern dynamic industrial economy will be examined. Our general conclusion will be that a stringent anti-merger and anti-monopoly stance will be supportive of our broader aims, but there may arise situations where, in order to achieve our broader strategic aims, mergers may be agreed subject to certain contractual conditions. We end up by briefly contemplating and speculating on the European scene.

Democracy and the concentration of economic power

The dominance of the giant corporations has advanced considerably in recent history. This has mainly come about via large-scale merger activity, which in Europe at least has been principally horizontal in character. The situation in the United States was somewhat different: merger activity was still commonplace, but usually conglomerate. We in Britain are now in the middle of a further merger wave of immense proportions, which is likely to have a similar impact to the merger wave of the late 1960s and early 1970s which completely transformed the industrial structure of the UK economy.[1] Economic power is being concentrated in fewer and fewer hands.

The growth of such power raises many issues but the fundamental one is that of the ability of people, and the communities of which they are part, to assert their right to determine their own future. This is the essence of democracy – the ability of people and their communities to allocate resources in the way they choose. Thus economic democracy is fundamental to maximizing a community's economic welfare. To begin to achieve economic democracy, people and communities have to possess some significant degree of direct control over the dominant centres of economic power. Lying behind this requirement is the fundamental asymmetry between the locational mobility of the giant corporation, in terms of its production and investment strategies, and the locational rigidity or inflexibility of people in general, and the communities of which they are part. This asymmetry implies a basic asymmetry of power which can only be curbed by direct intervention by communities and nation states in the activities of these giants. The mobility of capital gives it power over cities, regions and nations and the creation of giant transnational corporations not only provides the necessary conditions for the use of such power but also adds to such power the ability to determine how markets are allowed to work and the environment within which they operate. Leaving mergers to the market means that the only people involved are shareholders, and the effective decision-makers are the shareholders of the acquired firm, and those shareholders are the only group which gains from an acquisition. The wider involvement of workers, consumers and local communities can only be ensured through government legislation and intervention.

Whilst the incompatibility of democracy with the capitalist organization of production is a feature of any capitalist system, since equal participation of all involved in the economic enterprise would undermine the essence of a capitalist firm, the incompatibility is particularly marked as economic power becomes more concentrated. So long as capitalist enterprise remains small-scale its power to subvert the system of democracy remains circumscribed. So long as any degree of economic inequality exists then political equality will generally not exist, but the extent of political inequality will be related to the degree of economic inequality. The evolution of capital has led to the growth in the concentration of control over economic resources. As a result many people have lost their economic independence and therefore some degree of control over their own lives, others have had some degree of autonomy taken away from them, and centres of economic power have grown up which are capable of subverting the political process. In addition, as argued in Chapter 1, the centripetal tendencies within the merger process and the giant firm also raise major issues of democratic control. Large numbers of small firms have become agglomerated into large multi-plant firms which has, in many cases, led to the loss of a degree of local and regional autonomy. Higher level decision making and associated higher level occupations have been pulled to the centre and the periphery has developed all the characteristics of a branch plant economy. As the economic base of an area is taken over by outside interests, so the profit share is extracted for use at the centre and lost to the control of the local community.

A policy on merger

Merger activity normally leads to the acquisition of economic power, but this may be balanced, in an economic welfare sense, by the possibility of real resource savings following from the more efficient organization of resources. This requires us to know more about any cost savings which might result from merger and provides a justification for much of the empirical work on the impact of merger. Such investigations have revealed a very consistent picture in which it is difficult to sustain the view that merger is in fact a necessary or sufficient condition for efficiency gain. Results for the UK have shown that merger was generally consistent with either no change in profitability or with its decline (see e.g. Meeks, 1977[2]). These results are also consistent with those obtained for the conglomerate merger waves of the US (see e.g. Ravenscraft and Scherer, 1989[3]). Given that merger can be expected to lead to greater economic power, and therefore greater profitability, these various observations on declining or constant profitability must be construed as a strong indication of declining efficiency. Other work attempted to break down changes in profits following merger into efficiency and market power effects (see Cowling et al., 1980[4]). The message is the same – in general there is no evidence of significant efficiency gain following merger.

These results, and additional concerns about the broader consequences of unfettered merger activity[5] would indicate that a rigorous anti-merger policy is called for. There is much to be said for a complete ban on mergers where either participant is of significant size. This would have the additional beneficial effect of shutting-off an obvious avenue for circumventing restrictive practices legislation – if you are not allowed collectively to fix prices you merge your interests – and would, therefore, contribute to the efficiency of existing legislation.

To many observers such a policy may appear unattractive. Why not let the existing Mergers Panel (a group of civil servants from the various interested departments) or the Monopolies Commission assess each case on its merits? Surely it is irrational simply to apply a blanket refusal? After all we can all think of cases where firms are ineffectively managed by those who run them. Why not allow the more thrusting managements of other corporations to acquire and reorganize them?

Our first response to this argument would be to recall that the evidence does not support this view. The evidence suggests that bad decisions have been made in the past: mergers have been allowed which in some cases have been disastrous and in other cases have simply allowed the emergence of substantial monopolies without any significant, offsetting benefits. More fundamentally the whole approach has been biased in favour of acceptance since the parties involved have not been required to demonstrate that social benefits will result. Even where it is possible to identify a more effective management group anxious to take over a less effective one, it may still be the case that the agglomeration of their interests will leave those in control with a problem of managerial overload. Management revealed as effective with one level and variety of problems and resources may fail to operate effectively when faced with a very different level and variety. The argument can be extended to say that scarce management resources would be better employed in promoting the internal growth of the firm, which would also involve the creation of new resources: takeovers merely represent the rearrangement of ownership and do not in themselves promote the creation of new resources. More positively we can seek remedies for sleepy monopolies in terms of facilitating divestiture (the break-up of existing corporations) and management or employee buy-outs (see later).

The implication of these arguments is that the array of policy options should be confined to a range, with an onus of proof on the merging firms to demonstrate social benefit at one end defining the mildest policy, and an outright ban at the other end defining the toughest policy. Social benefit would be interpreted in a way that is consistent with the broader industrial strategy.[6] Within this range a variety of types of ban could be identified which might relate to the size of firms involved and their joint market shares. That is, both size and market share would make a ban more likely.[7] As a provisional guideline we would suggest that any merger involving the one hundred largest corporations, or any merger taking firms into the top one hundred list, should be subject to an outright ban.[8] Mergers involving other firms of significant size, or creating firms of significant size, would be subject to the onus of proof regulation. This could include the next 400 firms. In these cases we would want to ensure that there was full consultation with the workers involved before such mergers were allowed to go ahead.

A straightforward ban on acquisitions by giant firms would have a further advantage. If the merger is important to the firms involved, and the evidence suggests this would not normally be for reasons of productive efficiency, then under existing arrangements considerable effort will be expended in convincing the appropriate people within government, whether 'sponsoring department' (each industry has a sponsoring department within the existing government apparatus), Mergers Panel or Monopolies Commission, that it is indeed in the public interest: this effort being in addition to the private effort involved in the market operations to secure the acquisition. Both forms of waste, in terms of managerial effort, would be avoided by a tight ban on acquisitions. It should be noted that simply the fees of merchant bankers and institutions for their involvement in British mergers totalled £300 million in 1985 and more than £600 million for 1986 (see *Acquisitions Monthly*).

But what about the impact of a ban, or the prospect of a ban? Insofar as firms are restricted from doing what they would otherwise do, then it may be optimal for them collectively to invest in attempts to secure the removal of the ban. They would undoubtedly do this, but it would be unlikely to amount to significant waste. However if the ban is accompanied with 'let-out' clauses then each firm with a merger in mind will invest resources in convincing the appropriate authority that their case falls under at least one of these clauses. The looser the rules, the greater the social waste.

A policy on monopoly

However, even if strict controls were established over future mergers, such that only a minority were allowed, this would still leave a highly concentrated industry structure, itself primarily the legacy of the permissive merger policy of the past.[9] A hard-line merger policy, although important, would still have to be seen as peripheral to the central issue of the concentration of economic power. This will be even more so in the future given the enormous, and largely unfettered, merger wave we are currently experiencing. Recent evidence consistently suggests that there is little to be gained by increases in the size of individual corporations, but potentially much to be lost. Given this, the question of divestiture or demerger has to be raised. Under existing legislation it is clearly within the power of ministers to order such action, although it has never been taken, nor likely even threatened. It should now be presented as a policy which will be systematically considered in the case of the whole spectrum of major corporations.[10] It could also be used as a declared sanction in cases where mergers have been conditionally approved.

However, there may be cases where divestiture is not desirable, in which case controls over the behaviour of such organizations has to be considered. Despite the existence of the Monopolies Commission there would seem to be compelling reasons for an additional institutional framework for the regulation of the major centres of economic power. Society needs an institution to monitor their activities; to regulate the corporation as a whole and to bring more of the evidence into the public arena (see also Chapter 9). This could be achieved by parliamentary committees or by some commission, like the Monopolies Commission, but operating in a very open and public way. Such institutions would provide a focus for the harnessing of public opinion to the aim of effective control of these major corporations.

Nevertheless such policies could be undermined within the government apparatus. Within the government, industry and the consumer have unequal access and influence. The notion of 'sponsoring department' is a case in point. It is one of the specific functions of departments of state like Industry, Agriculture and Transport, to represent the interests of their associated firms and industries within the government. The permissiveness of past and current merger policies, and the unwillingness to contemplate more effective ways to monitor and control monopoly behaviour may be partially explained by the existence of 'sponsoring departments'. It would seem important to challenge this institution. 'Industry's' case should be made openly as written or oral submission to the Merger Panel or to the Monopolies Commission, so that everyone can see clearly where the view of vested interests is being put.

However a basic asymmetry remains, given the fact that final consumers are not organized or represented in as efficient a manner as 'industry'. This becomes more and more the case as industry becomes more and more concentrated. The bigger firms become, the more dominant they are within individual industries, the more incentive they have to represent 'industry's' view, in aggregate or as a specific industry. The benefits from lobbying activities accrue more completely, and more directly, to the firm in question the bigger or more dominant that particular firm. Given this it becomes more and more crucial to develop new methods of democratic control of the operations of government and Civil Service as concentration increases. The achievement of an effective merger and monopoly policy will be crucially dependent on opening up the government apparatus to such control.

Thus we have returned to the requirement of an extension of democracy to secure economic efficiency, which we analysed in general terms earlier in the chapter. We now turn to the question of linking our policy on merger and monopoly with our broader, strategic aims for British industry.

Links with the broader industrial strategy

We will now seek to identify the complementarities or inconsistencies which may exist between such a strategy and the policy on merger and monopoly we have previously outlined.

Our view is that the inconsistencies are minimal. A stringent merger policy coupled with the tight regulation of monopoly power will also serve our strategic ambition for industrial dynamism, and, in turn, an industrial strategy aimed at creating new firms and encouraging new entry via public intervention across a spectrum of strategic industries, will serve to moderate the monopoly power of extant corporations. Indeed, we will, in our industrial strategy, need to avoid what happened in the case of the Industrial Reorganization Corporation (IRC), a creation of a former Labour government, where, rather than the IRC picking winners, the 'winners' were picking the IRC (see Hindley, 1983[11]). That is, some firms saw the IRC primarily as a means of short-circuiting the monopolies and merger legislation, and their resultant profitability had more to do with greater monopoly power than greater efficiency. Thus, whilst we are not contemplating a new IRC, we have to guard against inconsistencies within our overall strategy which will inevitably be exploited by those with much to gain.

On what basis can it be concluded that a much stricter policy on merger and monopoly will in general contribute to our objective of greater industrial dynamism in the British economy? First, there is the evidence of the many studies of mergers within this country and elsewhere. As mentioned earlier, the results of such studies point fairly unambiguously to a lack of improvement in profitability following merger, and in many cases substantial reductions. Given that the mergers in Britain and in Europe were essentially horizontal in character, this points to a reduction in efficiency. When efficiency was directly measured (as in Cowling *et al.*, 1980, op. cit.) this implication was apparently borne out. More recently, a major and important work has been completed on conglomerate merger in the United States (see Ravenscraft and Scherer, 1989, op. cit.). This research traces through the impact of merger on the specific companies acquired, and is of interest in the UK context as the balance of merger activity shifts somewhat toward conglomerate acquisitions and away from the dominant horizontal merger of the past. The results are striking. Acquired companies' pre-merger profitability was substantially above manufacturing sector norms but, following merger, profitability declined and fell well below 'normal' levels, even after large numbers of companies, with negative profitability on average, had been sold off. Case studies of acquisitions that ended in sell-off revealed substantial control loss problems. Mueller (1985)[12] also discovered that market share declined precipitately among lines of business that were acquired, as compared with a minimal-acquisition control group. We must conclude that restricting merger will serve generally to protect relatively small, efficient firms from the predatory attentions of other, normally much larger firms, and that the consequences of this can be expected to be greater efficiency in general. The market share consequences may be interpreted as implying a greater resistance to import penetration by an economy which effectively protects its dynamic smaller firms in this way.

And yet, confronted with this sort of evidence, some will undoubtedly argue that although operational efficiency may suffer, and monopoly power may increase, as a result of a merger movement activated by the industrial giants, nevertheless in the long run the giants will win out, given their greater capacity for innovation. Given this response the first point which has to be made is, why does this not show up in profitability or market share over an extended period? But we should also look more directly at the evidence on innovation. An analysis of this evidence suggests that technological progressiveness will not normally be promoted by the monopolization of the system, nor the creation of large conglomerate-enterprises (see, for example, Scherer[13] and Stoneman[14] for surveys). A recent investigation of innovations in the UK over the period 1945–1983 gives strong support to the view that industrial dynamism will be retarded by high levels of concentration and restrictions on entry (Geroski and Stewart, 1986[15]). Despite controlling most of the recorded research and development, the giant corporations have not provided the origins of the major technological innovations. These are often appropriated from much smaller firms, or even individuals, and in many cases their innovation is suppressed or delayed (see, for example, Mandel, 1968[16]). However, it may still be the case that once innovation has taken place, diffusion across the economy may be more rapid in a world of giant firms. But we must be clear about the purposes and consequences of such diffusion. The innovation of new products by these firms is an attempt to secure and enhance their market positions and hence will contribute to the general tendency for the degree of monopoly to increase over time. Similarly with process innovations. Although those who control the giants will be motivated by the search for efficient techniques, this will include the 'efficiency' provided by control over the workforce. Thus new technology will tend to reflect the search for such control, which inevitably will have distributional implications. In addition there will be a bias in the new technology favouring a system of production and control suited to the giant. Thus process innovations will also tend to sustain the monopolization trend previously identified. We conclude that most evidence would suggest that the further extension of the dominance of the giant corporations would not contribute to industrial dynamism but, where it might, it serves to push us even further away from the democratic economy we seek and which lies at the root of social efficiency.

One further point which is sometimes raised in favour of merger and the creation of the giant corporation is in terms of power and the ability to compete against foreign giants. We have already noted that efficient firms can be absorbed by giants, who themselves fail to maintain previous levels of efficiency within their acquisitions. We have also noted that such companies appear to lose out to rivals in terms of their market share (Mueller, 1985 op. cit.). And yet it may still be argued that within export markets the position of such firms is strengthened by their being part of a larger and more powerful enterprise. We can accept this as a possibility, although we may doubt that it is the usual outcome, given the market-share evidence. However, this does not mean that it is the best outcome so far as a national industrial strategy is concerned. If indeed efficiency is promoted by restricting the predatory takeover activities of giant firms and yet the resultant industrial structure is inimical to our national ambitions regarding exports, then new institutions can be created which preserve operational efficiency whilst at the same time serving to promote exports. Export co-operatives, for example, would offer an alternative to the supposed superiority of the giants in foreign markets.

The last basis on which we can conclude that a stricter merger and monopoly policy may serve to enhance our industrial dynamism relates to the present dominance of the short-term view within the financial institutions and, therefore, within industry. An active market for corporate control, as argued in Chapter 1, allows the short-term perspective of the financial institutions to impinge much more decisively on the perspective of industry, which must of necessity be long-term in terms of its own industrial logic. This was rightly a central concern and a central focus of Labour's Policy Review[17] (see the section on relieving short-term pressures, p. 11). The financial environment is not conducive to the rational planning of the long-term future of our industrial base. But that environment can be crucially changed, at a stroke, by removing the present lax system of control over merger and substituting one in which a ban on any merger involving a major participant is the first reaction of the regulatory authority. It will, of course, remain possible for the financial institutions to try to maintain their control by directly intervening in industry, but if this happened we might also move to a more appropriate position where financial capital becomes more involved and better informed about the imperatives of industrial logic as is the case in both the Federal Republic of Germany and Japan. This would be entirely in line with the objective of raising the quantity and quality of real investment in Britain.

Removing management from the constant threat of takeover and, equally, removing from management the ability to grow by takeover, will act as a liberating force in British industry. The existing system produces two sorts of social waste: the managerial effort spent by the bidders on non-productive activities (growing by acquisition, given that the efficiency of acquisitions is apparently not improved by the change in control), and the managerial effort wasted in trying to avoid the attention or undermine the success of the raider. Thus managerial effort can be redirected toward operational efficiency and organic growth within a long-term context more suited to industrial realities. To prevent lapses into lethargy and inefficiency requires a watchful and tough monopoly policy coupled with a commitment to encourage new firms and new entrants.

Nevertheless, there will undoubtedly be cases where either we see merger as contributing to our industrial strategy, or alternatively where, to get the necessary compliance, something has to be given up on the merger front. However this should not extend to the establishment of national champions and in any situation we need to be wary of merged firms' power and sceptical of their efficiency.[18] This suggests those engaged in operating the merger and monopoly policy should be infused with the thinking and objectives of the industrial strategy, and vice-versa. This could be achieved by appropriate cross membership between the two sets of institutions, e.g. planning agency and Merger Panel, and NEDC and Monopolies Commission.

Conclusions

We have considered merger and monopoly policy within the context of economic democracy. We see the central question of social efficiency as being intimately bound up with economic democracy. Only with democratic control can we begin to move towards a socially efficient economic system. We have examined the links between democracy and the concentration of economic power and we have made suggestions for the control of the latter. We have also examined some links which are likely to exist between merger and monopoly power and a broad industrial strategy aimed at a more dynamic economy. We find that a stringent policy on merger and monopoly will generally serve the objectives of industrial strategy.

As far as Labour's Policy Review is concerned, we feel the general thrust on merger policy is correct, but we feel the actual recommendations do not go far enough in two senses. First, simply reversing the burden of proof '. . . so that the predator must show that the takeover is positively in the public interest' (p. 11), is unlikely to be sufficient to attain the objective sought. Firms in such a position will undoubtedly make a powerful case for what they have decided on and the regulators will not normally have access to the information necessary to adequately evaluate such cases. The history of business regulation in Britain also is not reassuring. There would seem to be too many sympathetic voices within the range of public institutions – too many people too easily convinced by the Big Business case. If our view is reasonably accurate then adopting non-discretionary public policy rules, along the lines we advocate, would seem justified. Of course where mergers are allowed by the rules then we would wish to consult those workers who are involved, as the Review suggests. These matters receive some attention in the next chapter. Where we do rely on reversing the burden of proof, then such proof should be demonstrated to pass the test of time. We therefore suggest that a contract be formalized with accompanying penalty clauses.

The other sense in which the proposals do not go far enough is in the relative neglect of monopoly policy as such. Whilst the regulation of public enterprise monopolies does receive some attention (see Chapter 9) the document is largely silent on the regulation of private monopoly except via merger policy. Given the extreme laxity of merger policy now and in the past it is absolutely essential that we formulate a policy on monopoly in the broader context of our industrial strategy to allow us to appropriately handle the substantial positions of economic power which now exist within the industrial economy. This chapter has sought to offer a way forward on this front.

Lastly, the questions raised for merger and monopoly policy by Europe. The Single European Act and '1992' will inevitably have an impact on the conduct of mergers and monopolies policies. Hitherto, the policies of the EC on monopolies, mergers and restrictive practices have only applied to inter-state trade, have had only a minor impact and have only recently begun to raise questions of jurisdiction between the Commission and national governments. At the time of writing, bargaining between the Commission and national governments over the boundary of responsibilities, particularly over merger policy, is still continuing. It is, however, likely that the Commission will acquire the power to decide on proposed mergers involving large firms with significant inter-state trade (with the bargaining concerning the definition of large and significant). Thus, it is likely that a merger which in previous years would have been seen as a matter for the British government will in the future fall under the auspices of the Commission.

There has been a wide variation in the mergers policies pursued by member states, with many states having no explicit policy towards mergers. In a number of countries, though, there are constraints on hostile takeover bids. This suggests that the forging of an explicit Community-wide policy on mergers (other than for a few large cross-border ones) may be a long process, and one which could be strongly influenced by a British government. The previous discussion clearly advocates a mergers policy involving the prohibition of large mergers; and we see good reason for seeking to extend this to the Community level.

There will, however, be substantial battles to be fought between a future British Labour government and the EC. The policy proposed above would probably be much more stringent than the policy on mergers of the EC, and thus there will be mergers which we would wish to ban but which would be permitted by the EC. Further, many of the supposed benefits of the Single European Market are said to arise from the exploitation of economies of scale, which would imply the encouragement of mergers and the growth of concentration. We take a much less ebullient view of the prospects of the gains from economies of scale and of the use of mergers as a means of achieving greater efficiency and lower costs. But the view of encouraging large European firms to compete with American and Japanese firms does appear to infuse much of the EC thinking. Thus there may well be a basic conflict of approach between our thinking and that of the EC.

The policy of the present British government and to some degree of the EC stresses the role and benefits of competition. In respect of mergers policy, the present policy (sometimes called the Tebbit doctrine) 'has been and will continue to be to make references [of mergers to the Monopolies and Mergers Commission] primarily on competition grounds' (speech by Norman Tebbit reported in *British Business* 13 July 1984). However, the notion of competition has been rather flexibly applied, and has meant allowing the vast majority of mergers to proceed. The essential dilemma for a market enthusiast is that 'market forces' implies permitting all mergers to proceed (since they are sanctioned by the financial markets), and yet recognizing that mergers are a major factor in the rise of concentration and monopoly. The dilemma facing the EC will be greater since they will be advocating both the role of competition and of large size for exploiting economies of scale. Our view is that little benefit in terms of the exploitation of any economies of scale comes from merger, so that dilemma does not normally arise.

Notes

1   Taking a peak year in the early seventies, 1972, the *Business Monitor* M7, Department of Trade and Industry, records the number of acquisitions as 1210 with a value of £2531.6 million. The latest local peak, 1988, has 1224 companies acquired with a value of £22,122.6 million. Deflating by the FT 500 Index (Financial Statistics) suggests that 1988 merger activity, in terms of real expenditure on acquisitions, was close to double that in 1972 (see Malcolm Sawyer, 1989, 'Industry' in M. Artis (ed.) Prest and Coppock, *A Manual of Applied Economics*, London). Of course the economy has grown substantially since 1972, but the figures suggest that the current merger wave, relative to the size of the industrial economy, is at least as important as it was in the previous merger boom.

2   G. Meeks, 1977, *Disappointing Marriage: A Study of the Gains from Merger*, London, Cambridge University Press. The results of the various studies are summarized in Malcolm Sawyer, 1981, *Economics of Industries and Firms*, London, Croom Helm, 222–229.

3   D. J. Ravenscraft and F. M. Scherer, 1989, 'The Profitability of Mergers' *International Journal of Industrial Organisation*, 7, 101–116.

4   K. Cowling, and P. Stoneman, J. Cubbin, J. Cable, G. Hall, S. Domberger, and P. Dutton, 1980, *Mergers and Economic Performance*, London, Cambridge University Press.

5   Broader consequences would relate to the income distributional and possible stagnationist tendencies induced by the monopolization of markets, see K. Cowling, 1982, *Monopoly Capitalism*, London, Macmillan. They would also, of course, relate to the more fundamental issue of democracy itself.

6 The present policy of only competition matters is ill-defined in the sense that competition is not defined, though it would seem to be a smoke-screen for allowing virtually any merger through. The policy we are proposing is more stimulating of competition than the present policy. Further, our industrial strategy would mean that the promotion of investment and research and development would be more to the forefront.

7 Dennis Mueller – 1986, *Profits in the Long Run*, London, Cambridge University Press – proposes a flat ban on acquisitions by the 500 largest corporations in the United States subject to an efficiency defence. Whilst this may be appropriate in the US context, we can't help but feel that within the British context it would be only too easy for the big corporations to convince the regulators of the validity of their cases.

8 The two authors would adopt different stances at this point. Cowling would be relatively unyielding in the application of such a ban, while Sawyer's approach would be much more in terms of bargaining for future behaviour consistent with the overall industrial strategy. Any such assurances would be formalized and be the subject of a contract between government and company, with penalty clauses in the event of non-performance.

9 Less than 3% of mergers which could have been referred were actually referred to the Monopolies Commission.

10 Both Oliver Williamson – O. E. Williamson, 1975, *Markets and Hierarchies: Analysis and Antitrust Implications*, New York, Free Press – and Dennis Mueller – D. C. Mueller, 1986, *Profits in the Long Run*, London, Cambridge University Press – advocate self-suggested dissolution of dominant corporations subject to an efficiency test.

11 B. Hindley ed., 1983, *State Investment Companies in Western Europe: Picking Winners or Backing Losers*, London, Macmillan.

12 D. C. Mueller, 1985, 'Mergers and Market Share', *Review of Economics and Statistics*.

13 F. M. Scherer, 1980, *Industrial Market Structure and Economic Performance*, Chicago, Rand McNally.

14 P. Stoneman, 1983, *The Economics of Technological Change*, Oxford, Oxford University Press.

15 P. A. Geroski and G. Stewart, 1986, 'Competitive Rivalry and the Response of Markets to Innovative Opportunities', University of Southampton.

16 E. Mandel, 1968, *Marxist Economic Theory*, London, Merlin Press.

17 Labour Party, 1989, *Meet the Challenge, Make the Change – A New Agenda for Britain. Final Report of Labour's Policy Review for the 1990s*, London, Labour Party.

18 One of the interesting features of Japanese industrial policy is that they have been able to develop a coherent industrial strategy with a marked deconcentrating tendency, and thereby have created an extremely dynamic industrial system. In contrast, the present British government, although extolling the virtues of competition, is presiding over a merger boom which is decisively eliminating competition and creating a much more concentrated market structure in this country.

5　K. G. Knight and Roger Sugden

Efficiency, economic democracy and company law

Whilst post-war Labour politics has tended to be characterized by a faintly patronizing statist tradition, recently there has been more emphasis on the libertarian element in socialist thought. This is seen in Labour's 1989 Policy Review,[1] for example. The Review stresses the need to democratise the institutions of our society to give individuals greater freedom and control over all aspects of their lives.

Part of the case for greater democracy is political[2] but there is also an economic justification based on efficiency;[3] institutions in which participants share both power and responsibility work better, and nowhere is this shown more clearly than in the production of goods and services.[4] This economic justification and the policies it implies are the concern of this chapter (see also the discussion of democracy and the concentration of economic power in Chapter 4).

More specifically, the first section details the evidence on efficiency. It concludes that industrial performance can be given a real boost if there is a significant shift in the balance of power within firms. The means of achieving this is the subject of the second section. It examines possibilities for the radical reform of company law, suggesting a new Company Act which rejects archaic and inefficient hierarchy in favour of something fit for the twenty-first century.

Efficiency and economic democracy

Researchers from a wide variety of disciplines have examined the impact of various forms of economic democracy on performance and efficiency. One pioneering study by students of management is

that by Peters and Waterman (1982). They examine the performance of 36 top US firms selected from a much larger sample. In
order to qualify as a 'top' firm a company had to perform in the top
half of its industry on the basis of indicators measured over a full
twenty-year period beginning in 1961. The indicators include
measures of technical progressiveness, asset growth and the average
return on capital and sales. In fact, 17 of the 36 companies ranked in
the top half on all the indicators of performance. One of the
principal characteristics of these companies identified by Peters and
Waterman is that 'they do not foster (negative) we/they labour
attitudes'. Instead they adopt decentralized and progressive labour
policies in which informality is prized and in which workers develop
self esteem through peer review and by being involved in company
decision making.

This study is not a socialist treatise. In it the creation of positive
attitudes by greater employee involvement is generally achieved by
paternalistic styles of management, with information sharing rather
than power sharing as the prescription favoured by Peters and
Waterman. However, this work demonstrates clearly that
companies perform well if they foster positive worker attitudes by
listening to the views of their employees and seeking to
accommodate them.

Moreover other studies have suggested that these positive
attitudes are more likely to emerge in firms in which there is some
degree of genuine power sharing via employee participation in
corporate decisions, rather than mere involvement. Indeed a
substantial body of evidence now exists on the impact of employee
participation in decision making (power sharing) which encompasses a wide variety of arrangements from the rights of
consultation enjoyed by trade unions in a capitalist firm to full
blown worker management.[5]

The evidence on the effect of union presence on firm and industry
performance in both the US and the UK is extensive and
illuminating. The seminal works that inspired much of the
literature of the last decade are those of the 'Harvard School',
notably Freeman (1976) and Medoff and Brown (1978). In the
empirical paper by Medoff and Brown a production function is
estimated using data from US manufacturing industry. They test
for productivity changes resulting from union presence by
including a variable that effectively displaces the intercept term in

the production function. Having made some correction for the higher quality of workers employed they find that labour productivity is 22% higher in unionized firms. This approximately offsets the higher wages paid to unionized workers in their sample. Part of this (about one fifth) results from the more stable employment and longer job tenure that characterizes the unionized firm (Freeman, 1980). This enables employers to derive the productivity benefits arising from 'learning by doing' and from higher levels of firm-specific training justified by the greater ease of amortizing human capital investments.

The bulk of the efficiency improvement, however, occurs because of the direct effects of workers having a 'voice' in company affairs. Freeman (1976) and more extensively Freeman and Medoff (1984) argue that unions establish rules which reduce corrosive rivalry between workers. They also provide channels of communication to speedily resolve grievances and negotiate over work conditions. They negotiate higher wages, which, in itself, may have a beneficial 'shock' effect on management and they also improve fringe benefits. In short, when unions are involved in decision making, especially that pertaining directly to employees, the surrender of management prerogative in the capitalist firm results in higher productivity.

With few exceptions more recent work in the US (Clark, 1980, Allen, 1984, 1986 and Ichniowski, 1984, for example) has broadly confirmed Medoff and Brown's results. However, the consensus view is that the positive productivity effects associated with union presence are rather smaller than they suggest. The main reason is that Medoff and Brown employed a measure of value rather than physical productivity. Insofar as unionized firms pass on higher wages to prices this value measure will be inflated and needs to be corrected as a result. Allen's (1986) study illustrates the point. He found his estimate of the positive effect of unions in the US construction industry was halved when value productivity measures were replaced by physical equivalents. Not surprisingly these positive productivity effects are confirmed by studies of industrial costs. Allen (1986) estimates a translog cost function for US construction projects. He finds lower costs exist among union contractors.

A further feature of the US work has been to explore the impact of the use of union sanctions on productivity. In general this aspect of union presence has no significant effects, as Neumann and Reder

(1984) show. In only six of the 63 industries studied by these authors does the use of the strike sanction have a significant adverse effect on output. This is more than offset by the 19 where there is a positive effect arising from the role strikes can play as a safety valve for corrosive tension caused by long standing or deeply rooted grievances. In the remaining majority of industries union disputes have no significant effect either way.

Given the effects on wage and productivity levels recent attention has focused on the impact of union presence on profits in the US. All the studies have shown that the wage effect dominates so union presence erodes profits, notably where firms enjoy some degree of product market power. Voos and Michel's (1986) study is typical and particularly good, not least because it models union presence endogenously. They find profits are reduced by 35% of which four fifths is caused by the redistributive effects of higher wages.

With these strong effects in mind US research has recently been examining the dynamic effects of unions on investment, technical change and productivity growth. A survey by Addison and Hirsch (1989) of the existing evidence concludes that union presence appears to lower firms' investment in physical capital, as well as to decrease R & D and other innovative and risk-taking activities. As a consequence, productivity growth tends to be slower in unionized firms and industries.

Power sharing with unions by capitalist firms in the US appears, on this evidence, to have a 'shock' effect, raising labour productivity levels, but these beneficial effects are eroded through time. Trade unionism by itself has not in the US produced a sustained improvement in productive efficiency though it has clearly helped.

The UK evidence is not so extensive but some conclusions are possible. Firstly, the strong positive effect of union presence on the level of labour productivity has not been replicated. Neither, on the other hand, has the popular view that unions impede performance been generally confirmed. Machin's study (1988) is especially valuable since it employs measures of physical productivity to pinpoint the effects of unions in a sample of firms in the engineering industry. It uses the same production function approach adopted in the US studies so comparisons can also be made. It also employs an indicator of union presence that incorporates a wide variety of institutional features. It finds that in roughly 25% of the sample trade unions effects are adverse. These are generally large firms with more than 1000 employees where other evidence (Wadhwani, 1989) shows the incidence of restrictive work practices is greatest. In a further 20% of the firms the effects are similar to those found in the US, namely positive. However, in general, the impact is insignificantly different from zero. This confirms the findings of other recent studies including that of Knight (1989), which also finds (like Neumann and Reder in the US) that strike activity improves the level of productivity in some industries, reduces it in others but has a small overall effect.

The UK evidence also suggests the impact of unions on profits is, broadly speaking, the same as in the US. Machin (1988a) investigates a sample of 145 companies from the Datastream and Exstat databanks. He finds profits are lower in unionized firms especially where they possess product market power. This is consistent with studies that find that the impact of unions on wages in the UK is largest[6] in firms that possess market power. It is also clear that this wage effect of union presence clearly dominates the neutral productivity effect.

In contrast, the evidence on the dynamic effects of union presence clearly differs from the US. Surveys by the PSI[7] have shown that, on balance, unions do not impede the introduction of new technologies and, in many cases, actually encourage it. Daniel (1987) examines responses to the 1984 Workplace Industrial Relations Survey (WIRS) and also finds that the pace of technical change is higher in unionized plants in Britain. Recent work by Machin and Wadhwani (1989) using the 1984 WIRS data has shown unions have no significant influence on company investment plans. This confirms the results obtained by Wadhwani and Wall (1989) using company accounts data for the 1970s. For the 1980s the results show the investment rate of highly unionized firms is higher than in comparable low unionized firms. This mirrors the findings of Nickell, Wadhwani and Wall (1989) in respect of productivity growth and clearly contradicts the US evidence.

It is clear from this survey that power sharing with workers and their trade unions offers many potential opportunities for increased and increasing efficiency. It is also clear that neither in the UK nor in the US has this potential been fully realized. In part this reflects the unwillingness of management to share power, especially over matters that do not bear directly on workers. Moreover any tendency in the 1980s for the emphasis on macho management's right or duty to manage makes this worse (see McCarthy, 1988, on the attitudes of Margaret Thatcher and her ministers). It may also reflect the reluctance of workers to participate in performance enhancing activities in a capitalist firm in which they have no direct stake. The task for industrial policy in Britain is to secure these benefits from power sharing and that requires overcoming all these obstacles. The crucial question now is how can this best be done?

The evidence from the US and the UK suggests that further extensions of union presence in capitalist firms may help to reap the efficiency gains from power sharing but, alone, are simply not enough. More formal changes in the internal organization of firms and perhaps in the system of rewards are needed.

One currently fashionable proposal is to introduce profit sharing schemes on a widespread scale. Part of the case for profit sharing is that it provides workers with an incentive to co-operate in measures designed to improve company performance. This kind of consideration persuaded the Thatcher government to strengthen the tax concessions for this kind of scheme. As a result they are now commonplace in the UK. The 1984 WIRS shows 40% of all plants operated at least one form of profit sharing, including schemes that involve some degree of share ownership via Employee Share Ownership Plans (ESOPs). In general, however, the evidence suggests that profit sharing schemes by themselves have actually had very little impact on company performance. Studies, notably those of Blanchflower and Oswald (1987, 1988), using the WIRS data for 1980 and 1984, show that the existence of profit sharing (including ESOPs) in a plant makes little difference to employment or investment or to overall indicators of financial performance. These types of scheme appear to be largely cosmetic and introduced to take advantage of the tax concessions on offer. There has been little benefit from income sharing for company performance in practice in Britain.

The study by Cable and Wilson (1989) is especially important in finding an explanation for this fact. It uses a sample of engineering companies that is smaller and narrower in its coverage than WIRS but there is a lot more detailed and reliable data on company performance in the survey. Cable and Wilson use the production function approach adopted in much of the empirical literature that examines union effects on productivity. However, the model they employ is more subtle and allows for the possibility that profit sharing interacts with factor input levels in a way that changes productivity. In fact the model selection tests they use reject the usual assumption made in most other work, that productivity increases arise from disembodied, Hicks-neutral shifts in the production surface, and supports their more subtle effects. They find the existence of a profit sharing scheme raises productivity by between 3% and 8% (with beneficial effects on profitability) but only in certain well defined circumstances. The favourable effects depend on the firm's technological progressiveness, its internal organization and its forms of power sharing. Increases in productivity occurred in firms characterized by a strong collective (union density) voice, and by the occurrence of joint consultation committees in which employees participate to some extent in corporate decision making. In addition the existence of formal job evaluation schemes was conducive to efficiency gains. One explanation for this result is that job evaluation helps to provide a reasonably objective way of monitoring and rewarding the contribution made by individual workers and reinforces peer group pressures (articulated partly by unions) to prevent shirking. It confronts and overcomes the theoretical objection to profit sharing made by some free market US economists[8] that there will be an uncontrollable propensity to shirk in participatory firms and beneficial effects will hence be small.

Cable and Wilson conclude from their study that 'profit sharing, ceteris paribus, will not necessarily have productivity enhancing effects; accompanying changes in other dimensions of organizational design are important'. It is the widespread failure to make these necessary accompanying changes, including the introduction of a complementary system of power sharing, that explains the small beneficial effects of current schemes of profit income sharing on overall British economic performance noted above.

Another paper using the same sample is Estrin and Wilson (1986). This focuses on the employment generating effects often cited as a reason for the tax concessions for profit sharing schemes in Britain. It finds, using a simultaneous equation system that determines pay and employment, that the occurrence of profit sharing increases employment by 13%. Thus a surprising but encouraging feature of the Estrin and Wilson/Cable and Wilson papers is the finding that both productivity and employment are raised by employee participation in capitalist firms. Productivity increases require power sharing but a number of authors, including

Weitzman (1984), have argued that employment generation will only take place if workers are given a share of profits without any rights to influence corporate policy, i.e. there is no power sharing. Employees wishing to maximize their income share have a vested interest in limiting employment in their firm so must not be given any opportunity to do so. However, this takes a rather static view of the firm and its response to employee participation. If power sharing improves firm performance, including raising profits, any tendency to limit employment will be weakened. Moreover, if increasing employment is an objective of workers or their collective representatives the apparent choice that needs to be made between employment and productivity increasing policies is not important in practice. Profit sharing is not an alternative to power sharing as an instrument of industrial policy. This is the important conclusion derived from the studies of UK engineering firms by Estrin, Cable and Wilson.

Studies from the US are also interesting. One important recent study is that of Conte and Svejnar (1988). It examines the impact of profit sharing and various forms of employee participation (including union presence) on productivity in a panel of US manufacturing firms. Using instrumental variable estimation (to allow for endogeneity in the regressors) of a translog production function they find profit sharing *per se* does not lead to higher productivity. It is when it is combined with some degree of power sharing that significant efficiency gains are observed. Interestingly they also find that additional increases in productivity occur when other forms of power sharing are accompanied by strong trade union presence and involvement in pay (but not production) decisions. In general this result is typical of the US work.

Despite the strength of the theoretical arguments in their favour[9] empirical studies of partially employee owned firms and of producer co-operatives are a little mixed in their conclusions but still offer some general support for power sharing. Conte and Tannenbaum (1978) investigated employee owned firms in the US and find that the good industrial relations climate that prevails contributes to higher levels of profitability than in comparably sized companies in the same industry. However, the use of profitability as an indicator of performance may pose problems of interpretation when the tax advantages of employee ownership are as important as they are in the US. An alternative measure is productivity and this is explored in the Conte and Svejnar study referred to above. They find the productivity benefits of employee owned firms mainly arise from the extent of power sharing that exists. In fact the impact of very high levels of ownership *per se* is actually weakly negative but as the authors emphasize this may reflect the particular and peculiar situation of the industries (plywood and veneer manufacture) in which these firms are located.

In the UK there are a number of relevant studies. Bradley and Estrin (1987) examine the performance of the John Lewis Partnership and find an impressive record equalled by few other firms in the retail sector. In the manufacturing sector Jones and Backus (1977) examine producer co-operatives in footwear and using the production function approach find support for the proposition that the high level of participation in corporate decision making in these firms raises productivity levels. Jones (1982) extends the empirical analysis to clothing and printing. The results are very mixed and, not surprisingly, differ by industry group but in general they do show that the combination of profit sharing with share ownership and participation does improve company performance. However, this is not a universal effect. In clothing, for example, it is detected in large firms but not small.

To understand the lack of unambiguous support for the efficiency gains from these US/UK studies of employee ownership it is important to recognize the unfavourable and hostile climate in which these untypical firms function. For example there are legal restrictions which limit the access of UK co-operatives to outside finance for investment; preference share issues, for example, were not allowed for much of the period Jones considers and banks have not always been helpful in offering overdraft facilities. This is changing but recent developments of employee ownership and democratic control in both the UK and the US have relied more on specialist financial institutions than those employed by capitalist firms. In contrast, in political and economic environments in which employee owned firms are perceived positively (or just neutrally) the evidence is more clear cut. In the Mondragon region of northern Spain, for example, a large group of co-operative firms, in which the workforce has a considerable say over its activities, has grown up since 1943. Of vital importance to these firms is the supporting structure of banks and training and educational institutions, including a university. Using a variety of financial and economic performance indicators Thomas (1982) finds the co-operatives to be more productive and profitable than conventional capitalist firms.

A new Company Act

Our review of the evidence clearly suggests that policy should follow the general direction of greater power sharing but we still need to be more specific about how this is to be achieved.

Fiscal incentives of the type introduced by the Callaghan government in the 1970s to encourage profit sharing may help. But as the experience of the 1980s indicates, they alone are not enough (see Blanchflower and Oswald, 1988). Unless they are conditional on plans for increased worker participation in corporate decision making, the potential for efficiency gains is not realized. US experience confirms this. Congress has given substantial and growing tax incentives to employee share ownership schemes. As a result by the mid 1980s 7% of workers belonged to an ESOP but few had any say in the management of their firms. Rather voting rights have been generally exercised by management on behalf of an ESOP trust, see Lusk (1989). There are also real dangers that tax incentives alone induce an incentive to cheat as both economic theorists like Wadhwani (1988) and trade unionists like Bill Jordan have emphasized. To avoid this and to get the benefits of power sharing a new industrial policy will require something more.

An obvious area of concern is the legal framework within which firms operate; this is extremely influential on the entire structure of a firm and will therefore be central to the possibility of introducing genuine worker participation. Indeed the search for an appropriate Company Act and all that this entails seems to us a vital issue and accordingly we will focus on it in the rest of this chapter.

The issue is the subject of existing literature. For instance it is discussed by Wedderburn (1985), who includes a comparison of Britain and the US, and by Goyder (1987).[10] Its significance is recognized but unexplored in Labour's Policy Review. There is also a very interesting recent discussion by Snaith (1988), which (includes some useful references and) concludes that it would be wrong to assume the same method of power sharing should be imposed on all companies. Charkham (1989) is another interesting paper. It discusses the roles played by executive and non-executive directors, shareholders' use of exit and voice to exert influence, and the importance of share markets. These are factors which need to be pursued in greater detail if the democratization of British industry is to be as well founded and successful as possible.

However they will not detain us here. Although we will refer to some comments by Snaith (1988) and Charkham (1989) in due course, our particular focus is to draw heavily on the texts by Mayson, French and Ryan[11] to characterize the existing legal position and to indicate possible changes in the light of the previous evidence.

Existing British law sees firms as extremely hierarchal. This alone suggests the need for new legislation. For instance Mayson *et al.* note that 'Managers occupy a somewhat ambiguous position in a company – somewhere between directors responsible for the formulation of policy and employees responsible for the execution of policy'. This notion of employees as mere executors of company policy, not formulators, at best sits uneasily alongside the need for genuine power sharing. So too does the in between position of managers.

In line with this an interesting possibility is the broadening of 'membership' of British companies. Membership is very important because it confers 'the right to influence the conduct of the company's affairs' (Mayson *et al.*). For instance a firm's directors may be dismissed by a majority vote of members; the significance of this is that directors are at the pinnacle of a firm's internal hierarchy and it is out of their meetings that a firm's strategy is given substance. Yet current law focuses on investors as members. This seems to be the result of its explaining the existence of corporations by the desirability of limiting investors' liability. Separation of business and personal affairs is felt to be essential where a business requires lots of capital from many investors who cannot all participate in the internal management of a firm; the basic problem is that 'an investor may put money into a business run by others if offered a share of profits in return, but not if faced with unlimited liability for the debts the managers may incur in running the business' (Mayson *et al.*). This problem can be overcome by investors becoming members of a corporation and by the corporation being responsible for debts. In the law's eyes this is why there are corporations.[12] However this is a very narrow, technical approach. More specifically, whilst it focuses on investors having rights via membership, the implication of the evidence in the first section is that sharing their rights with employees may yield benefits (see especially the discussion of profit sharing and share owner-ship). Hence it is sensible to consider broadening the notion of membership.

There are several options here. The simplest and for that reason an appealing approach is to make individual producers (all of those working in a firm) members in their own right – i.e. to introduce the notion of 'producer members' alongside 'investor members'. This raises some tricky practical problems like the distribution of votes between the two groups in a way that shares power effectively without significantly undermining the incentive to invest. For instance, if each producer and each investor were simply given one vote to exercise individually, the chances are producers would be swamped. Associated with this is whether the extension of membership to producers should be done on a collective basis. Some degree of participation in the corporate planning exercise is currently enjoyed by large institutional shareholders in this country and in West Germany by banks who represent sizeable blocks of individual shareholders by proxy (see the discussion in Charkham, 1989). With this experience in mind – and given our earlier comments on the role of trade unions – perhaps it is essential to devise a system giving producers a collective voice and an incentive to participate as individuals in the exercise of that voice. For example, one way to do this is to introduce an appropriate form of producer co-operative to exercise producer members' collective vote. Another is to establish a trust to exercise the vote. All producers (subject to a qualifying period of employment) under a scheme of this kind would be entitled to equal voting rights in the election (by secret ballot) of the trustees. The accountability provided by this structure would need to be reinforced by regular trust meetings and a communication system linking trustees to individual employees would be essential. Clearly this would require the trust to set up its own secretariat to do all this properly and that may require public support.

An alternative approach is to extend membership by issuing shares to a firm's producers, possibly by the creation on a much wider scale than at present of ESOPs. This provides producers with an even stronger incentive to participate in the formulation of company policy because it gives additional financial interest. They gain if strategic plans succeed and lose if they do not. Furthermore the evidence surveyed in the first section on existing schemes for profit sharing and/or share ownership suggests that they really do improve economic performance if an intention of them is to increase involvement in decision making (and they are successful in this), which is precisely what we are seeking. Again there are delicate problems like the proportion of shares producers should receive and again the idea of a producer co-operative or trust to exercise the collective vote of producer shareholders could be pursued. Indeed the co-operative idea is currently being promoted in the US, see Lusk (1989). He reports that the Boston-based Industrial Co-operative Association is promoting the notion of 'democratic ESOPs'. The aim of these is for the voting rights attached to shareholdings to be exercised collectively according to the instructions of a producer co-operative. More generally, any mechanism for exercising the collective vote of producer shareholders should not be confused with Thatcherite proposals for wider share ownership as these inhibit a major shift in corporate power.

However a potential problem with the shareholding route is the importance of recognizing producers' interests *qua* producers, not simply as shareholders. For instance the evidence on trade unions suggests that benefits arise from producers sharing power as producers, not investors. In this respect the shareholding route can be deceptive, diverting attention from the real issues. For example, the traditional view in British law is that directors have a duty to act bona fide in the interests of the company, which effectively means the company's shareholders. This sits comfortably alongside a policy which simply makes producers shareholders. Yet if the crucial need is for producers to be members because they are producers a more appropriate duty for directors must be recognized: to act bona fide in the interests of a company's shareholders and producers. This does not pose insurmountable difficulties. For instance, a redrafted Company Act could recognize two classes of investor members – 'producer investors' and 'non-producer investors' – and burden directors with a duty towards producers *qua* producers, among other things. The vital thing is to be conscious of such issues so as to avoid inadequate reform and not be deceived into something inappropriate.

More generally there are issues beyond mere broadening of membership that need to be addressed in reforming company law. One is the entire question of directors' duties, which are currently very limited. For instance Mayson *et al.* note that directors face 'the relatively light duty of care', a duty not to be negligent; but whilst a company has redress against negligent directors it only remains a possibility that members can take action – the law is simply unclear. If membership is broadened as a means of power sharing this needs to be altered. Members must be owed duties which they can enforce.

A further problem is that if power sharing is not to be a sham it is essential for members and their representatives to have access to the kind of information on which corporate planning is based. Merely being able to vote (even as a group) is a very limited power if there are severe constraints on information. For instance, under the current system it is customary for members to receive a circular – paid for out of company funds – explaining the directors' views on proposed resolutions at members' meetings. As Mayson *et al.* argue, this gives directors 'a significant advantage because, since they control for the most part the timing of any meeting, they will be able to prepare a well-argued circular'. Even now this advantage is, to some extent, offset by provisions allowing a group of members to have their views circulated – e.g. if the group has at least 5% of total member votes. But whilst such provisions could be maintained with a more broadly defined membership, they are clearly very limited and their imaginative extension is needed. This requires the incorporation of a right to information in a new Company Act.[13] Furthermore access to information is useless without an ability to act on it. This requires expertise and to provide this substantial public provision of training and education in the relevant disciplines (like accountancy) will obviously be necessary. The aforementioned experiences of the supporting structure in Mondragon are especially relevant here. In addition there must be access to high quality and independent sources of 'know-how'. This may also require public support but the expenditure is necessary if a viable system of power sharing is to be established in the corporate sector of the British economy.

There is also the difficulty that greater power sharing within companies may lead to the improved position of 'insiders' being used to the disadvantage of those continuing to be 'outsiders'. For instance, local communities, the unemployed and consumers have an interest in company's decisions but if they remain outside their interests may suffer. There is therefore a need to enhance the accountability of a company to the wider community. This point is recognized in several respects within Labour's Policy Review (especially in the reports of the Productive and Competitive and Consumer and Community Review Groups) even if its complementarity with power sharing is not. More interestingly, Snaith (1988) is very useful on the point; he examines the pros and cons of various options for increasing accountability to different groups, suggesting that each may be best served in different ways. See also Wedderburn (1985) and the discussion of regulatory bodies in Chapter 9, relevant because, for example, there are similarities between regulating a major utility in the interests of consumers and in general enhancing the accountability of companies to outsiders.

Yet another issue concerns the relationship in the unionized sector of the economy between the new and the traditional trade union mechanisms of representation. Many trade unionists will feel uneasy at suggestions that they fear may usurp their role and undermine the effectiveness of the union voice. This knee-jerk response is misplaced, if understandable in the light of the history of profit sharing in Britain (see Hatton, 1988). The intention is to augment their collective representation of employees and to give workers a voice in new areas of company decision making. The objective is to increase social benefit and to increase productive efficiency by complementing existing channels and not replacing them. Indeed we reported evidence from Cable and Wilson (1989) that the productivity gains of introducing profit sharing schemes are greater in firms where unions are best organized (see also the discussion of Conte and Svejnar, 1988). Furthermore the complementary objective is especially seen in the idea of trusts being used to represent members collectively; trade unionists would presumably be very actively engaged in trust affairs.

What may surprise many people is that the discussion thus far has not mentioned employee directors, a favourite in discussions of this sort (see for example the Bullock Report (1977) and the discussion of it in McCarthy's (1988) analysis of industrial democracy). This is because we believe such a solution may create unnecessary problems. True employee directors would have the opportunity to challenge management's view of the strategic direction of a company and to initiate proposals of their own in the central decision making forum of a company. On the other hand, for example, there are clear conflicts of interest for employee directors who as representatives of a particular interest group may also find themselves collectively responsible for the decision of the board as a whole. This may persuade some employee directors to pursue the interests of groups other than those who elected them. Such problems would need to be clearly addressed if employee directors were introduced.[14] But they are an unnecessary complication because the whole idea misses the point, which is that companies should be operated with employees having their full share of power. Once this is accepted, why should any director be exempted from responsibility to employees?

Finally, it is worth considering Britain's membership of the European Community *vis-à-vis* our discussion. Taking a narrow perspective of this membership – seeing it simply as a potential constraint on desirable action – it is reassuring to know that at the time of writing the sort of changes discussed in this chapter seem to be legally feasible. There are moves towards harmonizing company law across members but there is still some way to go. In particular there is a draft directive dealing with worker participation, for instance. According to the 1988 edition of *Farrar's Company Law*,[15] the current proposal was put forward in 1983, is still being given 'preliminary consideration' by a working party and 'it is anticipated that discussion of the draft will take several years'. Similarly there are draft proposals in other relevant areas – such as directors' duties – and binding directives elsewhere, see the review of adopted and proposed measures as of 1 January 1989 in Commission of the European Communities (1989). But all in all it seems that up to now the Community has had relatively little consequence for company law (so far as we are concerned) and that our discussion raises nothing to infringe any existing or imminent legal constraints.

But far more interestingly other Community members are sympathetic to the idea of power sharing. Indeed they seem to have a real commitment to worker participation. In contrast Britain has lagged behind and indeed put a brake on Community progress. For instance the draft Community Charter of Fundamental Social Rights[16] states among other things that: 'Information, consultation and participation for workers must be developed along appropriate lines and in such a way as to take account of the laws, collective agreements and practices in force in the Member States'. It seems other members are very keen to endorse the Charter, but not Britain. (See for example Buchan and Burns (1989) and Palmer

(1989), reporting the opposition of Britain's Employment Minister in the face of unanimity amongst the other eleven governments.)

The implication of this for the Labour Party – both now and when it forms a government – is that whatever course is taken as regards power sharing it should be pursued at the European level. There is a great deal to learn from Britain's neighbours and – given current uncertainty and flux over future directives and so on – there is an important opportunity to positively influence events. Indeed, bearing in mind that the European Community has been especially concerned with employee directors, this may be an area where Labour can lead Europe.

Conclusion

This chapter attempts to explore an economic justification for greater democracy and the policies that this implies. More specifically, the survey of evidence in the first section concludes that industrial performance can be given a real boost if there is a significant shift in the balance of power within firms. The second section examines possibilities for the radical reform of company law, suggesting a new Company Act which rejects archaic and inefficient hierarchy in favour of something fit for the twenty-first century.

The survey of evidence concentrates on the US and UK. It encompasses a wide variety of arrangements, from the rights of consultation enjoyed by trade unions in a capitalist firm to full-blown worker management. The effects on such things as productivity, technical change and employment are considered. It is clear from the survey that power sharing offers many opportunities for increased and increasing efficiency but that these opportunities are not being fully realized in either the US or UK.

In rectifying this, an obvious area of concern is the legal framework within which firms operate. Accordingly, the chapter characterizes the existing legal position in Britain and indicates possible changes in the light of the previous evidence. We argue that broadening membership is a sensible option to consider and in the light of this also suggest changes to directors' duties, access to information and so on.

There is undoubtedly more work that can be done on these issues. For instance, an even closer look at firms' experiences may reveal more detailed information on what is and is not most appropriate; and a detailed new Company Act could be drafted. However it should be clear from this chapter that there is a need for power sharing and for a careful consideration of company law reform.

Notes

We would like to thank Angelo Forte and Bob Lane for their very helpful discussions.

1   Labour Party, 1989.

2   The political case for a shift in Labour policy is clearly put in the Policy Review: the preamble to the report of the Democracy Review Group argues that 'the true purpose of socialism is the creation of a genuinely free society in which a more equal distribution of power and wealth extends the rights and choices of the whole community'. There is also throughout the Policy Review an acceptance that this can only be done by securing (paradoxically by collective action) a significant shift towards the individual citizen in the balance of power within the institutions which establish and entrench our individual and collective rights. Only by this means can the degree of genuine control exercised by the individual over their everyday lives be enhanced. This is crucial because the recognition of the need for a fundamental shift in power is distinguishing the libertarianism of socialists from the Thatcherite alternative.

3   Political principle and economic benefit are not all that matters; see for instance our later comments on Goyder (1987).

4   By improved efficiency we mean improved company performance in terms of productivity, technical change, employment and so on. Thus 'efficiency' is being used in a general sense and not to describe a narrow, technical concept.

5   In what follows our main focus is the UK and US. There is also a voluminous literature on other countries. Recent examples are: Fitzroy and Cable (1980), Cable (1988), Fitzroy and Kraft (1987) for Germany; Jones and Svejnar (1985) for Italy.

6   Mark Stewart (1989) using the WIRS data shows this.

7   There are a number of surveys. Typical is that reported in Northcott, Fogarty and Trevor (1985).

8   The most vocal advocates of this view are the Texas school. The paper by Jensen and Meckling (1979) gives a flavour of this school of thought.

9   The recent paper by Ireland and Law (1988) sets out some of the arguments.

10   Goyder (1987) argues that a system denying employees 'the right to participate in the formulation of corporate purpose in the company to which they may have devoted most of their working lives . . . is morally indefensible and opposed to the natural law'.

11   All of our quotes are from Mayson *et al.* (1987) but see also the more recent Mayson *et al.* (1989).

12   The Thatcher years have seen a boom in liquidations which suggests there is increasing abuse of the privileges arising from limited liability. This suggests a strong case for making incorporation more difficult.

13   The circulation of information may be facilitated by the use of a broad band cable network, discussed in Chapter 10. More generally, successful democratization of firms clearly requires effective communication between

various parties and the use of modern technology will therefore be vital.

14 Snaith (1988) argues that nominee directors are commonly used by merchant banks and holding companies, and that they have raised problems of conflict of interest. This experience would help to solve problems that might arise from having employee directors.

15 Farrar *et al.*, 1988.

16 Commission of the European Communities, 1989a.

Bibliography

J. T. Addison and B. T. Hirsch, 1989, 'Union Effects on Productivity, Profits and Growth: Has the Long Run Arrived?', *Journal of Labor Economics*.

S. Allen, 1984, 'Unionized Construction Workers are More Productive', *Quarterly Journal of Economics*.

S. Allen, 1986, 'Unionization and Productivity in Office Building and School Construction', *Industrial and Labor Relations Review*.

D. Blanchflower and A. Oswald, 1987, 'Profit Sharing; Can it Work?', *Oxford Economic Papers*.

D. Blanchflower and A. Oswald, 1988, 'Profit Related Pay: Prose Discovered?', *Economic Journal*.

K. Bradley and S. Estrin, 1987, 'Profit Sharing in the Retail Trade Sector: The Relative Performance of the John Lewis Partnership', Centre for Labour Economics, London School of Economics Discussion Paper 279.

David Buchan and Jimmy Burns, 1989, 'Storm Gathers Over Social Charter', *Financial Times*, 30 October.

Bullock Report, 1977, *Report of the Committee of Inquiry on Industrial Democracy*, London, HMSO.

J. Cable and F. Fitzroy, 1980, 'Production Efficiency, Incentives and Employee Participation; Some Preliminary Results for West Germany', *Kyklos*.

J. Cable, 1988, 'Is Profit Sharing Participation? Evidence on Alternative Firm Types from West Germany', *International Journal of Industrial Organization*.

J. Cable and N. Wilson, 1989, 'Profit Sharing and Productivity: An analysis of UK Engineering Firms', *Economic Journal*.

Jonathan Charkham, 1989, 'Corporate Governance and the Market for Control of Companies', Bank of England Panel Paper 25.

K. Clark, 1980, 'Unionization and Productivity; Micro-Econometric Evidence', *Quarterly Journal of Economics*.

Commission of the European Communities, 1989, *Harmonization of Company Law in the European Communities. Measures Adopted and Proposed. Situation as of 1 January 1989*, Luxembourg, Office for Official Publications of the European Communities.

Commission of the European Communities, 1989a, *Community Charter of Fundamental Social Rights*, Brussels, Commission of the European Communities.

M. Conte and A. Tannenbaum, 1978, 'Employee Owned Companies; Is the Difference Measurable?', *Monthly Labor Review*.

M. Conte and J. Svejnar, 1988, 'Productivity Effects of Worker Participation in Management, Profit Sharing, Worker Ownership of Assets and Unionization in US Firms', *International Journal of Industrial Organization*.

W. Daniel, 1987, *Workplace Industrial Relations and Technical Change*, Frances Pinter/PSI.

S. Estrin and N. Wilson, 1986, 'The Microeconomic Effects of Profit Sharing: The British Experience', Centre for Labour Economics, London School of Economics Discussion Paper 247.

John H. Farrar, Nigel E. Furey, Brenda M. Hannigan and Philip Wylie, 1988, *Farrar's Company Law*, London, Butterworths.

F. Fitzroy and K. Kraft, 1987, 'Cooperation, Productivity and Profit Sharing', *Quarterly Journal of Economics*.

R. Freeman, 1976, 'The Exit-Voice Tradeoff in the Labour Market', *AER Papers and Proceedings*.

R. Freeman, 1980, 'The Effect of Unions on Worker Attachment to Firms', *Journal of Labour Research*.

R. Freeman and J. Medoff, 1984, *'What do Unions Do?'*, New York, Basic Books.

G. E. Goyder, 1987, *The Just Enterprise*, London, Deutsch.

T. Hatton, 1988, 'Profit Sharing in British Industry', *International Journal of Industrial Organization*.

C. Ichniowski, 1984, 'Industrial Relations and Economic Performance', NBER Working Paper 1367.

N. Ireland and P. Law, 1988, 'Management Design under Labour Management', *Journal of Comparative Economics*.

M. C. Jensen and W. H. Meckling, 1979, 'Rights and Production Functions: An Application to Labor Managed Firms and Codetermination', *Journal of Business*.

D. C. Jones and D. Backus, 1977, 'British Producer Cooperatives in the Footwear Industry: An Empirical Test of the Theory of Financing', *Economic Journal*.

D. C. Jones, 1982, 'British Producer Cooperatives 1948–68: Productivity and Organizational Structure' in D. C. Jones and J. Svejnar, eds., *Participatory and Self-Managed Firms: Evaluating Economic Performance*, Lexington, D. C. Heath.

D. Jones and J. Svejnar, 1985, 'Participation, Profit Sharing and Efficiency in Italian Producer Cooperatives', *Economica*.

K. G. Knight, 1989, 'Labour Productivity and Strike Activity in British Manufacturing Industries: Some Quantitative Evidence', *British Journal of Industrial Relations*.

Labour Party, 1989, *Meet the Challenge, Make the Change – A New Agenda for Britain. Final Report of Labour's Policy Review for the 1990s*, London, Labour Party.

Paul Lusk, 1989, 'Worker Control or Just Another Way of Controlling the Workers?', *The Guardian*, 7 August.

S. Machin, 1988, 'The Productivity Effects of Unionisation and Firm Size in British Engineering Firms', Warwick Economic Research Paper 293.

S. Machin, 1988a, 'Unions and the Capture of Economic Rents: An Investigation Using British Firm Level Data', University College London Discussion Paper 89–02.

S. Machin and S. Wadhwani, 1989, 'The Effects of Unions on Organisational Change: Evidence from WIRS', Centre for Labour Economics, London School of Economics Discussion Paper 355.

Stephen Mayson, Derek French and Christopher L. Ryan, 1987, *A Practical Approach to Company Law*, London, Financial Training.

Stephen W. Mayson, Derek French and Christopher L. Ryan, 1989, *Mayson, French and Ryan on Company Law*, London, Blackstone Press.

William McCarthy, 1988, 'The Future of Industrial Democracy', Fabian Tract 526.

J. Medoff and C. Brown, 1978, 'Trade Unions in the Production Process', *Journal of Political Economy*.

G. Neumann and M. Reder, 1984, 'Output and Strike Activity in US Manufacturing: How Large are the Losses?', *Industrial and Labor Relations Review*.

S. Nickell, S. Wadhwani and M. Wall, 1989, 'Unions and Productivity Growth in Britain, 1974–86: Evidence from UK Accounts Data', Centre for Labour Economics, London School of Economics Discussion Paper 353.

J. Northcott, M. Fogarty and M. Trevor, 1985, *Chips and Jobs*, PSI.

John Palmer, 1989, 'UK Isolated on Charter for Workers', *The Guardian*, 31 October.

T. Peters and R. Waterman, 1982, *In Search of Excellence*, London, Harper & Row.

Ian Snaith, 1988, 'Companies to Serve Society: Opening up Debate on the Reform of Business Structures', paper submitted to the Productive and Competitive Economy Policy Review Group.

M. Stewart, 1989, 'Union Wage Differentials, Product Market Influences and the Division of Rents', Warwick Economic Research Paper 323.

H. Thomas, 1982, 'The Performance of the Mondragon Cooperatives in Spain' in D. C. Jones and J. Svejnar, eds., *Participatory and Self-Managed Firms: Evaluating Economic Performance*, Lexington, D. C. Heath.

P. Voos and L. Michel, 1986, 'The Union Impact on Profits: Evidence from Industry Price-Cost Margin Data', *Journal of Labor Economics*.

S. Wadhwani, 1989, 'The Effect of Unions on Productivity Growth, Investment and Employment', Centre for Labour Economics, London School of Economics Discussion Paper 356.

S. Wadhwani and M. Wall, 1989, 'The Effect of Unions on Corporate Investment: Evidence from Accounts Data 1972–86', Centre for Labour Economics, London School of Economics Discussion Paper 354.

Lord Wedderburn of Charlton, 1985, 'The Social Responsibility of Companies', *Melbourne Law Review*.

M. Weitzmann, 1984, *The Share Economy: Conquering Stagflation*, Harvard, Harvard University Press.

Macro-economic policies and inflation

Introduction

Keynesian economics rightly teaches that there is little reason to believe that the level of aggregate demand in a capitalist economy will be sufficient to maintain full employment. There may be times when aggregate demand is greater than that required to secure full employment; but a more usual occurrence is that demand is inadequate for full employment. During the 'fifties and sixties, Keynesian economists argued that unemployment (at least on the mass scale experienced in the thirties) was a thing of the past since governments now knew how to act to ensure adequate demand for full (or at least near full) employment. However, the mistake frequently made by many Keynesian economists was to ignore the supply-side of the economy. Indeed, many of them could be accused of believing that the major macro-economic problem was to maintain high levels of demand, and that the supply-side would largely look after itself. There were also a range of other constraints on the achievement of full employment, such as avoidance of large trade deficits and containment of inflation, which were not faced up to and to which we return below.

The widespread acceptance of the Keynesian message by the Left in the post-war period represented a drastic change from the pre-war position. Previously, economic problems such as unemployment and business cycles were seen as derived from the anarchy of production under competitive capitalism, which could be solved by socialist planning and nationalization. But the approach to industrial strategy developed in this book represents a welcome return to traditional socialist concerns over the supply-side of the economy, and a considerable downgrading of concern over the level of aggregate demand.

Whilst this chapter focuses on the demand-side, with the rest of the book being more concerned with the supply-side, it should be seen as arguing for a macro-economic policy guiding aggregate demand etc. in a way which is complementary to and supportive of an industrial strategy.

An appropriate level of aggregate demand is a necessary but not sufficient condition for the achievement of full employment. In addition, there must be sufficient capital equipment for the workers to use, and a lack of capital equipment may well be a significant constraint at the present time (in part reflecting the general low level of investment in the British economy which has been particularly acute during the eighties). Further, the work-force must have appropriate skills and training, the lack of which again is likely to be a major problem. The economy must be internationally competitive so that the demand for imports resulting from full employment can be matched by exports, and thereby a balance of trade crisis avoided. The balance of trade position in 1988 and 1989, and the deteriorating balance on manufactured goods during the 1980s clearly show that the British economy continues to be severely constrained by an inability to match exports to imports. The inadequacy of the stock of capital equipment, the low levels of skills and training and an internationally uncompetitive economy are all problems which have to be tackled from the supply-side. The role of macro-economic policies in these circumstances should be seen as supporting as far as possible the operation of those supply-side policies. A buoyant level of demand helps to stimulate investment but macro-economic policies can help to ensure that investment is not crowded out by consumer expenditure if there are binding constraints on total expenditure. The two roles for macro-economic policies are then:

(1) to ensure the correct balance of and level of demand. The appropriate level of demand would be that which leads to the highest level of output which the economy is currently capable of sustaining, bearing in mind constraints from the balance of trade, inadequacy of capital equipment. This would serve on the one side to limit any inflationary pressures arising from demand running ahead of effective supply. But on the other side, a high level of demand encourages investment. The composition of demand has to

be shifted in the direction of investment and exports (and import substitution). A major problem confronting an incoming Labour government is likely to be a substantial balance of trade deficit (even if deflationary policies have reduced the deficit from its current level of over 4% of GDP). Further, the stimulation of investment and research and development will be a major policy objective.

(2) to help the economy cope with short-term pressures and shocks. These pressures could range from foreign exchange crisis through to sudden rises in price of commodities. Policies designed to strengthen the supply-side will take many years to come to fruition. The clear danger (of which the effective abandonment of the National Plan in July 1966 is the best-known example) is that these long-term plans will be jettisoned in the face of short-term pressures.

This general approach to the design and purpose of macro-economic policies stands in sharp contrast with those associated with monetarism. The doctrine of monetarism combined two notions of relevance to our discussion. The first notion was that the level of demand could look after itself without any guidance from government. The present government's view has been that '[t]here is no basic lack of demand . . . the reason why we cannot use our full labour force is that we have not adapted well enough, particularly in our jobs market' (Department of Employment, 1985). The second was that the supply-side of the economy either was smoothly functioning or could be made so by the removal of impediments to competition and market forces). In contrast, we see both demand-side and supply-side policies as necessary for the achievement of full employment and a strong economy.

An economic theory can have influence well outside the academic sphere, and such influence can arise from the use which powerful groups can make of the theory. This has been the case with monetarism (Bhaduri and Steindl, 1983). Monetarism, along with changes in the financial system, has promoted the interests of the financial sector rather than the interests of the industrial sector. The treatment in the media of economic news is indicative of the attention given to the needs of the financial sector over those of the industrial sector. Economists interviewed on radio and television are generally employed by City institutions, and their answers reflect the interests and concerns of finance rather than industry (and more generally of working people). Indeed, it would be rather strange if the employees of City institutions did not reflect in public the interests of those institutions. The present government's medium-term financial strategy (MTFS) has been to focus on financial rather than real aspects of the economy, on the use of (narrowly interpreted) monetary rather than fiscal policy for short-term adjustments, and on the balance between government expenditure and taxation. There has also been an obsessional concern with the views and power of the financial markets.

A major feature of financial markets is that the vast majority of transactions are concerned with the trading of existing financial assets. The attention of the participants in financial markets is directed to the current level of prices (e.g. of equities) and interest rates, and even more so with the change of prices and interest rates. In other words, the concern is with the short-term, often the very short-term. Further, much of the income of financial institutions depends on the volume of transactions, and as such their interests are helped by more and more transactions in the existing financial assets. In Chapter 1, Keith Cowling identifies short-termism of markets as a major reason for the need for an industrial strategy, with much short-termism arising from the financial sector. Whereas the financial sector is largely concerned with exchange of existing financial assets, the industrial sector is involved with the production of goods and services. Production inevitably takes time, and particularly the development of new products and processes requires substantial periods of time and planning. The exchange of existing assets does not create wealth, whilst production does create wealth. When Mrs Thatcher talks of governments not being able to 'buck the market', the market which it is said cannot be bucked is the foreign exchange market. But it is not only governments which appear to have to accept what happens in the foreign exchange markets, it is also consumers, workers and industry. A major underlying purpose of economic policy should be to enable people to indeed 'buck the market' when markets do not serve their interests well.

It is well-known that the volume of transactions in foreign exchange markets is many times (of the order of 50 to 100 times) the volume of international trade. Thus the vast majority of foreign exchange transactions are related to financial transactions: that is money moving from one currency to another is search of higher interest rates and gains from exchange rate fluctuations. The determination of the exchange rate (in a floating exchange rate system) is then dominated (at least in the short run) by financial considerations. The experience of the floating exchange rate has clearly been that of highly volatile exchange rates with significant periods of time during which a currency has been substantially overvalued and others when it has been undervalued. '[F]oreign exchange markets behave much more like the unstable and irrational asset markets described by Keynes than the efficient markets described by modern finance theory' (Klugman, 1989). Whilst there is an element of 'what is gained on swings is lost on the roundabouts' here, nevertheless the uncertainty generated by volatility is harmful for planning by firms and others, and tends to discourage investment and trade.

The thrust of our earlier discussion has been that macro-economic policies should be designed to support the industrial supply-side strategy. In the words of the Labour Party's Policy Review (Labour Party, 1989), the 'strengthening [of] our productive base requires that macro-economic policy should serve our general economic and industrial objectives. We shall therefore change the balance of that policy in favour of wealth creators rather than the holders of assets.' This would represent a welcome shift away from any concern over the views expressed by (a small group of politically motivated) participants in the stock and exchange markets to a concern with those of workers, other producers and consumers. A realization by the City that when there was a conflict of interest between the production side of the economy and the financial side a Labour government would favour production over finance may well mean that the prospect of the election of a Labour government would lead to falls in financial markets. Falling Stock Market prices may make the headlines, but as the Stock Market crash of October 1987 indicates, are otherwise of little significance.[1] A falling exchange rate is of much greater significance, and we return to discussion of that below.

It would be trite to say that the conduct of economic policy faces a variety of constraints, from the finiteness of existing resources through to the requirement that government expenditure is financed (by taxation, borrowing and money creation). But one major aspect of economic policy should be concerned with the easing of crucial constraints. The present government has often eagerly accepted the constraints posed by the financial (particularly the exchange) markets. Whilst there are of course many situations in which a government has to accept the constraints imposed by the financial markets, the thrust should be towards the formulation of policies which will ease such constraints. Thus, rather than arguing that it is not possible to 'buck the market', it should be a matter of striving to 'tame the market' in the social interest.

A particularly important idea in the Labour Party's Policy Review is that of a Medium Term Industrial Strategy (MTIS) with a strengthened Department of Trade and Industry (DTI) placed on at least a par with the Treasury. This should help to promote long-term strategic thinking within the government machine, and to help to reduce the influence of the short-termism of both the financial markets and the Treasury. It would also help to promote greater interest in production and wealth creation and to reduce interest in finance and the exchange of existing pieces of paper (and entries in computer memories). However, an industrial strategy is a long-term project and needs some protection from short-term pressure. This suggests that the DTI budget should be given protected status; that is if short-term pressures require a reduction in public expenditure, such reductions should not fall on the DTI budget. However, the other side of that proposition is that reductions should fall on other budgets, nearly all of which would have their champions in the Labour Party and elsewhere. Thus there will be considerable political difficulties in maintaining the DTI budget in such circumstances.

Short-term pressures

The short-term pressures are most likely to arise from the foreign sector, and there are of course plenty of examples of Labour governments being blown off course by foreign exchange crises. Exchange rates under a floating rate system have exhibited wide fluctuations which probably inhibit international trade and intro-duced major problems into the conduct of short-term economic management. The foreign exchange markets provide a clear example of the need for government intervention in markets; in this instance to provide some stability. Interest rates are a blunt instrument for dealing with this problem, and have adverse side-effects on the rest of the economy. The election of a Labour government, which will probably be combined with a substantial balance of trade deficit, is likely to place heavy pressure on sterling. Each past Labour government has experienced at some stage a sterling crisis. The crisis may reflect balance of trade difficulties (as in the first months of the 1964 Labour government) or come about without any such difficulties (as in 1976).[2] Whatever the cause of a run on sterling, there should be policy instruments to hand to minimize the damage.

A successful industrial policy would eventually aid balance of trade difficulties by reducing the propensity to import (especially the tendency of imports to grow faster than income) and encouraging the growth of exports. But in the interim some reduction of the value of sterling will probably be required. There is a clear danger that the reductions in living standard and rising inflation consequent upon a declining exchange rate will threaten the Labour government's programme at the start. Thus, an incoming Labour government must have at its disposal a range of policy instruments (other than raising interest rates) to cope with an exchange rate crisis. But even a successful industrial policy and a much improved balance of trade would be no guarantee against a sterling crisis, given the economic influence and collective irrationality of the exchange markets.[3] It is then clearly necessary to design policy instruments to deal with an exchange crisis. It is debatable whether such policy instruments should be publicly discussed, for it could be argued that such discussion may make an exchange rate crisis more likely. But, the reverse argument is at least as plausible, namely that market participants are less likely to generate a run on the pound if there are credible policy instruments ready to deal with such a run.

At the time of writing, Britain's membership of the exchange rate mechanism (ERM) of the European Monetary System (EMS) is a matter of intense political debate. It may well be that Britain will be a member by the time of the next election (or even by the time of publication of this book), in which case some limited protection against a run on the pound will already be in place. If Britain is not already a member of the ERM, then the suggestion here is to join early as a means of stabilizing the value of the pound (at least against other EC currencies) at a reasonable level. The longer-term implications of such membership are considered below.

Membership of the ERM raises the question of what rate should be set for sterling. We do not intend to provide any specific figure since movements in inflation rates etc. between the time of calculation and the time of publication may well invalidate such figures. Below we indicate the factors to be taken into account when the rate is set, and these factors change over time. We would argue that if the 'correct' level of sterling is seen as that which is consistent with elimination of the balance of trade deficit then at the present time such a 'correct' level would probably mean a drastic reduction in the value of sterling with a significant impact on living standards and the rate of inflation. Further, British industry would probably find it very difficult because of capacity constraints to supply the higher demand for exports which would be generated by a depreciation. In any event we would argue that the specific level may be of less significance than the fact of membership itself. Variations in the exchange rate may have little impact on the balance of trade for the combination of two reasons. First, prices of (internationally) traded goods may not fully reflect the change in the exchange rate. For example, importers into the UK may not raise prices by the full extent of an exchange rate change because they wish to maintain their market position built up over the years.[4] Second, the sum of the relevant price elasticities of demand may be rather low. Some evidence on the elasticities of demand for imports and exports (Smith, 1988, Turner, 1988) places the sum of those elasticities as little above unity. Other estimates place the sum rather higher. Barker (1988), for example, suggests a sum of just below 2, but with a high income elasticity of demand for imports.

An important factor in setting an exchange rate on entry into the ERM of the EMS is that the rate is regarded as sustainable. Given the volatility of the exchange markets, at the time of entry, the value of sterling could be particularly low so a value of sterling above the previous rate may be reasonable. The other factors to be borne in mind are the effect on living standards and on inflation resulting from any depreciation, and the stimulus to exports in conjunction with industry's ability to supply further exports.

The gyrations of exchange rates to some degree reflect the dominance of flows across the exchanges related to financial deals over those related to financing international trade. The benefits of involvement of a country in the international economy arises from trade and real investment (even though the advantages are often overstated). The benefits do not arise from the movement of finance from one country to another in pursuit of higher interest rates and gains from exchange rate movements. The resulting volatility of the exchange rate may indeed cause damage. There are then reasons for reducing the financial flows. One suggestion for reducing the flows across the exchanges (and hence intended to reduce the gyration of exchange rates) is for a transactions tax on the exchange of currencies. There may be insuperable practical difficulties with this suggestion (e.g. the UK government could only levy the tax on transactions within the UK). These difficulties would be less if a transactions tax (or other instruments designed to reduce financial flows) were imposed at the EC level.

As argued above, there is a need for government to make short-term adjustments to the level of demand in response to economic events. These events may range from changes in international interest rates, pressure on sterling, changes in commodity prices, variations in the rate of inflation etc. Some adjustments can be made in the annual budget, but obviously there is no reason to think that adjustments will only be required at the time of the budget. Some instruments of policy (e.g. interest rates) are easier to vary quickly than others (e.g. rate of income tax), though quick adjustment may be quite different from quick impact.[5] Different speeds of adjustment and of impact, as well as doubts about the size of impact,[6] suggests that a range of instruments should be used to control the economy, rather than any reliance on a single instrument. The standard argument since Tinbergen (1952) has been that a government should use a number of instruments equal to the number of policy objectives.[7] The present government has unnecessarily foregone the use of a range of instruments, notably fiscal policy and a range of monetary policies (other than interest rates). A range of policy instruments are needed where there are numerous policy targets. The possibilities of variations of tax rates between budgets and the forms of credit control as instruments of short-term policy will be discussed. It can then be argued that credit controls present less difficulties when viewed as short-term policies than if the intention was to operate them on a permanent basis.

It is probably right to avoid extreme fine-tuning of the economy, the failure of which helped to give Keynesian economics a bad name. Adjustments to policy stance are regularly made in the annual budget, and adjustments at other times are necessary when short-term pressures are particularly strong or when there is some large and unexpected change in the economic environment. The attraction of interest rates as a short-term policy instrument appears to be that it can be quickly and frequently adjusted. However, there are political constraints to the extent of interest rate adjustments, and there may be considerable lags between interest rate changes and their effects. But there must be doubts on the use of interest rates in other ways. If the purpose of a variation in interest rates is to influence the level of demand then there have long been doubts especially from Keynesians as to the extent of such influence.

A sudden rise in interest rates obviously acts to the detriment of borrowers and to the advantage of lenders, and the effects are particularly pronounced when borrowing has been undertaken on a variable interest rate basis. Much of the international debt crisis of the eighties can be traced to the unexpected rise in interest rates starting with a tightening of American monetary policy. At a domestic level, recent borrowers (especially those with mortgages with variable interest rates) are particularly affected. The impact on different groups of people and firms of a rise in interest rates is essentially arbitrary and unplanned, whereas deflation through tax and expenditure adjustments can to some degree be targeted.

The major influence of the level of interest rates probably comes through its influence on the exchange rate. A rise in UK interest rates (relative to overseas interest rates) is usually seen to make sterling more attractive and sterling appreciates (relative to the level it would have otherwise attained). However, with internationally mobile finance capital, it would be anticipated that the interest rate differential (between the UK and say West Germany) would be equal to the expected rate of depreciation of sterling relative to (in this example) the DMark (which in turn may be influenced by the expected difference in the inflation rates of the two countries). Thus high UK interest rates would signal a rapidly depreciating value of the pound sterling.[8] On this argument, high interest rates are not a method for squeezing inflation out of the economy, but rather a signal of future depreciation of the pound, which will usually be associated with faster inflation.

Two sets of policy instruments which have been overlooked in recent years are credit controls and variations in tax rates. A wider selection of policy instruments would probably include these, and we now discuss them in turn. Credit controls can take many forms ranging from the imposition of minimum repayments on credit cards, through conditions on loans (length of repayments etc.) to

instructions to financial institutions and calling in of special
deposits from banks. Most forms of credit control have the
advantage of speedy adjustment. Some developments in the
financial sector (over something like the last twenty-five years) have
made the effective use of some forms of credit controls more difficult
than it used to be. But that does not mean that all forms of credit
control are impossible to use effectively. As in many other areas of
policy, a Labour government would have to construct new agencies
and instruments for the implementation of their policies.

It is often argued that credit controls can be circumvented and
eventually become ineffectual, with one route being borrowing from
abroad. But it must be said that whilst this argument has some force
when considering borrowing by large corporations, it has much less
force when borrowing by consumers is considered. Borrowing from
abroad is not something which most consumers are likely to rush to
do. A government which sought to encourage investment (to some
degree at the expense of consumer expenditure) would be applying
credit controls to households rather than to firms. But when
borrowing abroad is possible, then a high UK interest rate policy, as
well as credit controls, can be circumvented.[9] However, if credit
controls are seen as short-term measures only, then the
circumvention argument becomes less persuasive. For example, if it
were felt necessary to take some consumer demand out of the
economy, credit controls related to consumer expenditure could be
used initially; tax increases could be used on a longer-term basis to
pursue a similar end.

There has clearly been an explosion of credit, particularly
for households, during the eighties. The calculated propensity
to save by households refers to the balance between those who are
saving and those who are dissaving (by incurring debt and by
depleting their past savings).[10] The amount of outstanding personal
debt more than doubled between the end of 1984 and the end of
1988, though the bulk of personal debt is accounted for by loans for
house purchase. The rise in borrowing by households has been
reflected in a drastic decline in the propensity to save by households,
down from 14 % in 1980 to 4½% in 1988, and undermines the
Conservative government's claim of financial rectitude.[11,12] The
social dangers of rising personal debt have become readily apparent
in the past few years, when unexpected unemployment and rises in
interest rates can force individuals (and countries) into a position

where debt repayment becomes virtually impossible. However, credit controls are not well designed to tackle those particular problems and policies such as government information, codes of conduct by financial institutions are likely to be more appropriate.

Fiscal policy is a potent weapon for the guidance of the economy in both the short term and the long term.[13] Some elements of fiscal policy are not well suited for use in the short term: it makes little sense to interfere with most public expenditure for short-term management purposes. Public expenditure (as discussed below) requires careful planning to fulfil social objectives. Taxation is better suited than public expenditure to quick adjustments, and this applies particularly to taxes such as value-added tax and national insurance contributions. This is not to advocate that these taxes are frequently adjusted but rather that these are potent instruments to be added to the list of possibilities.

However, the general point here is that the short-term guidance of the economy should utilize a battery of instruments. The choice of instrument should depend on the specific circumstances (e.g. credit controls may be more potent than tax changes in some circumstances but not in others), with due consideration being given to the distributional and inflationary effects of the instruments under discussion.

The emphasis in macro-economic policy should be on the objectives of policy rather than the means of achievement. The relevant policies will change as the economic situation changes. However, it should be possible to explore (e.g. through simulation of macro-econometric models) the ways in which economic policy should respond to a range of possible circumstances. Given a history of Labour governments being blown off course, it is imperative that a future Labour government is prepared with responses to economic problems which maintain the long-term priorities of the policy. In order to do this, it is useful to have relatively formal responses tailored to the different sources of problems and equivalent reactions if events go better than expected. It is also argued by many economists that making the form of such responses publicly known will improve the credibility of policy and effectiveness of macro-economic intervention. This would represent a development of the conditional tax changes which were used during the 1974/79 Labour government.

Exchange rate systems

Britain's membership of the ERM was seen above as helpful in reducing the volatility of the exchange rate which has been observed in the near twenty years of floating exchange rates.[14] In particular, it is important that a Labour government is not blown off course by a sterling crisis, and this possibility is reduced by ERM membership. In effect, membership of the ERM is the only present feasible option for some move back towards fixed exchange rates. A system of fixed exchange rates is clearly undermined by differences in national inflation rates. Relatively small differences can be tolerated in the short term and met by adjustments to the exchange rates. But large differences will mean frequent adjustments and expectation of adjustments, thereby undermining the whole concept of fixed exchange rates.

Britain's membership of the ERM would pose two particular problems. The first is that, as indicated above, there has been a long standing tendency for the British inflation rate to be above average and specifically above the German inflation rate.[15] If attempts are made to deal with this inflationary tendency by holding down the level of economic activity (i.e. raising unemployment) the costs will be considerable.[16] The continuing divergence between national inflation rates was a major factor in the eventual collapse of the Bretton Woods system in the early seventies. The second is the balance of trade position and the tendency for the UK's position to worsen through a propensity to import which is much higher than the propensity of other countries to import from the UK. A British economic growth rate which is much below that of many other countries has been a major way by which the balance of trade deficit has been held in check.

The specifically British problems in joining the ERM arise from these tendencies towards faster inflation and a trade deficit. These are not problems which can be overcome by any co-ordination of fiscal and monetary policies. Membership of a fixed exchange rate system does impose limitations of domestic policies, though it is arguable whether these are more constraining than those imposed by the exchange markets under a floating exchange rate system. Thus British membership of the ERM needs to be backed up by industrial and other policies to strengthen the competitiveness of the UK economy.

Composition of aggregate demand

Through most of the post-war period, the British economy has tended to under-invest in people, capital equipment and ideas (as compared with its international rivals) and to run into balance of trade difficulties. The share of GDP devoted to gross fixed capital formation in the UK has generally fallen below that of our main rivals. For example, in 1987, gross fixed capital formation represented 17% of GDP in the UK, whilst the corresponding figure for the rest of the EC was 2½ percentage points higher.[17] Investment in manufacturing has been particularly poor during the 1980s. Gross investment only recovered its levels of the late 1970s in 1988, and net investment was negative each year from 1981 to 1986 (with the exception of 1985).[18] The balance of trade position for the past decade or more has of course been greatly aided by the arrival of North Sea oil, but it is now clear that the basic balance of trade problems have not been solved but merely masked by the bonus of oil.[19] A major purpose of the industrial strategy developed in this book is to raise the level of investment (in people as well as in capital equipment) and to improve Britain's international competitiveness. The implication of seeking to reduce Britain's balance of trade deficit[20] and of a shift towards investment is that the composition of aggregate demand moves away from consumer expenditure towards investment and exports. Whilst it may be possible to avoid a reduction in consumer expenditure, a growth rate of such expenditure much below that observed in recent years will be necessary.

Thus an industrial strategy involves the government taking a view on the appropriate balance between consumer expenditure, investment and exports as well as on government expenditure. This would represent the reintroduction of macro-economic planning, and would require the development of policy instruments able to influence consumer expenditure etc. But the immediate prospect is that such planning would have to point in the direction of raising investment and exports, and it is usually rather overlooked that this may involve the restraint of consumer expenditure.[21] The Labour Party's Policy Review rightly points to the importance of raising investment and exports, and that a credit-financed consumer expenditure boom has generated some of the present economic difficulties. There is a danger that the restraint of consumer expenditure will mean the restraint of wages, and the stimulation of investment higher levels of profits. These dangers could be reduced (at least in the longer term) by the encouragement of workers' funds. The restraint of consumer expenditure would then arise through the stimulation of savings by workers through the media of workers' funds. This would provide the finance for investment, and would open the way for the growth of worker ownership of industry. In other words, constraint on wages and consumer expenditure would not be equivalent to an increase in profits for shareholders, but would rather represent collective savings by workers.

Inflation

Discussion of inflation and policies towards the control of inflation faces two prior questions – what are the costs of inflation and what are the causes of inflation? The general failure by economists, commentators and others to provide convincing answers to these questions means that most discussion of inflation takes place in a kind of vacuum. The stated concern of the present government with inflation as the number one economic problem is frequently enunciated, though its record in the past few years (especially its own contribution to inflation through raising nationalized industries' prices and interest rates) must cast doubt on its sincerity. There is a lack of reasons given as to why control of inflation should be given absolute priority in light of the many other economic difficulties. Further, there is a general lack of analysis as to how raising interest rates is to bring down the rate of inflation, and no discussion of other instruments of policy.[22]

When inflation threatens to explode with the danger of hyper-inflation and the breakdown of the use of money, the focus of political attention is on inflation, and there are good reasons for treating inflation as a severe problem. But when inflation is relatively low the dangers of hyper-inflation are not imminent, and the control of inflation should receive lower priority (as compared with unemployment, improving the regional balance of economic activity etc.). Some aspects of industrial strategy (improved training, more economic activity in the regions) will help reduce inflationary pressures by easing bottlenecks and improve the operation of the supply-side of the economy. Many would advocate higher levels of unemployment as a means of constraining inflation. In contrast, we would see such a policy as inefficient, not only for the substantial costs for those made unemployed, but also as eventually unsuccessful. There are doubts as to the short-term impact of unemployment on inflation, and any effect may be short-lived (depending on rising unemployment rather than a higher level of unemployment). It would also be preferable to focus on restraining prices over which government has an influence rather than raising unemployment as an inefficient attempt to constrain inflation. Further, we would argue that if inflation threatens to become a serious constraint on policy, that it should be tackled head-on by price control.

The control of inflation has not proved easy in the past, and policies adopted towards the reduction of inflation have their own substantial adverse effects. These may be those arising from unemployment and excess capacity (when deflationary policies are used to try to damp down inflation) through to the difficulties of implementing and maintaining a prices and incomes policy. The attention paid to the control of inflation should then be commensurate with the costs of inflation. Economists have found considerable difficulty in identifying the costs of inflation *per se*, especially in a world of floating exchange rates. The move towards fixed exchange rates which is involved in joining the ERM of the EMS would mean that some difficulties would arise when the UK's inflation rate was substantially out of line with the average for the the rest of the EC, which would suggest a target of bringing the UK inflation rate in line with the EC average. But this should be seen as a target, along with other targets such as low level of unemployment, improved distribution of income and a more competitive British industry.

The considerable public concern with inflation, taken with the dangers of inflation slipping into hyper-inflation, means that attention has to be given to the control of inflation (and particularly to the prevention of the acceleration of inflation). But it may be that the expressed concern with inflation arises from other problems which often go alongside inflation, such as enhanced struggle over income shares, worsening economic performance (as during the early seventies).

The discussion of the causes of inflation (and the implied policies to control inflation) suffers from an urge to find a single cause. This was most apparent in the monetarist theory where increases in the money supply were seen as the unique cause of inflation with the implied policy of control of the money supply. It is evident from the

events of the past decade that this view was incorrect both in terms
of the causes of inflation and of the possibilities of control of the
money supply. In recent times, the emphasis has switched, with
'overheating' of the economy being frequently cited. This cor-
responds to the Phillips curve view of wage inflation, whereby the rate
of wage inflation depends on, *inter alia*, the level of unemployment.

The view of inflation advanced here has a number of elements.
There are many causes of price and wage rises, and it is folly to
search for a single cause or a universal theory. The multi-cause view
implies that a search for a single cure would ultimately be doomed.
Further, insofar as 'overheating' is a cause of inflation, it is the
change in economic activity rather than the level of activity which is
relevant. There is considerable empirical and theoretical support
for the view that any effect of unemployment on the pace of inflation
comes from change in unemployment (or the closely related
variable of unemployment relative to its recent levels) rather than
the level of unemployment, though it is not always found that there
is an effect of unemployment on inflation.[23] Thus, increases in
economic activity may bring with them some 'blip' of inflation, but a
sustained higher level of economic activity does not immediate pose
an inflationary threat. However, prolonged full employment does
change the balance of economic power between workers and
employers and may involve inflationary pressures.

Conflicts over the share of income (wages vs. profits, maintenance
of differentials etc.) can often trigger off and sustain inflation. Periods
of social consensus reduce the conflicts, whilst periods of high
unemployment and low capacity utilization can suppress the
conflict. However, high unemployment hits some groups more than
others, and during the eighties there has been a substantial shift
from wages to profits. Further, unemployment usually hits the less
skilled harder than the more skilled and there may be effects on wage
differentials (which have also tended to widen during the eighties).
When unemployment declines, as is now being observed, inflationary
pressures arise from attempts to restore differentials.

Increases in money and credit are not generally the cause of
inflation but rather the monetary and credit conditions respond to
the prevailing rate of inflation. The causes of inflation should then be
seen as arising on the real side of the economy, and the monetary
side of the economy accommodates to the prevailing rate of inflation.
There are (relatively rare) occasions when credit expansion triggers

off an episode of inflation, and this generally shows up initially in a rise in the price of houses and other assets.

Finally, the British rate of inflation tends to move in sympathy with, though usually somewhat above, the OECD rate of inflation. An important common influence on the UK and other OECD countries is the rise and fall of commodity prices[24]. Thus a part of inflation comes from outside of the British economy, and that aspect of inflation would be reinforced under a fixed exchange rate regime.

This line of approach leads to a number of policy conclusions. The reflation of the economy may stimulate some rise in the rate of inflation, but this may be a necessary cost of falling unemployment. These inflationary consequences may place a limit on the speed of reflation, but not on the process of reflation. However, the inflationary consequences can be reduced by targeted reflation, and this would mean, *inter alia*, at the present time directing the reflationary effects towards the more depressed regions. But the inflationary consequences of reflation should not be overestimated for reflation contains elements which help to restrain inflation. The greater use of existing capacity helps to lower unit costs of production. Higher real wages can ease some of the pressures for wage increases. When reflation is directed towards, for example, education and training, there will in time be an easing of supply constraints, helping to lower inflationary pressures.

Inflation is viewed here as more of a real phenomenon rather than a monetary one. In other words, it is the real side of the economy (level of economic activity, changes in distribution of income etc.) which generate inflation, and not the monetary side of the economy which largely passively provides the required finance for the inflationary process.

Attempts to change the distribution of income (e.g. by raising low pay through a national minimum wage) can have inflationary consequences. But those consequences are largely a reflection of the ability and willingness of groups in society to offset the proposed changes. The appropriate response is to campaign to convince people of the justice of the proposed distributional changes and to phase them in during periods of growing prosperity. There are clear examples where considerable changes have been made (some reduction of male/female differentials in the seventies, worsening inequality in most dimensions since 1979) without great inflationary consequences. But in order to avoid inflationary consequences, the changes have to be generally accepted or those adversely affected lack the power to respond. However, many of the policies advocated by the Labour Party would shift income from the more to the less powerful, whereas the policies of the present Conservative government have been designed and had the effect of shifting income to the economically (and politically) powerful. The less powerful are not able to offset income gains of the more powerful, whilst under Labour policies the more powerful would be able to offset gains by the less powerful. However, in a longer term perspective, a national minimum wage may help build a consensus on a desirable distribution of income and limit inflationary pressures (as discussed further below).

A certain amount of luck is also involved. The British inflation rate may rise or fall for reasons quite outside the control of the British government. The Labour government of the seventies suffered in this respect, whilst the Tory government benefited through the mid eighties. The general world inflationary climate, the level of economic activity at a world-level etc., considerably influence the British inflation rate, and this would be reinforced under a (quasi) fixed exchange rate.

In the short term (i.e. the first parliament of a Labour government), much will depend on the inherited inflationary climate. If the present government is successful in reducing price inflation back to say 3%, there may be a 'window of opportunity' during which inflation can be given low priority, and attention given to reducing unemployment and inequality. These will have some inflationary consequences, but these could be absorbed without creating a hyper-inflationary environment and the expectation of high and rising inflation. But, if as is more likely, the present government is not successful in reducing inflation, then it is likely that inflation would be a key election issue, in circumstances of relatively high and perhaps rising inflation. An incoming Labour government might then be faced (in a way comparable to 1974) with an inflationary climate. There would be much to be said in such circumstances for an immediate price freeze to quickly break the inflationary climate. The share of profits has risen substantially in recent years, and should be able to absorb the impact on profits which a price freeze would initially entail (in some contrast to the position in the mid seventies). But in any event some crash programme would be required in an inflationary climate for otherwise other policies will have to be delayed.

The experience of the Price Commission with intervention over prices and costs in the period 1977–1979 could be built on. During this time, it operated as an efficiency audit body, with a much greater case load than that of the Monopolies Commission. This would extend the proposal in the Policy Review to use a tighter competition policy to reduce monopoly power and prices to a consideration also of efficiency of operation and the reduction of costs.

In the longer term, the maintenance of full employment will be undermined by inflationary pressures unless some (implicit or explicit) agreement over incomes is in place. Such an agreement requires an underlying consensus over the distribution of income (both as between wages and profits, and within the work-force). The experience of the post-war period would suggest that it may take a considerable time before the inflationary pressures under-mine full employment (and there were other reasons why the post-war boom came to an end). In any future return to full employment, the length of time before severe inflationary pressures build up is likely to be less than in the post-war boom up to 1973 for in part inflation was largely a wartime phenomenon before World War II, whilst now it is a pervasive feature of economic life. Any consensus on income distribution is not easily achieved, and would have to be created after the years of Thatcherism which has gloried in growing inequalities. Further, previous incomes policies have been intro-duced as an emergency measure to contain rising inflation, which is perhaps the worst introduction for a proposed permament arrangement. The intention here would be the gradual build-up to a permanent consensus over incomes against a background of relatively low levels of inflation.

Finally, much inflation can be imported through a falling exchange rate. This would reinforce the discussion above on the need for policies which will help to control the speed of fall of the exchange rate.

This suggests that a three-pronged strategy is required. First, much thought has to be given to the nature of a socially acceptable distribution of income (again between wages and profits, and between workers). Clearly, this is an intricate subject, and also is not independent of other policies such as social security and taxation as well as the institutional arrangements referred to below. When we have some idea of an acceptable distribution of income, there would have to be a concerted effort to build a consensus around such a distribution.

Second, there are institutional changes which would enhance the building of such a consensus and which would aid the continuation of broad agreement over incomes. This would mean, *inter alia*, the encouragement of national bargaining and the growth of workers' and employers' organizations able to represent and bargain on behalf of their members. Third, incomes policies have in the past drawn heavily on a corporatist approach with the involvement of the central organs such as TUC and CBI. Tax-based income policies (TIPs) are one apparent solution to the problems of operating an incomes policy in a decentralized environment. But TIPs have many practical difficulties and are an attempt to impose the view that the existing income distribution is acceptable. However, there is a clear necessity to develop social and instituitional arrangements which will help to restrain inflation in a fully employed economy. In one sense there is plenty of time before any inflationary barrier to full employment will be reached, but the thrust of this argument is that the groundwork has to be undertaken before an era of prolonged full employment is achieved (and attention given to the many other constraints on the achievement of full employment).

It would be something of a pleasure to have to deal with the problems arising from prolonged full employment, and even under the most optimistic assessment such a situation is a long time off. The policies to be adopted in the meantime must depend heavily on the circumstances of the time. If the circumstances are initially of low inflation, then policies should be directed towards limiting inflationary falls in the exchange rate and avoiding policies which have a significant inflationary impact (e.g. avoid raising value added tax). But in an inflationary climate, 'short sharp shocks' such as a price freeze would be appropriate.

Public expenditure

Public expenditure cannot be judged solely in terms of its macroeconomic impact, even though public expenditure does have a significant impact on the level of employment and demand. The essential purpose of public expenditure should be seen as the public provision of goods and services to add to social welfare. This requires the effective and efficient provision of public services. It also implies that public expenditure should be considered primarily in terms of the economic and social welfare. It would also imply that public expenditure should not be used for short-term macro-economic purposes and in any event sudden changes in public expenditure are liable to be disruptive to its orderly planning. The most important feature of public expenditure is what it achieves. A clear statement of the objectives is required for each major area of policy against which the achievements of public expenditure can be judged. These should be defined in terms of ultimate targets and should relate where possible to measurable criteria. In education, for example, the aim should be defined in terms of the educational attainments of people rather than in terms of the inputs into education (e.g. number of teachers) or of the amount of money spent on education.

Public expenditure plans have to be modified in the light of economic developments. However, instead of supposedly fixed plans, derived from views on the ratio of public expenditure to national income, there is a need for a system whereby expenditure can be brought forward or delayed in response to the development of the economy. But the possibilities of using public expenditure as a short-term macro-economic regulator are limited. Nevertheless effective planning of public spending will need to recognize that there will arise circumstances when the problems of the economy will put short-term pressure on spending plans. It would be advantageous to identify in advance projects which can be held back or brought forward with relatively little disruption. The circumstances under which this might be done have been indicated in the kind of rule referred to in the section on short-term pressures above.

The level and mix of public expenditure have to pay regard to both the impact on the use of existing resources and on the social and economic benefits derived from public expenditure. The impact on the use of existing resources does not lead to the use of a target ratio of public expenditure to national income. It does mean, however, that public spending has to be set in the light of current economic position. This implies that due regard has to be paid to the overall level of public expenditure and to its composition since different types of public expenditure have quite different impacts on, for example, the level of demand and the balance of trade. The criterion for public expenditure which is then proposed is that the pattern of spending relates to what the economy can sustain.

Regional policies

Regional policies have not generally been considered part of macro-economic policy, but it is now clear that the regional balance of demand is an important component of macro-economic policy. The pressure on the capacity of British industry (and the resulting inflationary pressures and unemployment) is much more severe than it need be because the demand is so heavily concentrated in the South East. Macro-economic policy has an important role to play in balancing regional demand (along-side industrial policies to stimulate regional balance on the supply-side). There are many reasons for the adaption of a new approach to regional policy, and these are elaborated in Chapter 8. Here the simple point to make is that regional policies provide a good example of the role of the ways in which the strengthening of the supply-side can aid the achievement of macro-economic objectives.

Conclusions

There has been much talk of the overheating of the British economy, which compares rather strangely with the still high levels of unemployment and under-employment. It is a measure of the failures on the supply-side (especially in crucial areas of training, education and investment) and the unbalanced nature of the demand expansion that such talk is heard. A Labour government would be faced with the twin tasks of strengthening the supply side of the economy and with restoring some balance to the demand-side. The role of macro-economic policy would be to help the achievement of a balanced demand and to aid the meeting of the long-term objectives mainly pursued through industrial policies.

Notes

The authors are grateful to Philip Arestis for his comments on an earlier draft.

1 The main way by which a Stock Market crash could have some significance is when the purchase of equity on a rising market has been financed by loans. Then a fall in equity prices may lead to default on loans, and/or loans being called in. There is then the prospect as in 1929 of a failure to repay loans, bank failure etc. But the Central Banks now appear to operate in a way which has reduced the possibilities of such a collapse.

2   The sterling crisis of 1976 and the associated loans from the IMF took place against the background of an improving balance of trade and public expenditure coming under control. Visible exports grew 10% between 1975 and 1976 and grew a further 8% between 1976 and 1977. In contrast, visible imports which had fallen 9% between 1974 and 1975, only grew by 9% between 1975 and 1977. The current account position had been a deficit of over £3 billion in 1974, fell to £1½ billion in 1975, to under £1 billion in 1976 and virtual balance in 1977.

3   When the price of (say) sterling is rising, a profit-seeking individual who believes that sterling will continue to rise would buy sterling to gain from further price rises. This could be regarded as the operation of individual rationality. But the overall effect is to perpetuate a speculative bubble, and (in this example) a level of price for sterling which appears unsustainable.

4   See, for example, Cowling and Sugden (1989).

5   The impact of a change in an instrument of policy is likely to depend on expectations on the future changes in that policy instrument. A change in an instrument which can be quickly adjusted may have little impact if the general expectation is that there will be an early reversal. For example, high interest rates may not have much impact on borrowing on a variable interest rate basis if the borrowers expect interest rates to fall in the near future.

6   A quick glance at the experiments which have been carried out to compare the properties of a range of macro-econometric models would indicate that different models make quite different predictions on the impact of changes in, for example, interest rates. See, for example, Fisher *et al.* (1989).

7   There are many difficulties with this framework of targets and instruments. In particular, what some would regard as instruments, others would regard as objectives. For example, some would view unemployment as an instrument for the control of inflation, whilst others (such as the present authors) would see the reduction of unemployment as a key objective of policy.

8   Hence higher interest rates are associated with a currently higher (than otherwise) value of sterling and a more rapid expected depreciation. A rise in interest rates would then be expected to lead to a jump in the exchange rate, followed by a depreciation.

9   However, borrowing abroad incurs some exchange rate risk. When expected depreciation of exchange rate equals interest rate differential, the expected cost of borrowing is the same abroad as domestically.

10   A person may be both saving and dissaving at the same time. Savings may be compulsory (as under many pension schemes) and/or subject to long-term contracts (e.g. life assurance policies). Dissaving may occur to offset the compulsory nature of some savings and to avoid penalties which would arise from changing long-term contracts.

11   The information in this and the preceding sentence has been derived from *Economic Trends* and *Financial Statistics*.

12   National income accounts require that the net private savings (excess of savings over investment) plus net government budget surplus (tax and other revenues minus expenditure) plus foreign trade deficit (imports minus exports) sum to zero. From that perspective, it is not a great surprise that a budget surplus should be associated with negative net private savings. The unusual feature of the past few years is that the move of the government budget position from deficit to surplus has gone along with a worsening foreign trade position.

13   For some recent estimates see Fisher *et al.* (1989).

14   'The behaviour of exchange rates since 1973 has surprised both advocates and opponents of exchange rate flexibility. The large and

unpredictable exchange rate changes experienced since the breakdown of the Bretton Woods system had not been predicted. The expectation of continuous, small and predictable exchange rate changes has proved to have been ill-founded' (Zis, 1988).

The calculations of Zis (1986) (Table 3) indicates that the variability of exchange rates on a quarterly basis was substantially reduced for countries joining the EMS whereas there was an increase in variability for countries such as UK, USA and Japan. The comparison was made between the experience for the period 1975 (II) to 1978 (IV) and that for the period 1979 (I) to 1984 (IV).

15 In the years 1980–1988, the British inflation rate has been above the EEC average in six years out of nine (the three years of lower inflation in the UK being 1982, 1983, 1984). The British inflation rate has been above the German rate in every year.

16 We would have considerable doubts as to how successful such a strategy would be anyway for, as argued below, the impact of unemployment on inflation is rather limited and unsure (cf. notes 22 and 23).

17 Figures calculated from OECD (1989).

18 Based on statistics given in the National Income Blue Book.

19 The House of Lords Select Committee on Overseas Trade (House of Lords, 1985) expressed concern over the prospects for the trade position as North Sea Oil production declines, and pointed to the manufacturing trade position moving into deficit for the first time in 1983 (and that deficit has grown steadily since). The concerns of the Select Committee were summarily dismissed by the Conservative government (Department of Trade and Industry, 1985).

20 We do not accept the view advanced by the present government that a trade deficit is some kind of vote of confidence in the UK economy since foreigners have been prepared to lend money to the UK to finance the deficit. Interest rates have to be higher to secure the inflow of funds. The nature of the deficit problem is not that there is sometimes a deficit and sometimes a surplus (when the deficit could appropriately be met by borrowing to be repaid out of a trade surplus). The problem is rather the tendency of imports to grow faster than exports.

21 It would almost certainly involve increasing the proportion of national output which goes into investment and exports. It does not necessarily imply an actual reduction in consumer expenditure: that would clearly depend on the possibilities for the overall expansion of output.

22 High interest rates may lead to a higher (than otherwise) exchange rate, and thereby lower (than otherwise) import prices. But, as argued above, a large interest rate differential (between UK rates and those elsewhere) can be seen as a sign of depreciating currency. Higher interest rates may also be seen as depressing demand and economic activity, and leading through some type of Phillips' curve to a lower rate of inflation. We have considerable doubts on the empirical validity of the link from interest rate to the level of demand, and from the level of demand to the rate of inflation (cf. next note).

23 'There does not appear, therefore, to be a negative [wage change, unemployment] relationship in the UK and for the period since the mid-1960s. This should come as no surprise since other studies reach a similar result, notably the study by Henry, Sawyer and Smith (1976) and, more recently, Beckerman (1985)' (Arestis, 1986).

24 See, for example, Beckerman and Jenkinson (1986) for the argument on the importance of commodity prices for inflation.

Bibliography

P. Arestis, 1986, 'Wages and prices in the UK: the Post Keynesian view', *Journal of Post Keynesian Economics*, vol. 8.

T. Barker, 1988, 'International trade and the British economy' in T. Barker and P. Dunne (eds.) *The British economy after oil*, Croom Helm.

W. Beckerman, 1985, 'How the battle against inflation was really won', *Lloyds Bank Review*, no. 155.

W. Beckerman, and T. Jenkinson, 1986, 'What stopped the inflation? Unemployment or commodity prices?', *Economic Journal*, vol. 96.

A. Bhaduri, and J. Steindl, 1983, 'The rise of monetarism as a social doctrine', *Thames Papers in Political Economy*, Autumn.

K. Cowling, and R. Sugden, 1989, 'Exchange rate adjustment and oligopoly pricing behaviour', *Cambridge Journal of Economics*, vol. 13.

Department of Employment, 1985, *Employment: the challenge for the nation*, Cmnd. 9474, HMSO.

Department of Trade and Industry, 1985, *Balance of trade in manufactures*, Cmnd. 9697, HMSO.

R. Fisher, S. K. Tanna, D. S. Turner, K. F. Wallis, and J. D. Whitley, 1989, 'Comparative properties of models of the UK economy', *National Institute Economic Review*, no. 129.

S. G. B. Henry, M. Sawyer, and P. Smith, 1976, 'Models of inflation in the UK: an evaluation', *National Institute Economic Review*, no. 76.

House of Lords, 1985, *Report of the Select Committee on Overseas Trade*, HL 233.

P. Klugman, 1989, 'The case for stabilizing exchange rates', *Oxford Review of Economic Policy*, vol. 5.

Labour Party, 1989, *Meet the Challenge, Make the Change – a New Agenda for Britain. Final report of Labour's Policy Review for the 1990s*, London, Labour Party.

OECD, 1989, *National accounts: main aggregates 1960–1987*, Paris.

K. Smith, 1988, 'The UK economy in the late 1980s: trends and prospects', *International Review of Applied Economics*, vol. 2.

J. Tinbergen, 1952, *On the theory of economic policy*, North-Holland.

D. S. Turner, 1988, 'Does the UK face a balance of payments constraint on growth? – a quantitative analysis using the LBS and NIESR models', ESRC Macroeconomic Modelling Bureau Discussion Paper no. 16.

G. Zis, 1986, 'The European monetary system and the U.K.', *British Review of Economic Issues*, vol. 8.

G. Zis, 1988, 'Flexible exchange rates: the failure of a cure' in P. Arestis (ed.) *Contemporary issues in money and banking: essays in honour of Stephen Frowen*, Macmillan.

A proposal for monitoring transnational corporations

Introduction

It has been argued in Chapter 1 that problems of transnationalism provide a fundamental reason for a community imposing a coherent economic strategy on market forces. This clearly implies that it is desirable to develop a strategy for dealing with transnational corporations. Indeed Chapter 1 suggests that either Britain develops a strategy for intervening in transnationals' own strategy-making or it accepts their domination, their strategy and hence foregoes significant benefits. This is the starting point for the current chapter.[1]

We do not intend to pursue any further the pros and cons of transnationals' activities. Rather we will discuss the next stage of analysis, something which has received far less attention in existing debates. Whilst the idea of a strategy for dealing with transnationals is consistent with previous studies, there has been little attempt to actually explore a strategy. For instance the recent Labour Party Policy Review[2] recognizes problems posed by transnationals[3] yet makes no real attempt to explore mechanisms for handling these problems.[4] More specifically, our aim is to lay a detailed foundation for the first step which will ultimately lead to communities in Britain achieving their desires and attaining their goals rather than being subservient to the desires and goals of transnationals. We recognize that our ideas need developing and indeed we have some suggestions for the next stage of analysis. But for the moment the aim is to point to the right road without travelling very far down that road. The basic reason for this is the view that at this stage, excessive detail may obscure the need to accept some crucial foundations.

To this end in what follows we will first of all discuss a problem in developing any transnationals strategy. We then suggest some advantages of establishing a Transnationals Unit to monitor transnationals, including: first, it would provide a pool of knowledge for policy making; second, it would be an important institutional catalyst for dealing with transnationals; and third, it could affect the policies of transnational corporations themselves, as well as those of the public and government. Following our discussion of the benefits of a monitoring unit we consider the nature and form of the monitoring process, in particular the social audit approach. Finally we focus on the importance of European co-operation.

Overcoming traditional fear

In the past, often vague murmurings of discontent about trans-nationals have been followed by no real action; indeed the essence of Labour government policy has been identical to that of Con-servative, to give British-registered transnationals a free hand and to provide unrestricted welcoming and encouragement to foreign-registered concerns. This last point is explored in Sugden (1990). In Labour's case, we believe, the reason for the attitude has been fear. For instance, fear that if inward investment is not accommodated warts and all, it will be non-existent; i.e. that the cost of a country making any attempt to control foreign-owned firms is that the firms will take their investment elsewhere (and as their advantages are thought to outweigh the disadvantages this would be undesirable). Such fear can be seen, for example, in the comments of Sir Richard Clarke, then Permanent Secretary at the Ministry of Technology:[5] 'The government of the recipient country must accept that the multinational company must lay out its resources as it thinks right; and that if the performance of the local subsidiary is bad, nothing can stop the multinational company from drawing its own con-clusion . . . If governments get sensitive about this, they might be put in a quandary, if they put pressure on a multinational company and that company refuses to cooperate . . . The basic question is: do we want foreign investment? If we do we must accept the consequences.'[6] The suggestion from Hodges (1974) is that this characterizes an attitude of the 1964–70 Labour Government.

The presence of fear represents a problem for developing any transnational strategy because it will undermine any proposals.

This is important and we will return to it in the next section. For now, however, we will content ourselves with the knowledge that other countries – including the place many see as the economic success story of recent decades, Japan – have taken a different view. Whereas so-called developing countries have been far and away the most active in formulating policies with respect to transnationals, even many developed countries have not allowed them free rein (see the surveys in Safarian, 1983, United Nations, 1983, Dicken, 1986, and OECD, 1987). This is most notably true of France and Japan. The French government has simply made it clear, for instance, that it would happily discriminate against foreign investors when it came to granting official subsidies, loans or preferential purchasing agreements in order to maintain a domestic presence in areas where there was a fear of foreign dominance. At least before the 1970s the Japanese took an even stronger line; under the Foreign Exchange and Foreign Trade Control Law of 1949 and the 1950 Foreign Investment Law there was little investment from abroad. More recently Japan became more liberalized but in a way that could in principle very quickly return to a regime of tight regulation. Moreover even the USA – one of the most relaxed countries when it comes to worrying about trans-nationals – introduced the Office on Foreign Investment and the Committee on Foreign Investment to monitor, in a broad sense, their impact.

An important lesson from all this is that to confront transnationals would only be doing to a greater or lesser extent what other countries have been doing. If France, Japan and the United States can be more bold, why not Britain?

A Transnationals Unit

Bearing in mind this problem of fear, an obvious first step in dealing with transnationals is to set up a Transnationals Unit. The Unit would collect information,[7] prepare accounts and use these to influence economic policy and attitudes of and towards transnational corporations. This is an obvious step because of its simplicity, potential for significant benefit and its being the start of an evolutionary process of policy development, allowing a government to feel its way without trying to move too quickly too soon. These attributes should become clear as we proceed.

We would envisage two clear purposes in setting up the Transnationals Unit. First, it would have an important role to play in holding transnationals publicly accountable. However, as we explain in greater detail in the next section, we reject the sole use of traditional historic cost (or even current cost) accounts, such as those currently filed by some subsidiaries of transnational corporations with the Registrar of Companies, as the basis for adequate public accountability. We would propose that the Unit prepare social accounts, which encompass the wider economic and social consequences of transnational corporations' strategy, as well as more traditional accounting of transnationals' performance. Second, and another aspect of public accountability, we would see the setting up of a Transnationals Unit as a significant aspect of government industrial strategy, and as an important contributor to government policy making. It would provide information on individual transnational corporations and sectors. By making such information publicly available it would be possible to facilitate both government decision making and the decision making of those who are currently at a major disadvantage in their dealings with transnationals, e.g. workers, consumers and the public.

Before looking at the nature of the information to be collected and form of accounts to be prepared, we will deal briefly with some recent monitoring experience in other countries and explain in more detail some likely outcomes of setting up a Unit.

As we have already seen, the United States has monitored transnational corporations (see in particular Safarian, 1983). Its focus has been inward investment. The Office on Foreign Investment was established in the 1980s to bring together and study data that various agencies collected on foreign investment. In 1975 the Committee on Foreign Investment was created. It was given various functions, including: analysing trends in foreign investment in the United States; reviewing foreign investments which could have major implications for the United States' national interest; considering proposals for the control of such investments. Initially at least this Committee was not over-active. It met ten times in its first six years of existence. Since then it has become more active although when Safarian was writing it had still not used its powers to invoke relevant US legislation and thereby reject a proposed investment. More recently the activities of the Committee have been the subject of the Exon-Florio amendment to the 1988 Trade Act. According to Riddell (1989), the amendment is seen to strengthen official scrutiny of inward investment and some are proposing yet stronger action.

Other countries have also monitored transnationals (see again Safarian, 1983). For instance in 1973 Canada established the Foreign Investment Review Agency. It was charged with assessing inward investment with reference to, for instance, employment, exports, technological development, competition and Canadian participation as shareholders or directors. The Agency had a fairly wide remit, for example covering all new businesses and all but small acquisitions, and it was active. Similarly Australia created the Foreign Investment Review Board in 1976.

The point of all this is that by establishing a Transnationals Unit Britain would hardly be doing anything particularly radical. Rather it would be following in the footsteps of other countries. But in spite of this, it would be making a significant break from its past and be doing something extremely important – assuming that the Unit is given appropriately wide terms of reference and is vested with appropriate powers.

Clearly the Unit needs to be active; otherwise it would be a virtual irrelevance. Moreover it should be required to obtain and use information on the activities of all transnationals. This is crucial. For instance, there is evidence suggesting that transnationals pitch workers in different countries against each other to prevent collective action, thereby reducing worker bargaining power and adversely affecting worker utility (see for example Cowling and Sugden, 1987, and Sugden, 1990a). Indeed this seems to have been the strategy of General Motors in its recent dealings with Vauxhall workers over the siting of a new engine plant (see Clement, 1989). But it would be very naive to believe that foreign-registered firms play workers off whilst British-registered firms are innocent. Accordingly all transnationals need to be monitored. This monitoring should also be broad-ranging, hence maximizing the Unit's effect. For example the Unit should have the ability to investigate all activities by transnationals, be given wide powers to obtain information and be encouraged to discuss the information as broadly as possible; it should continuously monitor the activities of the largest corporations yet be free to randomly investigate others;[8] and it should scrutinize all inward and outward investments above a specified, small size. Do all of this and the Unit would prove valuable to the British people.

For one thing there is the significant advantage that any future policy-makers hampered by fear have little to lose by creating a Unit. We have argued that past Labour governments have been characterized by fear. Yet given their ignorance,[9] at worst they would have lost very little by establishing a Transnationals Unit; if the monitoring revealed that their fear was justified, the Unit could have been simply disbanded and at least their policy would have had a firm foundation. However, if the monitoring had shown the fear to be groundless, they could have developed a more appropriate stance. Clearly the same is true for similar policy-makers in the future; even if the knowledge that other countries have taken an approach different to that traditionally favoured by Britain is no comfort, they have either a little to lose by following our suggested strategy or – assuming the problems of transnationalism are sufficiently significant – a lot to gain.

More generally, if monitoring does not justify the sort of fear characterizing past governments, our suggested strategy has three other benefits. The first of these is a generalization of the advantage already discussed: it would provide a pool of knowledge enabling the formulation of coherent, detailed and successful strategies in the future. In the past lack of information on transnationals' activities has plagued British governments. For instance Hodges (1974) argues that to the extent investment by foreign-registered firms had its drawbacks, 'they were not readily apparent [to the 1964–70 Labour Government] particularly since there existed no machinery for giving special scrutiny to the activities of multinational companies, and in most areas there was inadequate information on which to base a coordinated policy toward them.' This has been a problem for as long as transnationals have existed and today knowledge of exactly what they are doing is very limited. Within the Labour Party, at least, it seems to be recognized that they pose problems – this is reflected in the Labour Party's recent Policy Review. But the precise occurrence and extent of those problems is unknown. Similarly we have seen that past Labour governments have relied on transnationals' alleged advantages, but the precise occurrence and extent of those advantages is unknown. Such ignorance is no basis for any sensible policy.

Another benefit of establishing a Transnationals Unit is that its discussion of transnationals' activities would be intended to provide a permanent catalyst and focal point for discussing strategy options, thereby leading to more detailed and complete strategies in the future. This is crucial to future industrial development. The Unit would stimulate a more detailed future strategy, something which goes beyond mere collation and discussion of information. It would be a co-ordinating unit, contributing to and initiating discussion of the different possibilities. Furthermore it would institutionalize concern with transnationals in a permanent body. This matters if it is assumed the problems they pose will not go away and will not remain static. Establishing an appropriate Transnationals Unit can ensure that a transnationals strategy remains prominently on the policy agenda.

Thus a Unit would provide the basis for more detailed and complete strategies in the future (by gathering information) and explicitly lead to the development of these strategies (by its discussion). It is in this sense that establishing a Unit is the first step to replacing transnationals' own strategy with a strategy of the British people.

Furthermore there is another benefit: the information a Unit provides could have some direct influence on transnationals' activities, especially insofar as the information is firm specific. The reason for this is that to a considerable extent transnationals trade on ignorance. Consider for example the story told in GLC (1985): 'Ford uses the relatively high prices prevailing in the UK car market to take higher profit margins on its imported cars. Yet at the same time they retain the significant advantage that consumers perceive Fords as being British cars. A typical instance is that of a major regional police force whose Police Authority refused to sanction the purchase of a fleet of BMWs because they were German made. Instead they ordered a fleet of Granadas. All Ford Granadas are now made in Germany.' If the Police Authority had been better informed Ford may well have lost a sale. More generally, by simply dispelling ignorance a Unit could influence public perception of a firm and thereby affect a firm's sales, at least on some occasions. This could sometimes cause firms to change their activities.

The social audit approach

We now turn to the question of what form the accounts prepared by the Transnationals Unit should take. Our discussion will begin with a brief review of traditional accounting. This is rejected as a suitable means of accounting for the activities of transnationals. Instead a social account by means of a social audit[10] is proposed. Although there are limitations to a social audit, it is argued that this approach offers a better solution to the problem than traditional accounting.

Our first task is to remind the reader that this is accounting. It is an attempt to find a suitable means for monitoring transnational corporations using a coherent framework, i.e. an appropriate method of accounting. Whereas it is often presented as a dry, technical subject, it should be clear to most readers that accounting is in fact highly political. The form accounting takes (what it focuses upon) is likely to be influential in matters such as resource allocation, income distribution etc. And the form of accounting, like the choice of economic system, or perspective chosen to analyse economic problems, is in part a political choice.

For many years there has been a debate in accounting as to the suitability of the traditional model based on historic costs (see for instance Tweedie and Whittington, 1984, and Parker, Harcourt and Whittington, 1985). This is heightened particularly during a period of inflation. Alternatives have been proposed and rejected, e.g. the current cost accounting of Statement of Standard Accounting Practice Number 16. What is often not clearly stated, however, is that the search is primarily for a model suited to the needs of owners of capital. Consequently there is little attempt to break out of the neoclassical, marginalist mould. At this point we should make it clear that we do not reject the usefulness of traditional accounting outright. It can help us assess return on capital and so may be useful in helping us understand the actions of transnationals. However, due to its reliance on market based transactions, and its failure to go far beyond transactions and events which affect the business bank balance, we believe that an alternative form of accounting is needed, which reflects the wider economic and social consequences of transnationals' actions. Thus we reject traditional accounting and all other marginalist alternatives as incomplete.

One means of capturing the wider economic and social consequences is the preparation of a social audit of the performance of transnational corporations. This involves accounting for financial and non-financial aspects of the economic and social performance.

Social auditing is not new. There are various accounts which can be seen as examples, although it is important to be aware of the

broad differences. Some have been voluntary, others arise due to
regulation. Some are independently prepared, others are prepared
internally. Some have been largely qualitative, others quantitative.
Sometimes the quantification has concentrated on financial figures
only, others cover non-financial. And some accounts have been
narrow in scope, featuring a single issue. Others have been more
wide-ranging. Few have been conducted regularly over a period of
time. All in all, some have been critical, whereas others have been
more like public relations exercises attempting to show business as
being socially responsible. (See Gray *et al.*, 1987, for further detail
of the scope and variety of practice.)

For our purposes two groups of social audit reports are worth
commenting on. The first reports have been selected because they
arose from the adverse consequences of decisions by transnational
and other corporations to close plants. These reports showed that an
alternative account of the consequences of corporate decisions
could be prepared (see Harte and Owen, 1987). Whereas companies
including transnationals like Ford, Smurfit, Metal Box, Vickers and
Rowntree Mackintosh were (presumably) making decisions based
on returns to capital (profit), social audit reports prepared by or for
local authorities revealed the wider financial costs, such as, to the
public exchequer, local economy and workers, as well as some non-
financial effects, such as unemployment (related to the local
situation) analysed according to age, sex, race, skills, etc. Some
reports also attempted to tackle the wider social consequences for
health, law and order, etc. For example, the social audit of the
Rowntree Mackintosh plc Edinburgh closure revealed that whereas
the corporation could expect to benefit from savings of £2.4 million
per annum, the cost to central government alone was estimated to be
at least £3.0 million in the first year and £12.3 million over the first
five years (see City of Edinburgh District Council and Lothian
Regional Council, 1985).

The second group of reports of note are those carried out by
Social Audit, the organization. These focused on individual
organizations, covering a wide range of issues, from health and
safety at work, product quality, advertising policy, wage rates, to
participation and alienation at work. Probably the best example of
these is the Social Audit of the Avon Rubber Co Ltd.[11] This was
funded mainly by the Social Science Research Council and Joseph
Rowntree Charitable Trust, following an initiative by Social

Audit's sister organization, Public Interest Research Centre. Researchers were originally given substantial co-operation by Avon's management and trade unions, as well as access to confidential files held by Government departments. Unfortunately the enquiry was cut short by Avon, whose explanation referred to a worsening financial position. Social Audit on the other hand suggested that it may have been halted due to the time taken up by the first round of interviewing. More generally the report illustrates that social auditing has many benefits but may also encounter problems, an issue to which we will return in a moment.

On the positive side, the detail contained in the 87-page Avon report is impressive, particularly as the introduction refers to the researchers' views that important information which would have reflected poorly on Avon may have been deliberately withheld, and outlines the outright refusal of one Government department to disclose pollution information concerning the firm. Despite these limitations the pioneering work of Social Audit indicates a wide-ranging approach which can be taken when looking at the overall performance of a transnational corporation. It offers a clear alternative to the Annual Report as a means of portraying the performance of a business.

Despite the independent approaches to social auditing to which we have referred, it is clear that a number of difficulties remain both with the concept itself and with the practical difficulties of measurement. At the more general level there is a danger in trying to prepare an account which attempts to satisfy too many interested parties, particularly where their objectives may be in conflict. For example there may be conflict between the interests of society and workers in a particular organization. However such differences could be accommodated by explicit references and alternative views being presented. Secondly, due to the overriding influence of profit as a measure of performance, it may be difficult, at first, to decide on objectives and concerns, and develop from these satisfactory indicators of performance. Clearly there will be no single-figure, all-embracing equivalent of profit. Yet it would seem more desirable to struggle with this problem than to ignore issues and concerns – as happens at present. Thirdly, social audits have in the past been accused of concentrating on the negative consequences of business actions. This need not necessarily be the case. Positive and negative things should be reported on. However, in addition, greater attention should perhaps be directed to estimating the resources etc. needed to repair damage done, rather than solely reporting on the adverse consequences. There is a positive role here for measuring performance.

A second group of limitations is more practical. First it is necessary to remember that since we operate in a capitalist society, which is made up of imperfect markets, the use of prices arising from these markets must be questioned. Otherwise the financial cost of, say, a closure to low paid workers will appear to be less significant than the cost to higher paid workers. Obviously in one sense, this is so, but the impact on these workers is not necessarily related to their wage level. This problem highlights the importance of developing non-financial accountings. Second, the social audit raises the problem of measuring things we may not be used to concentrating on. To that extent it will appear subjective. However exclusion of these largely non-financial issues is equally subjective. Some issues may be more difficult to measure than others. But some information may already be collected by transnationals themselves or by government. Third, the calculations involved are likely to involve subjectivity. However, such subjectivity should not be compared with an 'objective' traditional accounting model. As readers will know, profit calculations are riddled with highly subjective judgements, often involving the need to make forecasts of likely business actions.

These problems, we would suggest, are not insurmountable. Clear policy objectives and staff drawn from various scientific and social scientific backgrounds would be called for to staff a Transnationals Unit. There will be subjective choice involved and subjective calculation. This cannot be avoided. However, as we argue, traditional accounting is itself subjective both in choosing to focus on only some economic activity, and in how it chooses to reflect this.

European cooperation

Having said all of this it is not sufficient for Britain to merely establish a Transnationals Unit in isolation. There is another vital element in the Transnationals Unit strategy. This is because the potential rewards from countries collaborating over monitoring are very high.

Possible benefits that may arise are illustrated by the following three points.[12] First, collaboration could increase the quality and quantity of information. It could lead to a greater pool of data because various countries could be covered. This would be useful for interpreting the information on Britain. Moreover it could improve the actual data specifically concerned with Britain. For instance, firms may use transfer prices to hide the profits they obtain from British production but a co-ordinated effort by various countries might unearth the truth. Similarly information on transnationals' global strategies is best obtained by a collaborative effort. A second benefit is that co-operating monitoring bodies could stimulate each other's discussions. Co-operation could be a pooling of minds, hence ideas. This could lead to greater progress in dealing with transnationals by promoting more effective strategies in the future. Third, collaboration at the monitoring stage would be likely to lead to collaboration if strategies become more detailed. This could have enormous pay-offs, for example by totally undermining transnationals' attempts to play workers off against each other. Co-operation over monitoring would be an easy way for countries to become accustomed to collaborating over more detailed industrial strategies, perhaps paving the way for a time when roles are reversed and workers play transnationals off against each other.

The idea of collaboration over monitoring contrasts with the way countries have often behaved in the past. They have tended to see themselves as rivals in their dealings with transnationals and do anything but co-operate. Dicken (1986), for instance, refers to the ferocious competitive bidding between countries trying to attract an engine building plant for Ford's Escort model. However the argument in Chapter 1 is that problems of transnationalism give rise to a negative sum global game; this means that countries in general suffer from transnationals having a free reign. Accepting this implies that countries in general can gain by imposing their will on transnationals.

Moreover, analogy with the theory of the firm suggests that countries seeing themselves as rivals should collaborate. Cowling (1982) sees a typical firm's environment as characterized by the coexistence of rivalry and collusion. The argument is that oligopolists are rivals but that they recognize this, for instance realizing that an attempt by one firm to cut price and gain profit will generally be met by other firms retaliating, cutting their prices to defend their positions. But it is because they are rivals that firms tolerate each other's presence to avoid situations which leave each and every firm worse off, i.e. that firms collude. For instance they avoid price cuts leading to price wars and hence lower profits all round.[13] Similarly, wherever countries see themselves as rivals it makes sense for them to collaborate in avoiding situations which leave each and every one worse off, i.e. for them to collude. This suggests the need to coordinate strategies – for example to co-ordinate the monitoring of transnationals' activities.

Accordingly it makes sense to create a Transnationals Unit which works in co-operation with other countries. More specifically, Britain's most obvious action is to promote the formation of collaborating monitoring bodies[14] in the most sophisticated supranational institution with which Britain is involved: the European Community. In doing so it would undoubtedly find allies, as suggested by the fact that Britain has been the traditional barrier to a Community perspective on transnationals. For instance Dicken (1986) notes Britain's objection to the Vredeling Directive, which would have required transnationals to make information available to workers and so on. It is a paradox that although much about the Community is designed to suit these firms, there has always been rumbling discontent about their activities. This is clearly something that can be built upon and turned to Britain's advantage. In this sense membership of the European Community broadens the available strategy options and should be seen very positively; it offers exciting and useful possibilities.

Summary and conclusion

Without pursuing the pros and cons of transnational activities any further, we have attempted to focus on the first step down a road which will ultimately lead to communities achieving their desires and attaining their goals rather than being subservient to the desires and goals of transnationals.

An important lesson from the experiences of elsewhere is that if Britain confronts transnationals it will only be doing to a greater or lesser extent what other countries have been doing. We suggest the creation of a Transnationals Unit to collect information, prepare accounts and use these to influence economic policy and attitudes of and towards transnational corporations. This is not especially radical insofar as other countries have monitored transnationals but, if appropriately designed, a Unit would constitute a significant break from Britain's past and be extremely important for its future. For example, it would provide a pool of knowledge enabling the formulation of coherent, detailed and successful industrial strategies; it would provide a permanent catalyst and focal point for discussing strategy options, thereby leading to more detailed and complete strategies; and the information a Unit gathers could have some direct influence on transnationals' activities. This information should, we suggest, be gathered in order to prepare a social audit of transnationals' performance. A social audit account, as we see it, would incorporate traditional accounting as well as accounting for the wider economic and social consequences of performance. It would open up the agenda for discussion of industrial strategy beyond the scope set by the limited availability of traditional accounting reports. We also suggest that the Unit be created in collaboration with other countries, especially European Community members. This could increase the quality and quantity of information; could stimulate discussion of the information; and would promote co-operation if strategies become more detailed in the future.

Clearly there is a need for further research on the issue. More specifically, we suggest it is important to pursue two avenues. First, a detailed review of practices and proposals in other countries would provide invaluable insights from which important lessons could be drawn. Second, there is an urgent need to apply these lessons and indeed the arguments we have been developing in this chapter to a specific transnational case study. In other words, to monitor a transnational and thereby illustrate what can and cannot be achieved. In the meantime, this paper has laid some foundations for a transnationals monitoring unit.

Notes

We would like to thank our colleagues at a seminar in the Department of Business Studies and in the Department of Accounting and Business Method.

1 Problems of transnationalism are not identical to problems of sheer size simply because transnationals produce in various countries. Accordingly it is appropriate to focus on transnationals (as one aspect of an industrial strategy) and not large firms. As regards large firms more generally, see the discussion of monopolies and mergers in Chapter 4.

2 Labour Party, 1989.

3 This recognition represents a passing aside rather than genuine appreciation.

4 In line with the theme of this book, this chapter focuses on the future economic and industrial policies to be adopted by the 'Left'. Readers interested in developing economic and industrial policies from differentperspectives may nevertheless find the chapter interesting as the ideas presented are relevant to any government recognizing that transnationals have advantages and disadvantages.

5 This Ministry was introduced by a Labour Government in the 1960s, and in 1970 was merged with the Board of Trade to form the Department of Trade and Industry, see Hodges (1974).

6 From British North-American Committee (1970).

7 Some people may believe that establishing a Unit is doomed to failure from the outset, because of secrecy problems in gathering information and so on. This reveals the power they believe transnationals wield.

8 Chick (1990) discusses random investigation of monopoly abuse by firms.

9 This assertion will be justified shortly.

10 The term 'social audit' is used here to describe the accounts prepared which will reflect wider economic and social consequences.

11 Social Audit, 1976.

12 Obviously this analysis should be read in conjunction with our earlier discussion of a Unit's advantages.

13 For a more detailed discussion of this aspect of the theory of the firm, see Cowling and Sugden (1987).

14 We suggest collaborating monitoring bodies rather than collaboration to form one supranational institution because this leaves countries with greater degrees of freedom. For instance, one supranational unit would have to operate along lines acceptable to all collaborators and therefore may be less active than some countries desire.

Bibliography

British-North American Committee, 1970, 'Guidelines for Multinational Corporations: A Government View', British-North American Committee Paper, BN/M-12, July 1970, London.

Martin Chick, 1990, 'Information, Politics and the Defence of Market Power' in Martin Chick, ed., *Governments, Industries and Markets. Aspects of overnment-Industry Relations in GB, Japan, West Germany and the USA since 1945*, Gloucester, Edward Elgar.

City of Edinburgh District Council and Lothian Regional Council, 1985, *Rowntree Mackintosh plc, Edinburgh; The Consequences of Closure, A Social Audit*, Edinburgh, City of Edinburgh District Council and Lothian Regional Council.

Barrie Clement, 1989, 'Vauxhall Workers Given Ultimatum Over New Plant', *The Independent*, 1 November.

Keith Cowling, 1982, *Monopoly Capitalism*, London, Macmillan.

Keith Cowling and Roger Sugden, 1987, *Transnational Monopoly Capitalism*, Brighton, Wheatsheaf.

Peter Dicken, 1986, *Global Shift*, London, Harper and Row.

GLC, 1985, *London Industrial Strategy*, London, Greater London Council.

R. Gray, D. Owen and K. Maunders, 1987, *Corporate Social Reporting*, London, Prentice-Hall.

George Harte and David Owen, 1987, 'Fighting Deindustrialization – The Role of Local Government Social Audits', *Accounting, Organizations and Society*.

Michael Hodges, 1974, *Multinational Corporations and National Government*, Farnborough, Saxon House.

Labour Party, 1989, *Meet the Challenge, Make the Change – A New Agenda for Britain. Final Report of Labour's Policy Review for the 1990s*, London, Labour Party.

R. H. Parker, G. C. Harcourt and G. Whittington (eds.), 1985, *Readings in the Concept and Measurement of Income'*, 2nd edition, Oxford, Philip Allan.

OECD, 1987, *Controls and Impediments Affecting Inward Direct Investment*, Paris, OECD.

Peter Riddell, 1989, 'US Worries about Foreign Investment. The Task of Matching Sense and Sensibilities', *The Financial Times*, 5 September.

A. E. Safarian, 1983, *Government and Multinationals; Policies in the Developed Countries*, London, British-North American Committee.

Social Audit, 1976, *Social Audit on the Avon Rubber Company Ltd*, London, Social Audit.

Roger Sugden, 1990, 'The Warm Welcome for Foreign-Owned Transnationals from Recent British Governments' in Martin Chick, ed., *Governments, Industries and Markets. Aspects of Government-Industry Relations in GB, Japan, West Germany and the USA since 1945*, Gloucester, Edward Elgar.

Roger Sugden, 1990a, 'The Importance of Distributional Considerations' in Christos Pitelis and Roger Sugden, eds., *The Nature of the Transnational Firm*, London, Routledge.

David Tweedie and Geoffrey Whittington, 1984, *The Debate on Inflation Accounting*, Cambridge, Cambridge University Press.

United Nations, 1983, *Transnational Corporations in World Development. Third Survey*, New York, United Nations.

Regional renaissance and industrial regeneration: building a new policy perspective?

Introduction

Traditional regional policy attempts to redress the geographical inequalities which result from the uneven pattern of development of major industries. Inequalities between areas are seen as the unintended consequences of growth; they represent the outcome at any given time of a cumulative process in which agglomerations of productive capacity, finance, decision centres and infrastructure emerge, thus peripheralizing other locations. Intervention by the state, with its origins in the 1934 Special Areas Act and the 1940 Barlow Commission, is essentially concerned with the creation of counter forces capable of diverting growth to the periphery and away from the 'congested' metropolitan areas. Two overlapping approaches are apparent:

(1) The redirection of growth to designated Development Areas, originally through a system of controls on the location of new industrial development (Industrial Development Certificates) and subsequently through a combination of financial incentives to 'footloose' enterprises and the provision of industrial infrastructure.

(2) The use of these incentives and infrastructure provision to give indigenous firms in Development Areas a competitive advantage over enterprises elsewhere.

Development Area boundaries have been amended continuously to reflect economic and political circumstances, and recent policy has led to the designation of a further tier of priority areas, the inner cities, with their own separate framework of policy initiatives. But underlying these changes can be found a constant theme: uneven development is seen as the product of weakness in certain localities which can be remedied by geographically specific forms of intervention.

This chapter will argue a different case, one which identifies the source of weakness as lying within industries rather than localities *per se*. Local and regional economies rise and fall with the fortunes of the industries which underpin them. The absence of a coherent national approach to restructuring in industries, and of one which recognizes the spatial consequences of industrial change, is a central factor in explaining local and regional economic decline in many parts of the country. Regional policy as traditionally defined may therefore be less appropriate in the future than an industrial policy sensitive to the sectoral constraints and opportunities specific to the economies of particular areas.

To what extent can evidence for the emergence of a new approach to regional development be found in current policy debates? Labour's Policy Review[1] does not provide explicit and detailed answers to this question, though several indications are given that major new policy directions would be possible under a Labour government. Certainly the Policy Review appears to move some way away from the traditional separation of industrial and regional policy, a divide which has allowed recent government spokespeople to caricature regional intervention as social policy, and therefore as being of questionable status. While the 'revival' of traditional instruments of regional policy is designed to promote inward investment, two other dimensions are fairly prominent:

(1) The introduction of greater spatial equity in central government policy and expenditure, including investment, research and development, public sector employment and the regulation of monopolies and mergers.
(2) The enhancement of decentralized activity through the expansion of local authority economic strategies and the creation of a new tier of elected regional government.

A wide body of recent research into regional development appears to support this broad approach, though it will be argued below that discussion of the crucial organizational linkages in the Policy Review is somewhat sparse. It might also be seen as disappointing that the regional consequences of investment by the majority of public utilities and nationalized industries are not explicitly mentioned.

Defining the framework

A great deal has already been written on the nature of the regional problem in Britain, much of it characterizing the issue as that of a 'North-South Divide'.[2] Sensitive analyses however also concede that this characterization is too simplistic. While declining areas are concentrated in Scotland, the North of England or Wales, pockets of intense and persistent deprivation exist in the Inner London Boroughs, in the East and West Midlands, in Bristol and in the far South West.

This deprivation reflects both the high unemployment which results from industrial decline and the emergence of a secondary labour market in which disadvantaged workers are entrapped in low paid, casualized jobs. While such jobs increasingly constitute the reality of the 'service economy'[3] which some advocate as the salvation of cities and regions, they also indicate the extent to which the manufacturing sectors on which these economies traditionally depended have reverted to sweatshop practices in the absence of coherent industrial policies for modernisation and restructuring.[4]

In the remainder of this chapter the focus will therefore be on two principal areas of concern: the need for the effective restructuring of companies and sectors and the need for a critical assessment of the historical role of national industrial, regional and labour market policy. This will set the context within which a new policy framework can be outlined.

Regional regeneration: the transformation of sectors and companies
It can be argued that both the nature of the problem and the scope for the regeneration of depressed regional economies lies in the changing nature of markets.[5] Britain appears to start with major competitive disadvantages in relation to the mass production of standardized goods in many markets. Such products are highly price-sensitive and susceptible to competition either from low wage countries or from major overseas conglomerates capable of achieving substantial economies of scale. But many markets are becoming increasingly segmented, creating opportunities for the production of short runs of highly customized, high value goods. Manufacturers capable of high levels of flexibility, innovation, reliability and quality control can therefore seek profitable markets in which non-price factors are major determinants of competitiveness.

Competitiveness in developed economies appears to be the product of a tailored combination of easy access to investment capital, innovative technology, a high skills profile at all levels of the enterprise, new labour processes, and strategic market intelligence: in short a sophisticated organizational infrastructure which enables individual companies to evolve with their markets rather than simply to undercut their competitors.[6] It is the contention of this chapter that the development of such an infrastructure requires a crucial strategic role for the state, and that the way in which this role is fulfilled significantly affects the development of local and regional economies.

The move from mass production to customized production necessarily involves an enterprise in a comprehensive re-evaluation of its practice from product development and marketing through to training and job design. The concept of the 'new' firm clearly conceals a wide range of possible choices relating to commercial strategy, the selection and use of technology and the deployment of labour; nonetheless enterprises in this category stand in sharp contrast to 'traditional' firms seeking to survive in mass markets and trapped in a low wage, low investment, low profit spiral.[7] But what is the nature of the transition for firms and sectors seeking to move from the 'traditional' to the 'new' economies?

Traditional approaches to industrial restructuring have equated modernization with increasing scale and increasing automation. This is equally characteristic of the bland corporatism of the 1960s[8] and the more radically interventionist strategies of the seventies.[9] Certainly many people on the Left have not been unhappy with this equation: large firms were seen as susceptible to union organization and to state influence through planning agreements.[10] But it is clear that large scale producers have not escaped pressures to increase flexibility of labour through automation and deskilling, increased subcontracting and just-in-time delivery systems. As Scott points out, attacks on labour rigidities and entitlements secured in recent years by strongly unionized workers are now commonplace.[11]

Recently new perspectives have begun to challenge earlier axioms. As has been argued, competitive success in the 'new' economy is located within the producer's ability to adapt and innovate continuously, gaining an ever increasing awareness of the differences in the needs of each customer. The competitive advantage bestowed by economies of scale is much less significant and may even be counter-productive in markets based on small batches and customization. Smaller enterprises are in a position to challenge the large conglomerates in these new conditions, not in the traditional sense of undercutting through low overheads, but because they have the potential both for flexibility and for specialization. They are no longer confined to a small number of niche markets because many mass markets are themselves dissolving into a series of niches. But this challenge is predicated on co-operative relations between small firms, including shared resources and joint marketing ventures. Sabel and Zeitlin describe historical examples of 'industrial districts' in which versatility is achieved through the existence of networks of small, specialized, independent firms,[12] and accoding to Sabel[13] there is increasing evidence of the formation of new industrial districts in developed countries. Scott suggests that:

firms in flexible production sectors find it increasingly difficult to dispense with the intensifying agglomeration economies now available at particular locations in the new industrial spaces of North America and Western Europe. Each particular space is the site of an evolving polarised complex of production activities, local labour market phenomena and social life, in which each element (including educational institutions, residential neigh-bourhoods, the apparatus of local government, and so on) contributes in one way or another to the total process of local territorial reproduction (A. Scott, op cit).

The horizontal associations of small firms in the Emilia Romagna region of Italy, offer the best known examples of this.[14]

In terms of the organization of production, it can be argued that the value of traditional Taylorist work organization is diminished and a greater premium is placed on the creativity of each sub-contractor and each individual operative. Drawing on a comparison of the competitiveness of British and German manufacturing enterprises, Lane stresses the significance of a 'polyvalent' work-force able to adapt to continuous changes in production and to resolve the succession of different problems which this throws up[15]

Workers gain greater autonomy, trust and negotiating power, engaging in continuous dialogue with management on issues relating to production and product development. This of course is quite distinct from the strategies of flexibility which have so often characterized British management practice, particularly during the Thatcher era. Such strategies seek the 'liberation of capital from labour' through automation, deskilling, casualization and redundancy. Investment in technology becomes a means of disciplining labour, reinforcing authoritarian management practices on the shop floor. But as Lane and others argue, attitudes such as these are increasingly anachronistic within the demands of changing world markets for innovation and quality. (See also Chapter 5's discussion of democracy and company law.) While the model of segmented markets and flexible production described above is not unproblematic[16] the debate has largely been carried out at the level of theory: much systematic empirical evidence is still required at sectoral level. In some markets mass production and standardization remain relatively important, while in many consumer industries such as clothing[17] and furniture[18] available evidence on patterns of international competition suggests the emergence of new conditions. Scott points out that the situation is one of considerable complexity:

. . . for the old regime is far from having disappeared entirely and the new one by no means as yet universally regnant. Moreover the geographical outcomes proper to each regime intersect with one another in a sometimes disorderly and confusing manner (A. Scott, op cit).

However in markets where these new conditions do prevail, British firms in general, and specific regional concentrations of firms in particular, have been slow to respond. This has led to a rapid growth of imports from other developed countries where production is characterized by greater flexibility and innovation[19] Italy, for example, is now the second largest importer of fashion goods into the UK. In spatial terms it is possible to argue that declining localities and regions are precisely those in which concentrations exist of firms and sectors who have failed to make an effective transition to the 'new' economy and which are increasingly characterized by redundancies, closures, and sweatshop practices. As Tyler argues[20] such concentrations will be an important determinant of the pattern of regional growth and decline following the Single European Market in 1992.

As following sections will argue, this picture is one which generates extensive policy concerns. Where industries have been successful in crossing the threshold from the mass market, whether in the UK or elsewhere in Europe, state intervention is often a significant factor. As Best argues,[21] competitive advantage is defined by the effectiveness of organizational interrelationships: the ability of the enterprise to gain access to capital, research and development resources, specialist expertise and facilities, effective supply chains, strategic market intelligence and so on. For most companies this requires a degree of organization which must come from outside the enterprise itself. The roles of the Japanese Ministry of International Trade and Industry (MITI) – see Chapter 1 – or of the Italian State Holding Companies IRI and ENI, though not unproblematic, are the most frequently cited in providing this co-ordination.[22] However attention has recently been focussed on the complex networks of public and semi-public agencies in regions such as Emilia Romagna, Italy[23] The successful regeneration of industries like knitwear or ceramics, in which production is highly fragmented among many small enterprises, is closely linked to the development of sector specific agencies created jointly by local authorities, trade unions and manufacturers' organizations. In addition to their co-ordinating role, localized agencies exist to provide a comprehensive range of collective services geared towards enhancing the competitiveness of sectors operating in volatile world markets. Such services include research and development, design support, access to investment capital, quality control, technology transfer and training. Policies designed to tackle localized problems can therefore be integral to national industrial renewal processes.

The need to regenerate policy in Britain
Regional and sectoral concentrations of firms entrapped in mass market manufacture by a combination of failings in design, innovation, quality control, workforce training and investment levels therefore present a serious indictment of state policy at various levels. A later section argues that intervention must be diverse and pluralistic to reflect the complexities of industrial structures and restructuring: a system of decentralized policy production, but one that is located within a coherent strategic framework.

Though diverse in many respects, policy in recent decades has been essentially *ad hoc*, opportunistic, and lacking in co-ordination or coherence. The National Economic Development Council, created in 1963, had been designed as the central planning institution for the British economy. But as a tripartite forum, the Council 'perpetrated a voluntaristic tradition according to which the state left matters of industrial reorganization largely up to the private sector rather than try to impose its own plans'.[24] In this it differed markedly from the French Planning Commission, on which it was superficially modelled. The NEDC neither has an executive arm of its own, nor is it integral to the economic policy making process, and thus rarely succeeds in informing company strategies. No systematic surveys of industry are carried out as a means of identifying sectoral problems and issues, and thereby of informing the selective industrial interventions which take place under the auspices of the Department of Trade and Industry within S.8 of the 1982 Industrial Development Act. According to the National Audit Office 'lack of such analyses leaves DTI poorly placed under both past and current industrial policies to ensure that all appropriate areas for assistance have been identified, and to demonstrate that priorities for intervention have been allocated rationally'.[25]

The notable exception to this absence of direction is to be found in the Industry Schemes created by the Labour government during the mid-1970s.[26] These schemes sought to assist sectors in which the need for major restructuring had been identified, such as wool textiles, clothing, foundries and textile machinery. Their main features were:
(1) the formulation of sector specific goals to guide restructuring;
(2) the use of subsidized consultancy to translate these goals into individual company objectives;
(3) subsidies for capital investment undertaken in pursuit of these objectives;
(4) the full involvement of trade unions in the evaluation and implementation of proposals at company level;
(5) close monitoring of the effects of the schemes on participating companies and on the sector as a whole.
While these schemes were relatively short-lived and met with several difficulties in their implementation, their coherence and precision offer several lessons for the future development of policy. Improvements to the effectiveness of the Schemes – and perhaps in their level of accountability to shop floor workers – could undoubtedly have been made had their operation been decentralized to regional or local level.

Few other examples of co-ordinated intervention are to be found. Regional assistance, which dwarfs selective industrial assistance in terms of expenditure, was never targeted towards sectoral restructuring objectives. Assistance is granted automatically to most types of manufacturing (and more recently service sector) investment within designated Development Areas as a means of attempting to intervene in the locational decisions of firms. Criticisms of this system were widely disseminated following abuses by certain major companies during the 1970s. Fears also grew about the creation of 'branch plant economies' in which plants peripheral to the corporate strategies of their national or multi-national parents came to dominate local economies. The jobs they offered, moreover, were often poorly paid and tended to entrap women in traditional occupational categories. But three criticisms are particularly pertinent to the evaluation of regional policy in relation to industrial decline:

(1) That undue attention and resources are focused on the initial capital costs of development in the regions while ignoring the need for continuous reinvestment and renewal in many key industries.

(2) That assistance to individual firms allocated on the basis of spatial criteria ignores the circumstances of the markets in which they operate. Competitive distortions can occur by allowing subsidized firms to undercut enterprises elsewhere of greater strategic significance to the sector as a whole.

(3) That visible state policy towards the regions was undermined by other forms of state policy, notably that towards nationalized industries such as coal and steel, and in the regional distribution of government expenditure. Policy in these areas weakened regional economies severely, not just in terms of immediate job losses but by a negative multiplier effect across a wide range of manufacturing and service sectors.[27]

Since 1979, the NEDC has abandoned any pretence of playing a strategic planning role. Gone are the days in which strategy statements reflected a broad tripartite consensus across a range of sectors. The current organization is weak and ineffective, relying on a series of *ad hoc* projects to provide it with a continuing *raison d'etre*. Government policy for industry and the regions remains fragmented, and its overall inadequacy is compounded by the massive expenditure reductions of recent years. Current DTI schemes of assistance, while of some value in their own right, scarcely add up to a policy for enterprise.

Labour market policy provides another example of *ad hoc* intervention. During the eighties, massive expenditure by the

Manpower Services Commission on vocational training has tended to pursue short-term, opportunistic ends while ignoring the strategic issues affecting many sectors. Likewise urban policy under the present government has succeeded in targeting resources at the physical renewal of several inner city areas while ignoring or exacerbating the underlying dynamic of industrial decline.

Creating an alternative

The well documented and steady expansion of economic intervention by Labour-controlled local authorities during the 1980s is certainly related to the ineffectual nature of national industrial policy and to its failure to prevent the decline of the key manufacturing sectors on which many local economies depend. Despite government distaste, economic intervention is now an established part of local government activity, and is increasingly emulated by Conservative-controlled authorities.

The nature of local strategies varies widely from authority to authority, reflecting different circumstances and different perceptions of economic priorities. Principal categories of local authority industrial policy include:
(1) Direct investment in individual companies, through the provision of long term loans or the acquisition of equity. Several authorities have set up arms-length Enterprise Boards to undertake this activity, and the role of such agencies is discussed in Chapter 3.
(2) Collective Service provision to provide small and medium enterprises with access to specialist resources or expertise normally only available to companies enjoying substantial economies of scale. Fashion centres, for example, provide a range of design, marketing and technological assistance to local clothing firms.
(3) Infrastructure provision such as roads, factory units, etc., together with lobbying activity for improved transport facilities (e.g. rail freight access to the Channel Tunnel).
In industrial policy terms, the most significant dimension lies in the development of sector strategies. The analysis of principal industrial sectors within a locality provides the detailed framework within which specific problems can be identified and resources can be targeted effectively. Sector strategies may incorporate

elements of each of the above policy headings, informed both by
company level knowledge and by an understanding of broader
trends.

Textiles and clothing is one sector in which strategies are
emerging from several local authorities in England and Scotland,
and intervention includes the following examples:

(1) access to investment and working capital to enable companies to
     upgrade garment ranges in order to achieve higher value added
     production (e.g. West Midlands Enterprise Board);
(2) access to strategic market intelligence to provide a basis for
     business planning and for local lobbying activities;
(3) access to specialist equipment such as CAD/CAM to improve
     versatility and reduce material costs (e.g. Clothing Resource
     Centres in Coventry, Newcastle, Blackburn and Sandwell);
(4) access to specialist advice relating to technology transfer or
     production (e.g. Nottingham Fashion Centre, Coventry and
     Sandwell Resource Centres);
(5) access to marketing facilities and design resources (e.g.
     Newcastle and Nottingham Fashion Centres);
(6) provision of managed workspace with shared equipment and
     resources (e.g. Nottingham, Newcastle);
(7) support for young independent designers through the
     provision of Enterprise Workshops, shared equipment,
     specialist support and grants (e.g. Nottingham, Hackney).

Significantly some twenty local authorities involved in the
development of strategies for this sector have combined to form the
Local Action for Textiles and Clothing network. As well as
providing an information exchange, the network seeks to develop
collaborative projects around issues which cut across individual
local authority boundaries (such as training and fabric sourcing)
and to develop national policy proposals.

Local authority intervention is most effective in sectors which are
either dominated by small and medium sized firms, or where for
reasons of strategy resources should be concentrated on smaller
enterprises rather than the conglomerates. For one or other of these
reasons many consumer product industries could be included –
textiles and clothing, cutlery, furniture and specialist foods, for
example. Similar criteria also apply in parts of capital goods sectors,
such as motor vehicle components and machine manufacture,
where networks of smaller firms can provide the conditions for

efficient and flexible production, thereby playing a major role in regional economic regeneration.

An outline strategy

Traditionally, debates on regional intervention have been weak on the overall framework, both organizational and conceptual, within which individual policy measures would operate. The framework of policy production and implementation centrally affects the outcome of intervention, and this issue therefore requires further work and discussion at a very detailed level. In terms of organizational responsibilities the Policy Review makes a strong case for the transformation of the DTI into an agency capable of 'strategic interventions in key sectors', as well as providing support to small businesses at local level. At the same time, local authorities would be given greater competence in developing their economies through support for activities such as innovation and product development, and a new range of agencies such as Regional Investment Banks would be created.

But how are these agencies to relate to each other within such a model? Is each body to operate relatively autonomously, free to develop its own style of intervention within its general area of competence? Such a model has its attractions, but also appears to reproduce the lack of strategic co-ordination which has traditionally characterized the urban, regional and industrial policy process in Britain. It ignores the job displacement effects that can result from *ad hoc* intervention in particular companies or localities[28] and perpetrates the wasteful competitiveness that currently exists between different local authorities and development agencies in their scramble for inward investment. It also runs the risk of relegating local authority initiatives to the status of remedial measures for specific areas, whereas local intervention in particular sectors could add an important dimension to mainstream national industrial policy.

On the other hand, should national agencies orientate intervention towards the achievement of broad strategic goals for each sector, though in such a way which leaves scope for innovation and variation within different localities? If such a strategic framework is intended then it is surprising that the Policy Review makes no mention of the role of NEDO. Rather it falls to the DTI 'to work closely with industry, to develop strategies, to identify priorities, and provide the assistance, resources and organising capacity which industry will need', a theme which is discussed in Chapter 1. But if the DTI is to act as the central forum for the co-ordination of industrial policy, how will it inform and respond to the practices and experience of other agencies, including local authorities? And, crucially, will the transformed DTI retain its centralist orientation and commitment to uniform policy programmes across all sectors and regions? Or will it be prepared to devolve industrial policy expenditure and powers to the regional and local levels?

The extent of firms' ability to move from 'traditional' to 'new' market conditions has clear implications for national, regional and local economies, especially within the context of the Single European Market. In national terms whole sectors may prove themselves unable to make the transition as successfully as their competitors in other developed countries, and this will seriously affect the local and regional economies in which such sectors are clustered. But the problems of transition in any given sector vary both qualitatively and quantitatively between localities, depending on such factors as industrial structure, ownership, linkages, labour markets and regional infrastructure.

A policy framework capable of promoting the transformation of major industrial sectors therefore needs to be as diverse and complex as the sectors themselves. A decentralized framework would meet this condition, allowing strategic priorities to be set for each industry at national level while allowing the precise form of intervention to be determined by the specific problems and issues observable within local and regional economies. Accountability and accessibility must also be among the principal motives of this framework. Strategic institutions and practices must not only set the direction for action on the ground, but must be informed by it. Practices throughout the framework should be highly visible, and new means devised of encouraging criticism and involvement in the planning process from the shop floor and the community.

Central strategy and local empowerment

The relationship between central government and local authorities will thus be close to the heart of any discussions on the future of national industrial and regional policy. In the recent past there may have been a degree of overemphasis on the role of local authorities as instruments of reflation under a Labour government (spending to create jobs), rather than as instruments of wealth creation through the fostering of industrial and employment restructuring. But as a previous section argues, local authorities have begun to open up innovative and relevant new approaches to industrial policy. Under present circumstances, limitations on available powers and resources dictate that these initiatives fulfil an exemplary role with no more than a limited concrete impact on industry and employment. Moreover, in the absence of a national strategic policy framework, intervention by individual local authorities has been uncoordinated and unrelated to any national or regional policy objectives. At worst, local authorities often appear to be in competition with each other in attempting to attract or retain jobs, rather than operating as collaborators in tackling shared industrial problems. While some authorities have begun to recognize this problem, a set of ground rules is urgently required as a basis for good practice in the future.

What division of labour should be sought between central and local government intervention? This question can best be approached

(1) by identifying key issues which define the limitations of local action, namely
  (a) strategic planning and intervention
  (b) finance capital and investment
  (c) central resource allocation
(2) by examining areas of policy likely to operate more effectively on a decentralized basis, namely
  (a) sectoral intervention
  (b) skills and training provision

As this chapter will demonstrate, the aim is to produce a national strategic framework which offers concise objectives and a robust framework for the effective targeting of resources at all levels of governmental activity; at the same time such a framework should seek to maximize the ability of each locality to translate these broad objectives into actual policy measures which democratically reflect local concerns.

Strategic planning and intervention

As we have noted, market structures are more segmented and more changeable in the 1980s than in previous decades. These factors underline the growing need for strategic market intelligence as a

basis for informing investment and production decisions. Greater
uncertainty about market trends and customer demand affects most
firms, but small enterprises in particular lack access to sophisticated
market intelligence despite their growing significance in some
sectors. The knowledge demands which industrial planning and
intervention will put on a future government and on other public
agencies will be substantially greater than in the past. High quality
research and sophisticated data bases will certainly be required, as
will a high degree of co-operation between government, industry,
finance capital, academics and trade unions. While remaining
flexible, strategic market planning will also need to command
effective incentives and powers to achieve desired outcomes:
consensus between the various parties should be sought in the
planning process, but this should not be confused with the
ineffective voluntarism which has characterized the history of the
NEDC.

Whether the shell of the NEDC which the next Labour
government will inherit can be resuscitated to form the Strategic
Planning Agency discussed in Chapter 1 remains to be seen. The
new organization will need to represent a wider range of interests
than their predecessors, including local authorities and smaller
enterprises. This applies particularly to the Sectoral Agencies
located within the DTI (see Chapter 1) which would play a major
role (a) in setting strategic priorities and directions for key areas of
spending and investment susceptible to state control or influence;
(b) in acting as a channel through which national strategic priorities
are sensitized to local issues and concerns.

The operation of both selective and non-selective regional
assistance should be the object of particular scrutiny by the
Strategic Planning Agency. Neither form of intervention currently
appears able to guarantee additionality in job creation across the
UK economy nor is assistance targeted to meet clear sectoral
restructuring objectives. Regional assistance should be focused on
those projects capable of making a strategic contribution to key
sectors within a regional economy, but only where market conditions indicate little likelihood of job displacement elsewhere.

Based on their analysis of competitive advantage within particular markets, Sectoral Agencies would also play an innovative role in
relation to new areas of central government policy. In particular,
extra powers will be required to control dominant interests in

certain sectoral environments. Intervention at the level of the firm may be ineffective if, for example, access to raw materials is impeded, or if the dominance of a small number of retailers forces profit margins down to a level where overall investment is seriously curtailed. In fashion, for example, the ten largest retailers account for some 50% of garment sales. This oligopoly has damaged the UK fashion industry by its dominance over suppliers while making access to major market shares very easy for importers. Retailers must therefore be encouraged to build long term relationships with domestic suppliers, including involvement in both investment and training programmes.

Finance capital and investment

The successful regeneration of older industries will depend in no small measure on investment. As argued elsewhere in this volume, a central co-ordinating agency such as a National Investment Bank would be essential. However the principal locus of low interest, long term financing should be devolved to local and regional level through a network of industrial development banks and enterprise boards. This would have the following advantages (see also Chapter 3):

(1) while guided by national strategic priorities, local or regional bodies would have the industrial knowledge required to discriminate between firms and between projects in order to ensure a more effective distribution of funding;

(2) local or regional bodies aware of population structures or of the existence of particular centres of deprivation can fashion their policies to meet the specific needs of, for example, ethnic minority groups, women and the long term unemployed.

Government and local authorities have often sought to compensate for the deficiencies of the British financial system by offering grants to encourage investment. Experience suggests that these are often poorly targeted, provide no more than a temporary solution to the problem of under-investment, and offer little accountability compared with the provision of long term loans or equity. Grants can easily appear as a means of subsidizing inefficiency, while offering little positive benefit to the economy or workforce. While some grants would remain necessary – particularly in relation to training and regional development – the regeneration process should not be built on any substantial increase in grant aid. The focus on long term loan and equity provision allows for the maximum leverage in relation to business strategy, as well as to the improvement of working conditions, equal opportunities, training and so on. This leverage, including the appointment of directors where appropriate, should be seen as a central means for the achievement of sectoral objectives.

Central resource allocation

As this chapter argues, the transition to flexible and innovative production leads many firms to an apparently uncrossable divide. If industrial and regional policy is to provide the bridge, it must be adequately resourced. But this is not simply a question of increasing existing budgets, but of restructuring current financial mechanisms in order to achieve greater coherence and direction across a diverse range of departments and agencies involved in the process of economic development. The relationship between central government strategy and local policy is particularly important in this respect. The Urban Programme and the Local Government Act were never designed to provide surrogate funding for industrial policy and yet they have been the principal sources of finance for local authority economic initiatives. It would therefore be appropriate for the Industry Acts to be amended at the earliest opportunity in order to make proper budgetary provisions for local industrial policy. Effectively this would mean that powers under Section 8 of the Industrial Development Act 1982 (which allows the Secretary of State to devise schemes of financial assistance likely to benefit all or part of the UK economy) might be devolved to local and regional authorities. Given the appropriate structures, local and regional authorities would then be free to interpret national policy directives and guidelines in the light of local needs, experience and political choice, and thus to target resources in the most effective manner.

Local Sector Development Plans would be the principal instrument by which local and regional authorities could secure funding for intervention. Such plans would help to consolidate local knowledge and to direct research, and this would provide the basis from which integrated strategies could be developed. In spatial terms flexibility is essential. Plans could be prepared by a single authority or by a group of authorities with an interest in a particular sector or issue. Each plan would have to incorporate evidence of consultation with relevant interests before its submission. Plans would thus perform a double function: while ensuring a degree of co-ordination and compatibility with national sectoral priorities, they would also play a crucial role in informing and developing these priorities, assisted by the advocacy of local authority representatives on the appropriate Sector Working Parties.

This process, then, would seek to achieve strategically informed intervention at local level, and locally informed strategy at national level. Clearly it does not preclude direct intervention by national agencies, particularly in more concentrated industries. Rather, it proposes a set of partnerships between local, regional and central agencies which might vary considerably from area to area. For example, in a locality where a particular sector was dominated by large conglomerates, negotiation on corporate strategies could be led by national agencies. But this would take place within a context informed by an analysis of strategic options at plant level undertaken by the local authority. The problem of inactive or oppositional councils can also be seen in this context. The Secretary of State could be empowered to impose a statutory obligation on all authorities to produce plans for an industry in their areas or could intervene directly in pursuit of national objectives through consultation with trade unions and other local bodies.

Local sectoral intervention
The above paragraph has outlined a legal and financial structure for the empowerment of an effective industrial policy partnership between central and local government. But what type of sectoral intervention might we expect? Capital investment, dealt with above, is a necessary but by no means sufficient component in the process of restructuring, and cannot compensate for the lack of a supportive and well resourced environment. Small and medium sized enterprises are particularly dependent on various levels of external resourcing, lacking in-house expertise and facilities common to larger companies. While the 'industrial districts' discussed earlier provided small producers with a network of linkages able to solve problems relating to supplies, production, expertise and marketing, many firms now appear to operate in relative isolation, starved of vital sources of information and support.

The current government's 'enterprise initiative' attempts to resolve this problem by offering a programme of consultancy grants to individual companies. This grant-based approach is rejected (a) because it offers little accountability in relation to how the money is spent; (b) because these problems are recurrent for small companies and are not amenable to one-off solutions; (c) because grant expenditure is costly, yet provides no tangible cumulative gain for an industry, other than to the consultants themselves.

The forms of local authority collective service provision described above represent innovative attempts to update the concept of the industrial district by providing localized resources relevant to the intensive competitive conditions of the 1980s. But such services are unevenly developed across both sectors and localities. In textiles and clothing relatively sophisticated networks are being developed in traditional manufacturing locations across the country, despite austere resource provision and the marked absence of a national strategic framework. Other sectors are only sporadically catered for. A survey of collective service provision on an area-by-area, sector-by-sector basis should be sought from relevant Sector Working Parties in order to establish the magnitude and location of unmet need. In some sectors, active national organizations such as PERA (the Production Engineering Research Association) exist which might enter into partnerships with local authorities as a means of expanding their range of services and of decentralizing and targeting delivery to firms.

The following headings represent the categories of service which could be expected to develop with support from a Labour government:

(1) Strategic market information: a broad range of information targeted at the needs of specific sectors and groups of companies, covering the structure of markets, consumer profiles, principal trends, innovation, and assessments of competitive advantage within the local economy.

(2) Research, development and design: small units to provide firms with resources relating to product development and design innovation have proved extremely useful in many sectors. These include innovation workshops to provide expertise and equipment to smaller enterprises who lack in-house R & D facilities; fashion forecasting facilities for clothing designers; and design exchanges to put manufacturers in touch with outside design expertise on a consultancy basis.

(3) Technology transfer and work organization units: assistance to

overcome the profound ignorance of recent developments in process technology is urgently required in many areas of manufacturing. Such assistance should not seek to promote the dissemination of new technology as an end in itself, but should work with firms to achieve a proper balance between the human and capital investment required for flexibility and competitiveness. This would mean participation in the development of innovative new forms of work organization on the shop floor, based on multi-skilling and human centred methods of production.

(4) Technology resource centres: could provide access on a bureau basis to high technology plant such as CAD/CAM systems, which are normally beyond the reach of smaller firms.

(5) Quality control consortia: these have successfully developed among the small artisanal enterprises of Northern Italy and offer technical guidance to members on quality maintenance, plus a 'seal of approval' as an aid to marketing.

(6) Sourcing assistance is often needed to reduce bottlenecks in production, which prove to be a particular problem for small manufacturers who may require small orders of certain fabrics at competitive prices. This problem could be overcome through the development of on-line databanks updated to give information on available supplies, or by creating new marketing agencies for goods such as fabrics who could buy in bulk and sell in small customized batches.

(7) Collective marketing facilities such as showrooms, graphic design facilities, and NEDO-style 'Manufacturer-Retailer Panels' are helpful to small and even quite large firms. Active assistance should also be given to help smaller manufacturers gain joint orders through the creation of co-ordinated product ranges.

(8) Local authorities have already begun to create links with their counterparts in Europe, albeit on an *ad hoc* basis, usually in connection with a particular theme or industry. This is leading to the exchange of information on current trends and on policy initiatives, drawing on the enormous diversity of European experience. Such initiatives, especially with active support rather than indifference from central government, could open up new industrial linkages and could inform a new generation of Commission Programmes for Industrial and Regional Development.

The precise configuration of these agencies and services in a specific locality or industry would be the product of careful research combined with a degree of informed experimentation. Access to these services could be governed by some form of 'good employer' agreement, and in some instances membership fees could be levied which would offset a significant proportion of costs. The role of an enabling public sector in this process is envisaged as that of creating a climate in which it is widely accepted that the conduct of business should be highly visible and accountable to local communities.

Skills and training
Skills and training are clearly central to the operation of the strategy described in this chapter. The multi-skilling of the industrial workforce provides the route to productive flexibility, quality and innovation, and to the enhancement of occupational status and bargaining power. In contrast, education and training under the present government are characterized by:
(1) poor linkages to the economy;
(2) low levels of participation and poor achievements;
(3) restricted access and elitism.
The inability of individuals to develop their potential to the full is clearly reflected in the stunted economic performance of many sectors. A narrow conception of vocational training is simply a contradiction in an economy which seeks to place workers at the forefront of innovation and to give them greater control on the shop floor.

The principle of lifelong learning needs to underpin education and training structures. Such structures must recognize all the areas in which learning can occur, including the workplace, the community and the home. Providing the most effective context for learning is important to meet the needs of diverse individuals or groups, particularly in the case of adults who may possess a wealth of quite varied experience. A network of opportunity must be created which will be open to all, regardless of age, sex, disability, ethnic origin, social background or previous experience. The Open University and certain community-based schemes prefigure such a network, but its full shape has not yet begun to emerge. Within such a network, modular and credit transfer systems offer exciting possibilities for opening up access to certain areas of knowledge traditionally regarded the preserve of an academic elite. In the past education and training have been planned separately, reflecting in part the difference in status between the two areas. This separation needs to be broken down, creating new methods of planning based on comprehensive social and economic data. Employers' perceptions of short term skill requirements are a hopelessly inadequate basis for planning, a fact which is underlined by the poorly conceived and far from rigorous information systems developed by the Manpower Services Commission and its successors. Planners of education and training need to increase their understanding of the knowledge and skills required to perform certain jobs, but must also be prepared to enter into constructive dialogue with employers in relation to job design, particularly in questioning methods of applying new technology which might lead to deskilling. Within particular firms and industries, job design and work organization must be undertaken in close collaboration with trainers in order to find ways of improving access to career ladders and to new skill areas for workers at all levels of the enterprise.

Throughout, the emphasis must be on quality training to reflect the needs of the new economy. Current government schemes, which characteristically reduce skills provision to the lowest common denominator, must be rigorously examined and restructured around the principles described above. Locally based industry training plans could provide a major input into the sector development plans proposed above. Principal modes of industrial assistance might therefore be targeted at firms making significant efforts in skills enhancement and training, and this should be undertaken in ways which direct resources at the most disadvantaged groups in the labour market.

Conclusion

The above proposals have been put forward as a basis for discussion and refinement. They are radical because they propose a significant decentralization of policy making from the centre to local government, but within a widely agreed strategic framework; effective because they utilize local knowledge and understanding to pinpoint problems and target resources precisely and efficiently; practical because they build on several years experience of policy making and implementation within local authorities and could be developed as an immediate sign of a Labour government's commitment to economic regeneration at local, regional and national levels.

Notes

Earlier versions of this paper owe a great deal to contributions and criticisms from a number of individuals, notably Jonathan Zeitlin and members of Nottingham EcStra, especially Cathy Durucan, Chris Farrands and David Gillingwater.

1 Labour Party, 1989, *Meet the Challenge, Make the Change – A New Agenda for Britain. Final Report of Labour's Policy Review for the 1990s*, London, Labour Party.

2 Town and County Planning Association, 1987, *North-South Divide: A New Deal for Britain's Regions*, London, TCPA.

3 Sheffield City Council, 1987, *The Retail Revolution: Who Benefits?* Sheffield.

4 e.g. Greater London Council, 1985, *The London Industrial Strategy*, London.

5 P. Hirst and J. Zeitlin, 1989, *Reversing the Industrial Decline? Industrial Structure and Industrial Policy in Britain and Her Competitors*, Oxford, Berg/ St.Martin's Press; C. Sabel, G. Herrigel, R. Deeg and R. Kazis, 1989, 'Regional Prosperities Compared: Massachusetts and Baden-Wuerttemberg in the 1980s' in *Economy and Society* 18, 4.

6 M. Best, 1989 'Sector Strategies and Industrial Policy: The Furniture Industry and the Greater London Enterprise Board' in P. Hirst and J. Zeitlin, op cit.

7 P. Tyler, 1988, '1992 and the South Yorkshire region', Working Paper for Sheffield City Council, PA Cambridge Economic Consultants.

8 A. Knight, 1974, *Private Enterprize and Public Intervention*, London, Allen and Unwin.

9 S. Holland, 1975, *The Socialist Challenge*, London, Quartet.

10 J. Gough, 1986, 'Industrial Policy and Socialist Strategy: Restructuring and the Unity of the Working Class' in *Capital and Class*, 29.

11 A. Scott, 1988, 'Flexible Production Systems and Regional Development: The Rise of New Industrial Spaces in North America and Western Europe' in *International Journal of Urban and Regional Research*, 12, 2.

12 C. Sabel and J. Zeitlin, 1985, 'Historical Alternatives to Mass Production: Politics, Markets and Technology in Nineteenth Century Industrialization' in *Past and Present*, 108, August.

13 C. Sabel, 1989, 'Flexible Specialization and the Re-emergence of Regional Economies' in P. Hirst and J. Zeitlin, op cit.

14 S. Brusco, 1989, 'Local Government, Industrial Policy and Social Consensus: The Experience of Modena, Italy' in *Economy and Society*, 18, 4.

15 C. Lane, 1988, 'Industrial Change in Europe: The Pursuit of Flexible Specialization in Britain and West Germany' in *Work, Employment and Society*, 2, 2.

16 F. Murray, 1987, 'Flexible Specialization in the "Third Italy" ', in *Capital and Class*, 33; A. Pollert, 1988, 'Dismantling Flexibility' in *Capital and Class*, 34.

17 J. Zeitlin and P. Totterdill, 1989, 'Markets, Technology and Local Intervention: the Case of Clothing' in P. Hirst and J. Zeitlin, op cit.

18 Best, op cit.

19 P. Hirst and J. Zeitlin, op cit.
20 P. Tyler, op cit.
21 M. Best, 1989, op cit.
22 B. Majumdar, 1988, 'Industrial Policy in Action: The Case of the Electronics Industry in Japan' in *The Columbia Journal of World Business*, XXIII, 3; S. Holland, op cit.
23 S. Brusco, op cit.
24 Peter A. Hall, 1986, *Governing the Economy: the Politics of State Intervention in Britain and France*, London, Polity.
25 National Audit Office, 1987, *Report by the Comptroller and Auditor General; Department of Trade and Industry: Assistance to Industry under Section 8 of the Industrial Development Act 1982*, London, HMSO.
26 See, for example, J. Lambert, 1983, 'The Clothing Industry Scheme: An Assessment of the Effects of Selective Assistance under the Industry Act 1972', Government Economic Service Working Paper 61, Department of Trade and Industry.
27 D. Massey, 1984, *Spatial Divisions of Labour: Social Structures and the Geography of Production*, London, Macmillan.
28 J. Gough, 1986, 'Socialist Strategy and Local Economic Initiatives', Labour Economic Strategies Group Working Paper no 4.

The major utilities: ownership, regulation and energy usage

The theme of this chapter might be expounded as follows. The benefits of applying market mechanisms are widely appreciated, in the East increasingly, as well as the West. But we must not take it too far; the creation of market mechanisms is a means to an end, not an end in itself. The market is a good servant, but a bad master. In few areas is this more apparent than in the major utilities. Thus the free market is not an appropriate policy goal, but it is equally not sensible to see state ownership as an end in itself.

There are three fundamental reasons why a mix of instruments is required to achieve the efficiency and social desirability aims of a reasoned approach to the major utilities. First, these industries contain important elements of natural monopoly. In such areas, production by one firm is naturally more efficient than by two or more by virtue of the technology involved. Yet at the same time, a single firm in a reasonably entrenched position can charge prices substantially in excess of costs. A privately-owned firm in particular will have incentives to do so. And it is a central proposition of welfare economics (subject to some minor caveats) that, at prices in excess of marginal costs, a reduction in prices yields benefits to consumers in excess of the reduction in profits the firm thereby endures. State ownership or regulation are the traditional solutions to this problem. An alternative is to introduce competition. This can potentially be very wasteful given the technological considerations, yet at the same time it may generate pressures for cost-cutting and/or price reduction which would otherwise be absent. A trade-off is involved which may be best solved in different ways in different industries.

Second, several of the industries involve important externalities such as creation of pollutants which mean that market-led solutions do not take into account the full social costs of economic decisions. Again it is a fundamental tenet of welfare economics that in these cases, the invisible hand of the market left to itself will not lead to the correct decisions being taken. State ownership, regulation or taxation are standard alternative remedies. Third, in at least some of the cases, the time-scales involved in decision-taking, for example regarding new power stations, are extremely long, and in consequence difficult to handle through pure market mechanisms.

Nevertheless, the point regarding market failure and measures to correct it must not be overplayed. Individuals charged with making decisions in the public interest are not all-seeing either. It is very much the case of a choice between alternatives, none of which is perfect.

In what follows, I develop these points at greater length. I first consider briefly the question of ownership of the major utilities, then go on to assess regulatory frameworks for them, and subsequently move on to examine issues of planning and conservation. Some brief remarks on the special features of the individual industries involved close the substantive elements of this chapter.

The question of ownership

In 1979, the gas, electricity, rail, post and telecommunications industries were all in public hands, as was most of the water industry and many of the bus companies, most of the airport facilities and the major airline. Over the lifetime of three Parliaments, these industries have become very largely privately controlled. It would be a financially impossible, and in some cases perhaps counter-productive, task to buy them all back into the public sector. Priorities must be set and criteria for repurchase developed;[1] the Labour Policy Review makes a very sensible step in this direction.

Concerning the public-private ownership decision, there are two rather different underlying criteria – economic efficiency, and political and social desirability. For example if, as much of the evidence concerning the electricity industry suggests, there is little to choose on economic efficiency grounds between public and private ownership,[2] then the decision may be made on political and/ or social grounds with a clear conscience. If, to take the rather different example of waste disposal, not putting out to tender (whether the tender is actually won by an outside firm or by the inside team) leads to losses in efficiency,[3] then a political judgement may be made at the expense of economic efficiency. The strongest cases for repurchase for the public sector are those where economic efficiency arguments go along with political and social arguments.

The simplest cases arise in those concerns, not mentioned above, which are parts of an essentially competitive industry – Jaguar and National Freight are examples. In such cases it is difficult to argue that majority public ownership of itself would be economically efficient or socially desirable. By contrast, in the cases of the major utilities there is at least some argument for public ownership, so that priorities need to be applied.

Certain features of the privatizations which were the focus of criticism at the time are not relevant to current decisions. Many were bungled, with shares being priced too low (so as to ensure all shares were subscribed for) and with arguably entirely unnecessary large commissions being paid to underwriters. Indeed, the costs of flotation have ranged up to around 5% of total valuation. But these things are in the past and nothing can now be done about them. Like all sunk costs they should not, of themselves, affect economic decisions. However, there is one relevant lesson: since privatization and equally repurchase involve substantial costs, neither should be engaged in lightly. Thus the historical position does influence the direction which future policy can sensibly take. For example, to pursue the case of electricity generation, if public and private generation are equally efficient, then on economic grounds there is a case for leaving ownership as it is, whether it happens to be in public or private hands.

The ownership question is, in some respects at least, completely separable from the issue of regulation. It is possible (though perhaps undesirable) to have ownership without control. It is certainly possible to have a large degree of control without ownership. But this then raises the point that controls might attack many of the problems which repurchase is to deal with. In other words, the desirability or need for repurchase can be reduced by firmer control on private companies. Thus repurchase can be confined to those cases where regulation would not easily provide firm controls or where there are strong social or political arguments for public ownership, or where repurchase is relatively straightforward and cheap. Regulation issues will be covered below.

The other general consideration here is those peripheral areas of many previously state-owned enterprises which were hived off, for example British Transport Hotels, telephone receivers, etc. These again appear largely to be areas where competition brings consumer benefits and, where relevant, technical progress. They cannot be considered as potential targets for repurchase and, indeed, this would be extremely difficult given the number of companies in some areas (for example telephone equipment).

More detailed issues on priorities are reserved until the discussion of individual industries at the end of the chapter.

The issue of regulation

Traditional state enterprises in the UK have been controlled in four ways. The underlying framework was provided by a sequence of White Papers covering pricing, investment and financial targets, then latterly, 'non-financial performance indicators'.[4] As a result first of concerns over the public sector borrowing requirement, the Treasury has also imposed external financing limits – limits, that is, on the amount firms can borrow. More recently, the Monopolies and Mergers Commission has carried out efficiency audits on various aspects of the operation of nationalized and similar concerns, pointing in many cases to some changes in management practices. Finally, the tenure of the general manager has been fixed, and renewed only as a result of what was seen as reasonable performance.

A new tradition has quickly become established in the privatized industries with substantial monopoly power. This involves a regulatory office with a Director General in charge, specific to each case (Telecom, gas, with electricity and water to follow). Their major economic role is to administer a price-based formula imposed on the industry's major products.[5]

The Labour Policy Review proposes a further alternative, based upon a framework common in the United States. Each major industry is to have a Regulatory Commission charged with setting prices, establishing service quality standards, monitoring performance and assisting in laying down an investment programme. A major adoption from US practice (but previously anathema in the UK) is the proposal to make the Regulatory Commission hearings open.

Certainly the Regulatory Commission concept has much to recommend it. Many economists have criticized them for a tendency to allow 'padding' of the rate base, overcapitalization and the like, but it seems that the practice, in many States at least, is not such as to give force to this criticism.[6] Investments must be 'used and useful' and 'prudently' incurred, and there are examples of utilities making unwise decisions (e.g. about unsuitable nuclear plants in the electricity generation industry) which have led to severe financial constraints on them. 'Public image' advertising and charitable contributions are often disallowed.[7]

In this form of regulatory system, price is considered in relation to costs, so close scrutiny of costs is essential. The openness of the process is important here, to ensure that the Commissioners are seen not to be 'captured' by the utilities concerned, that is they do not become closely identified with the utilities' interests, at the expense of consumers.[8]

Arguably, openness is less important in a framework of price regulation without regard to costs, like that operating currently in the UK in telecoms, since the regulators have little discretion on pricing. However, as several people have pointed out, when the price formula comes up for renewal (every five years or so), costs do enter the picture, so that the regulatory body is more subject to capture and data manipulation at these stages, particularly if it has little experience concerning cost information.

Openness though, has a very important benefit. Information is required of the utility and is made public. One of the major problems for regulatory bodies is to discover enough about their charges' costs, quality of output and so on. There is a natural and evident tendency for the utility to conceal these things, to give access only grudgingly, and to claim commercial secrecy/sensitivity as an argument for not revealing information. Where the balance is changed to an open hearing, with open submissions, this problem of obtaining information from the utility is much reduced, since their own incentive is then much more in favour of revealing information in order to get what they want. Public justification is an extremely important mechanism in this area.

Individuals and responsible concerned organizations also of course have a far greater chance to represent their position within this framework. That is, the users of the service put their position directly in an open forum, if they are concerned about some aspects of the utilities' operation, rather than putting it indirectly through an office charged with regulation. Furthermore, this sort of forum would seem to be far more appropriate for raising issues like environmental impact than the regulatory framework, since the regulators have a less direct or prime interest in these issues.

At the same time, there are two potential problems with the Regulatory Commission framework. First, it is almost undoubtedly more costly than the regulatory office approach. Simple comparisons between the size of Oftel and of regulatory commissions in the US suggest the latter are at least double the size for an equivalent amount of 'business'. The direct costs are still low in relation to turnover, but it is clear in the US that there are substantial indirect costs on the companies involved in preparing their submission, and the judicial-style hearings are extremely lengthy. Considerable resources are devoted to these activities. Of course it could be argued that the US is a naturally more litigious country than the UK, and hearings would not reach such excesses here.

The other potential problem relates to the open hearing in areas where there is competition between utilities. It is likely that two companies operating in the same markets would be extremely reluctant to divulge accurate detailed cost information in a public manner, even more so if there were viable potential competitors. The public availability of detailed commercially-sensitive information required of this process may potentially be jeopardized by the presence of competition, or serious potential competition.

The experience of the regulatory offices to date has been mixed. Of course Oftel has been operating longest, so it has the most complete track record, but my casual impression is that it is also more successful in its tasks, for three reasons. First, by comparison with Ofgas, it has greater or freer access to information from BT than Ofgas has from British Gas, and it is also able to threaten BT with competition more convincingly. Second, the information requirements to operate the formula itself (though not its revisions) are inherently greater in gas (and electricity) than they are in telecoms, since they include cost as well as price factors. Thus gas is less suited to this form of control. Third, the style it has developed is a rather pugnacious one, which may come down simply to personalities.

The analysis above suggests that although the Regulatory Commission has much to offer, it also faces some difficulties by comparison with the regulatory office, under certain circumstances. Thus it might be sensible, initially at least, to experiment with different forms of regulation in different industries. For example, both because of its experience and the competitive situation existing, the telecommunications system might be best dealt with still by a regulatory office, whilst the absence of plausible competition to supply the vast majority of customers and the difficulty of getting cost information might point to the Commission being tried in the gas and water industries.

Experimentation of this type also seems sensible given the considerable effort required to establish a number of new institutions simultaneously. Thus a policy of retaining the best of the old institutions by testing the new in areas of greater need seems to me to have more to recommend it than a completely clean sweep.

Energy planning and conservation

Because of the range of energy sources, and their mixed ownership, energy planning is not straightforward. Co-ordinating the operations of a privately-owned oil industry, a publicly-owned coal industry, a private monopoly gas industry and a privatized electricity industry with elements of competition is probably an impossible task. Certainly, UK gas reserves and possibly also oil reserves, can be assessed with fair accuracy. But liberalization of coal sourcing resulting in substantial coal imports will probably be in place, so that the requirements of the electricity industry for UK-sourced inputs would be difficult to assess, even in the absence of competition in electricity generation facilities, and this makes things even more difficult. However, planning energy source requirements is an entirely different matter from planning energy-saving and environmentally-friendly measures, which is what is proposed here.

Privately-owned, market oriented companies in the energy field raise two major problems. First, much operation in energy involves production externalities which profit-centred companies have little incentive to correct. Second, competition between energy sources is likely to imply little if any incentive to encourage consumer conservation. Both these arguments will be examined in a little more detail below.

A classic example of an uncorrected production externality is acid rain due to sulphur-based fallout from conventional power stations.[9] This fallout means that the social cost of producing electricity by these means is in excess of the producer's cost, because the more that is produced, the greater the damage to the environment (and to forest-owners' assets), but this cost does not bear on the electricity producer directly. Hence the producer has an incentive to base production decisions on costs which, from a social point of view, are too low.

The strongly market-oriented economist's solution to this problem would be to say that, assuming the forest-owner could sue, the problem disappears. This is because the producer now has to take into account its losses from the court action in planning its production process. If it installs scrubbing equipment, this will add to production costs but is likely to reduce the expected damages to be paid out to forest-owners. However, there are severe problems with this argument. It assumes a high degree of efficiency in the legal system, together with a degree of certainty about the outcome. People affected who are not willing to bear the costs of extensive court representation will not pursue their claims. In addition, it assumes the forest-owner (say) can identify who to prosecute. In the situation where there are a number of competing electricity generators, even where it can be demonstrated beyond reasonable doubt that acid rain damage was due to power station emissions, it would be far more difficult to show which power station was responsible. Furthermore, it assumes there is a legal mechanism for Swedes (say) to prosecute UK power producers. These problems do not mean the legal mechanism will never affect production decisions – the fear of errors leading to nuclear accidents and consequent massive claims is probably one of the major reasons private producers are wary of running such stations (the other being the uncertainty whether those in the UK will ever be cost effective, even taking an extremely long-run view). But they do cast severe doubt on the efficiency of the legal mechanisms in securing the use of socially desirable production techniques.

In a country with a single energy producer, there would probably be some incentive for that producer to encourage conservation measures. For example, if the producer faces a potential difficulty in supplying its peak demand, then it could probably reduce overall costs and energy input, even given the same overall output, by encouraging people to shift consumption (e.g. by peak charging). Also, since energy conservation measures (e.g. loft insulation) add value to the units of energy purchased, this would provide an incentive by allowing the potential to add to the price per unit. Thus there may even be an incentive for the producer to subsidize the installation of things such as loft insulation which quickly pay for themselves yet which some people nevertheless neglect to install. Where there are several energy producers, the incentives to encourage conservation are likely to be largely absent. For one thing, increased competition among fuel sources is likely to take the form, at least in part, of competition for market share and thus encouragement of consumption. Also, since insulation, etc., has the property of benefiting all fuel sources used by the consumer, there is little incentive for one fuel source to supply insulation which benefits another. Moreover, there are incentives to push peakiness in demand off onto other sources of energy, which probably adds to uncertainty in demands, and so to costs. There will also be pressures within fuel sources, particularly electricity, where there is competition in generation, towards heavy utilization of facilities which have been constructed, and towards forward selling of new capacity and 'take or pay' contracts. These pressures go against energy conservation.

It should be said that some of the problems outlined and discussed above exist in a completely state-run system. For example, the electricity industry's record on pollution from coal-fired power stations is not a good one, though this is perhaps because the extent of the problem has only recently been fully appreciated. There has been competition between energy sources for market share, including over-promotion of expensive and inefficient methods of electrical central heating. For various reasons, untreated domestic coal is still consumed in 'smokeless' areas. To some extent, however, these points are irrelevant, for reasons explained earlier regarding sunk costs. The issue to be considered is how to deal with a privatized and decentralized energy system.

Thus, the fact that there is no overall control over energy sources makes it much more important that there should be an overarching mechanism to provide incentives for energy conservation, efficiency and reduction of external effects. This might take the form of an energy evaluation agency. Such an agency will need to act in a different way from a Regulatory Commission on price, and will need to have an overview of all potentially polluting energy sources, not just one fuel. On this issue of the mechanisms by which energy conservation measures are co-ordinated, the Labour Policy Review is curiously silent.

Energy producers will have, or can be given via strict 'yardstick' (comparative) regulation, their own incentives to be internally efficient and to avoid over-investment in production facilities and charging structures which encourage profligacy. The focus of attention on producers under this heading must therefore be on mechanisms to ensure the production of clean energy as far as possible, and if possible on renewable energy sources. Energy conservation measures are best directed at those with least information, or with little incentive to acquire information. This suggests a relatively heavy focus on domestic consumers, not least because producers will not provide the consumer with unbiased information.

One major lesson from environmental measures over the last few years is how often environmental pressure groups have been proven right in drawing attention to causes for concern which industry sources have minimized. Since so many sources of damage to the environment are cumulative, they must be dealt with swiftly once problems occur since doing nothing does not mean the problem remains at the current level. Doing nothing (a policy of no change) often means the problem gets worse. Planning is vital in order to conserve the environment for future generations. This necessitates developing methodologies to evaluate environmental benefits in a routineized way, so that evaluation of externalities can enter into decision taking without difficulty.

Remarks on individual industries

Telecoms
This industry is furthest down the track of regulation and of liberalization. There is also a measure of competition to BT (i.e. Mercury) in core business areas. Thus, to go back to a completely state-owned industry would be almost impossible, and probably counter-productive. People are used to being able to purchase their own telephone, answering machine, etc. Some business customers at least are now used to having a choice of telephone service suppliers. Although some problems with the regulatory system have emerged, in particular concerning the basket of goods which are in the pricing formula, and rebalancing within the basket, in

general the active pro-competitive stance of Oftel and its Director General has served the public interest well. One area which was a focus of public concern prior to privatization, namely call boxes, is now an area where service has much improved, in large part due to the DG's efforts. The ridiculously long wait for initial installation is now a thing of the past. At the same time, as BT is a strongly profit-oriented organization, there have been a number of areas of dubious public benefit or public detriment. The development of value added 'chatlines' and so on, and also 'enhanced' maintenance charges, can be instanced. Repurchase by the State would be expected to remove such difficulties as well as bringing back the concept of a universal service.

If repurchase is to be seen as successful though, the strong consumer and market orientation of much of Oftel's impact upon BT must be retained. The other sensitive issue is that alienation of management from changed objectives must be avoided. Privatization was in part secured by large 'payoffs' to management in the form of enhanced salaries and bonus mechanisms. Managers must continue to have incentives to provide good service if BT is returned to the public sector. This does not imply either a continuation of massive percentage pay increases, or pay being linked to profits. Indeed, the ideal link would be to social efficiency rather than private profitability, though under a tight regulatory regime where profit increases resulted in the main from efficient cost reductions, linking pay to profits may be a second-best approach to the problem[10]

Of course, all these remarks must be conditioned by the likely rapid pace of technological change in the area, particularly concerning developments in broad band cable, which are discussed in Chapter 10. If the nature of the industry changes, it is likely that the regulatory framework should also be modified.

Gas

Of all industries so far privatized, the gas industry has been the least subject to modifications to industry structure, though the imposition on it of a 'common carrier' obligation to transport other peoples' gas (at published tariffs) will have some impact in the future. British Gas has a good image in domestic consumers' eyes (though not those of small business) regarding charging, because of the real reductions in prices which have persisted both before and after privatization. Service on customer premises is a different matter, though again privatization has wrought no real changes for better or worse. Ofgas, the regulatory body, has had only a limited influence to date, though its role should increase as a result of recommendations in the Monopolies and Mergers Commission report on gas[11] One major problem on the horizon is that marginal costs of gas input are above average costs, as a result of rising extraction cost, lessening monopsony power, and the expiry of very cheap early North Sea contract sources.[12] This problem is exacerbated by the lack of information which the Director General of Gas Supplies currently is able to obtain concerning the cost structure of inputs.

Given that little competition is in prospect for supply to any but the largest customers, and given the opacity of input prices, a Regulatory Commission might perhaps be able to enforce more rigorous control over pricing, particularly concerning standing charges, charges to small business users, and other issues not fully treated in the present formulaic control. A more radical solution could involve some restructuring of the industry at its distribution end into separately constituted local distribution companies who would buy from a central supplier/transmitter. This would allow an element of 'yardstick' competition on costs through comparisons of area boards' prices and profitability.[13]

Electricity

This industry is currently the most uncertain of those considered here in terms of its future structure and performance. The current government plan has a semi-competitive generating arm to the industry, with two major companies (one much larger than the other) formed from the CEGB in potential competition with additional suppliers. Commitments to substantial nuclear generation capacity have been much reduced. Generation is to be separated from transmission (currently these are vertically integrated) and distribution, with separately-owned distribution boards having joint charge of the transmission company. It is true that generation is the only area where any real competition may be expected. Yet it is rather difficult to see how, and how well, the market will be able to co-ordinate the very long-run decisions involved in installing new generating capacity and in contracting for secure supplies. At the time of writing, privatization plans are being delayed by difficulties in agreeing on the new contractual relationships. In practice, the degree of vertical separation achieved may be modest. In Europe, a wide variety of ownership and control frameworks are in operation, with no clear leader in efficiency. The presence of a regulatory system may or may not help in this co-ordination: given the rather different structure of the US industry, co-ordination problems there are not as severe.[14] A Regulatory Commission, however, may be useful in reducing the likelihood of collusion between distributors under the proposed structure of the industry.

There are substantial arguments in favour of the transmission part of the industry (the National Grid) being in public ownership, even if private companies have a considerable proportion of the generation and distribution capacity. Otherwise the transmission facility will have an overwhelming strategic dominance which it may choose to use against the generator, or possibly its customers or the government. Unlike the distribution arm of the industry, there is not even the possibility of yardstick competition to facilitate effective regulation of private companies. Thus I believe the Grid is an important candidate for early repurchase and/or equity swapping to achieve the same aim. For example, if the government holds a minority stake in transmission and distribution jointly, this could be swapped for a majority in transmission coupled with a smaller share of distribution. This would necessarily involve separation of the distribution companies from the transmission company, but that may be no bad thing in any case, for reasons advanced above. The distribution companies could still be under the jurisdiction of a Regulatory Commission.

Water
The area of water supply and sewage disposal is the one which has quite rightly focused the greatest opposition to privatization, and where the arguments for repurchase are strongest. Loosely regulated private enterprise is likely to serve water badly for a number of reasons. One of the most important concerns charging: traditionally, rates of return have been low,[15] and the prospects thus 'unglamorous'. In order to attract investor interest and at the same time maintain significant investment in facilities, the industry is to be regulated lightly on prices, with increases in profit margins (implying prices trending above costs) possible in a range of circumstances, as well as prices trending above inflation. Also,

socially-optimal water quality will almost inevitably be above the companies' privately-optimal levels, in part because of the difficulty for the individual consumer in pursuing improved quality. Here the role of the National Rivers Authority will be crucial: it is as yet unclear how much impact this body will have on companies. Metering is likely to be forced upon consumers, for political and other reasons. Competition in supply is really not a practical proposition, and the takeover mechanism heralded as a substitute is a most dubious potential generator of economic efficiency. Indeed the threat of takeover may have its main impact upon the companies through their accountants' efforts to find ways round the price regulations to increase profitability in order to keep share prices high. Thus for example, Vickers and Yarrow[16] who take economic efficiency as their criterion, are strongly critical of water privat-isation, believing 'the existing proposals for privatization of the water industry will have several substantive detrimental effects on economic efficiency' (p. 422).

Assuming repurchase is adopted as a policy objective, the important issues focus upon the appropriate structure for the industry. It was never a Morrisonian-type corporation. Tradition-ally, local authorities played a major part, particularly in sewage disposal, but more recently the concept of integrated river basin management has come to the fore in the ten water authorities. This structure sensibly reduces the extent to which one group of people have negative impacts upon another (people downstream drinking upstream consumers' sewage, to put it crudely), and it does not prevent smaller bodies acting as agents to the authorities. These water authorities are the structures which are being privatized. Assuming they are repurchased, it seems sensible to keep the industry structure more or less unchanged, but to democratize the board structure to increase representation of consumer groups and local authorities. Immediately prior to privatization, the boards were rather small and unrepresentative (though this was not the historical tradition).

Repurchase does not reduce the case for a Regulatory Com-mission to oversee the industry, to evaluate one body by reference to another (yardstick competition) in order to gain experience of costs and so on. Nor does it reduce the case for a National Rivers Authority to monitor water quality and promote other environ-mental improvement. Indeed the introduction of an independent body to act as 'pollution policeman' to the industry is to be welcomed: the industry's record in policing itself is not unblemished! One open question is whether it is better to have separate bodies concerned with pricing and with water quality, or whether to combine these functions in one regulatory agency.

If repurchase should be infeasible for whatever reason, then an urgent priority for the Regulatory Commission should be to regain tight control over the industry in the interests of society generally.

Rail

It now seems unlikely that this industry will be in private hands by the next election. Its non-core businesses (Sealink, hotels and some catering) have already been privatized, and there is little chance or sense in reversing those decisions. My personal predilection regarding the remainder of catering is for one-person businesses or worker co-operatives to provide on-train services subject to contracts regarding security of supply written with British Rail.

Concerning the core business, the current government's plan seems to be to sell off individual sectors starting with those which are likely to capture investors' interest, namely Intercity and Railfreight. It is nevertheless clear that there are substantial system interdependencies, meaning that ownership of the track would need to be conditioned by guaranteed running rights for other sector businesses. In practice, separation of the industry into several sectors would lead to continuing administrative complexities which would appear to be far more problematic than those involved in separating gas distribution into twelve area distributors, for example.

In recent years, under existing management, considerable strides have been made towards providing a modern efficient customer-oriented service comparing well with that in other countries, with the exception that punctuality on intercity routes leaves something to be desired. Congestion is another concern, but this can be relieved by means of the extensive investment programme. In addition, there is the continuing impact upon services of inadequate pay in the South East of England. These issues should be the focus for attention by the Regulatory Commission, which could take the approach of writing a contract with BR, where the payment for service provision is dependent upon performance in specific respects (e.g. managerial salaries could depend upon non-financial performance outcomes). Reported managerial predilection for privatization may simply be a desire for performance-related pay and removal of artificial constraints on investment, etc.

The postal service
Here it is almost certain that the core mail delivery business will still be in public hands for the foreseeable future, though Post Office Counters may not be. As with British Rail, the main role for a potential Regulatory Commission will be to push for customer-oriented indices of quality to be set and rigorously enforced. This may involve statistical rather than post-office based performance measures, for example statistical sampling of delivery performance based upon posting to delivery (rather than collection to dispatch) times. As with other state-owned cases, ownership by itself does not imply control, and the control agency must have independence from the industry but also consumer representation. The industry has improved considerably in recent years in financial and volume terms, but perhaps not in customer perception, though it is becoming more responsive to private and commercial consumer needs.

Concluding remarks

The emphasis in this chapter has been very much upon policy towards the major utilities viewed from a standpoint of where they are now. To elaborate, one might take a view that ideally a particular industry or set of industries would best be located within the public sector under social ownership. However, what is ideal is not necessarily achievable, or not achievable without sacrificing some other objectives which are of at least equal importance, so that to attempt to put them back into the position they were in would be difficult, counter-productive and costly.

It is clear that very substantial changes have taken place in the major utilities over the last decade, by no means all of them for the worse. Yet there are some senses, or some cases, at least where ownership has been irrelevant to this process. Many of the industries have become more consumer-responsive, and this not as a result of privatization; the cases of the Post Office and British Rail on the one side, and British Gas[17] on the other illustrate the point.

Thus a pragmatic rather than dogmatic approach to reform of the major utilities has been developed here. This runs though ownership, regulatory frameworks and environmental protection.

In a similar way, the Labour Policy Review is indicative of a considerable shift of policy away from traditional, and in the main backward-looking, issues. Public ownership at all costs is abandoned in favour of a pragmatic policy of effective public *control* over important utilities. The Policy Review is rightly concerned with the design of mechanisms for effective control of the utilities in the public interest, though here my proposals differ somewhat. I argue that a wholesale abandonment of current regulatory office controls in favour of Regulatory Commissions would be too inflexible a stance. In the Policy Review, public ownership is reserved for specific cases, based upon specific argument. Energy source planning is dropped in favour of energy saving and environmental control issues. This latter is not, I believe, a cynical attempt to win the 'Green' vote, but rather a rational policy response to a changed framework of the energy industries coupled with increased knowledge regarding environmental damage. At the same time, I believe that more thought should be given to the agency or mechanism for developing this policy response. It is currently all too apparent that the Department of the Environment has a mixed brief, to say the least!

The overriding point is that in both major areas, the ownership/regulation issue and energy control, a judicious blend of the market and state intervention is appropriate. 'Social factors' in the major utilities are not nebulous excuses for doing anything one wants, but involve potentially quantifiable gains to society arising out of effective regulation leading to lower prices for example. They are no more intangible than the benefits in reduced travel times arising from the opening of a new motorway. The 'public interest' has been associated far too closely with 'what a freely operating market provides' by forces on the right of the political spectrum, but the world is too complex for a universal panacea to be applied.

Notes

1   Labour Party, 1989, *Meet the Challenge, Make the Change – A New Agenda for Britain. Final Report of Labour's Policy Review for the 1990s*, London, Labour Party.

2   See e.g. George Yarrow, 1986, 'Privatisation in theory and practice', *Economic Policy*.

3 See e.g. Simon Domberger, Shirley Meadowcroft and David Thompson, 1986, 'Competition, tendering and efficiency : the case of refuse collection', *Fiscal Studies.*

4 See e.g. Michael Waterson, 1988, *Regulation of the Firm and Natural Monopoly*, Oxford, Basil Blackwell, section 4.4, for an outline.

5 The first of these, on telecoms, was of an 'RPI-X' type, allowing price increases, on average, lower than the rate of general inflation. In the subsequent cases of gas and electricity, this was modified to 'RPI-X + Y', which allows some fuel cost influences in addition. See also Ian Bradley and Catherine Price, 1989, 'The economics of regulation of private industry by price constraints', *Journal of Industrial Economics*, for other points of comparison. In the case of the water industry, price increases will be allowed to run ahead of rises in the retail price index.

6 See e.g. I. Brown, 1986, *The Regulation of Gas and Electric Utilities in the USA*, London, Association for the Conservation of Energy; Sanford Berg and John Tschirhart, 1988, *Natural Monopoly Regulation*, Cambridge, Cambridge University Press, for more details on the operations of individual Commissions.

7 Compare this, for example, with the money spent by water companies on their so-called 'public image campaign' in the period prior to offical advertising for privatisation.

8 In addition, it is desirable that the relative flexibility particularly in the UK electricity tariffs reflecting different demand patterns over the day – e.g. 'white meter' tariffs – be retained in assessing pricing in relation to costs.

9 See e.g. Dieter Helm, John Kay and David Thompson, 1988, 'Energy policy and the role of the state in the market for energy', *Fiscal Studies.*

10 On this point, see Waterson, 1988, section 3.3.

11 *Gas*, Cm500, 1988 .

12 This is not incompatible with natural monopoly in the distribution of gas, evidenced by falling marginal distribution costs, given input prices.

13 On this see e.g. Michael Gibson and Catherine Price, 1988, 'Privatising the electricity industry: lessons from gas' in Saul Estrin and Christine Whitehead *Privatization and the Nationalized Industries*, London ST/ICERD, London School of Economics

14 See Paul Joskow and Richard Schmalensee, 1983, *Markets for Power*, London MIT Press .

15 In both the public and the previously privately-owned branches of the industry.

16 John Vickers and George Yarrow, 1988, *Privatization : An Economic Analysis*, Cambridge MA, MIT Press.

17 Despite its 'Banish Gripes' campaign.

Communications 2000: a broad band cable network for the UK

We live in an information society. Economic activity increasingly depends on knowledge as people work with numbers, facts and words rather than hammers, lathes and soldering irons. The successful economies of the 1990s will be those that fully utilise information technology and develop the skills of their citizens to harness the full power and capabilities of IT.

Many perceive the profound structural changes that are flowing from the spread of information technology as the beginning of a new epoch, making the same kind of break from the past as the industrial revolution achieved. From different parts of the ideological spectrum have come claims that we have now begun the next 'long wave' – a fifth Kondratieff cycle[1] – while others talk of the post-industrial society.

By 1981, according to an OECD study, between 40 and 50% of the workforce in its member countries were working in 'information jobs'.[2] Similar studies of the UK indicate that 58% of the Greater London workforce were in information occupations.[3] The EC expect telecommunications to be Europe's single biggest industry by 2000.

At the same time the internationalization of the economy, most sharply seen in the advent of the 1992 European Single Market, means that it is beginning to make more sense to think of the UK as a regional economy in a wider European market, or perhaps more accurately, as a number of smaller regional economies in a new 'Europe of regions'. (See Chapter 8). Labour's Policy Review[4] rightly warns that 'we risk a future as a depressed periphery on the edge of a Europe whose economic centre of gravity has moved decisively away from us.' Although it is possible to exaggerate the decline in autonomy of the nation state – the depth of the UK recession in 1979–81 and the economic problems of the late eighties, notably the trade deficit and high inflation, had a great deal to do with the actions of the Conservative governments in power at the time – there can be no dispute that the nation state is weaker than it once was, and that trend is intensifying.

National governments will therefore increasingly have to use economic policy measures more traditionally associated with regional economic development objectives. With access to an EC-wide market guaranteed from any location within EC boundaries, member countries, and the nations and regions within them, find themselves competing for inwards investment and finding ways to assist their indigenous companies that do not fall foul of the strict EC competition rules that forbid many of the subsidies and other measures traditionally used.

It therefore makes sense for Britain to fully embrace the information economy, and use the power of government not only to provide the infrastructure that will allow us to take full advantage of its capabilities, but also stimulate the production of information services and information technology equipment. In particular, information technology can overcome some of the geographical problems caused by the UK's peripheral position compared to the rest of Europe. The Cecchini report's much heralded, and rather optimistic, claims for the benefits of a single market flow to some extent from the concentration of production. This is likely to lead to two processes, already in evidence. Firstly a move in production towards the 'golden triangle' so that goods are produced in the centre of the most lucrative markets and secondly a trend towards the lower cost Southern economies, particularly Spain and Portugal. Neither of these trends benefit the UK. Therefore it makes sense to give a boost to an information infrastructure on which distance is a relatively unimportant concept.

Yet Britain's record in producing the equipment and exploiting the benefits of IT is poor. Fully one third of 1988's record trade deficit of £14 billion was represented by these high tech sectors. The promises on offer at the beginning of the eighties that Britain's 'sunset' manufacturing industries would be replaced by high tech 'sunrise' industries based on electronics and computers have proved bogus. Instead many of our competitors have not only achieved industrial restructuring with more concern for the social effects of change but, by applying new technology to older industries, have retained profitable traditional sectors as well.

The failures of British information technology have been well documented, most recently by the all-Party House of Commons Trade and Industry Select Committee. There has been a succession of government commissioned and quasi-official reports outlining British weaknesses, most noticeably in recent years the McKinsey report commissioned by NEDO, discussed in Chapter 2.[5] This stressed the over-dependence of the large British companies on defence and other government orders, rather than producing new products for the burgeoning consumer markets. British companies spend less on R & D than their competitors abroad and seem particularly poor at bringing new technologies through to production and market success. Industry is becoming increasingly vocal about skills shortages. Cuts in basic science and shortages of science teachers in schools further threaten our ability to innovate for the future.

The technology of fibre optic communications

There is however at least one area at the leading edge of technology in which Britain has a very real claim to be a world leader. This is broad band optical fibre for communications. The first proposals to use glass fibre as a substitute for copper cable were made by Kao and Hockham at STC's research labaratory in Harlow in 1966. Since then many of the technological advances that have made practical glass fibre networks possible – such as new kinds of glass that can be used for long runs with little loss of signal, optical amplifiers to boost signals through the network, and switching devices that allow the routing of signals to the desired destination, have been made in Britain – in particular at British Telecom's Martlesham research labs. Optical cable is now routinely in use for undersea cable, trunk lines and in the very high density networks required by the City of London. Indeed BT has proportionately more optical fibre in its network than any other operator in the world.

But optical fibre is far more than a clever way of replacing expensive and bulky copper cable with cheaper and much lighter glass fibre. It opens up a whole world of new communications possibilities. In the words of Labour's Policy Review 'It will bring great rivers of information, sight and sound, in and out of every living room, classroom and workplace. It will be the new electronic highway, providing a new medium whose full potential can only be glimpsed at present.' The key to this is its far greater bandwidth than copper cable.

Bandwidth is a measure of how much information a cable can carry. It is no exaggeration, at least for the lay-observer, to say that glass fibre has a near-infinite bandwidth compared to copper. The concept of bandwidth is best grasped by looking at the evolution of the telephone system. All telephones start by producing an analogue electrical signal, a small variation in voltage caused by sound hitting the microphone in the mouthpiece. In the simplest form of telephone system that signal is carried over copper wires to the exchange where it is routed to the desired receiving telephone whose earpiece will move in response to the original voltage and sound in sympathy with the originating phone.

This level of complexity works fine for a small number of local phones, perhaps in one office block. But it is no use for connecting calls over long distances. It would require an enormous number of cables to connect London and Manchester if each phone connection was going to be given its own individual copper cable. Various ways have therefore been found of combining phone calls – multiplexing as it is known – over one copper cable. But even using the most sophisticated techniques the limits of a copper cable are soon reached, and as multiplexing techniques are only in use between exchanges rather than between individual subscribers the benefits of the greater bandwidth achieved through multiplexing cannot be brought to each individual subscriber.

This problem becomes even more acute when we consider signals of greater complexity than simple phone calls. For example, the speed of a fax connection or computer-to-computer link using the ordinary phone system is limited by the amount of information that can be squeezed into the available bandwidth. The speed with which information can be exchanged on a line limited to the bandwidth required by a normal phone conversation, is much less than the speed at which a computer can generate it.

To solve this problem most developed countries, including Britain, are planning new Integrated Systems Digital Networks (ISDN) for the early nineties, specially developed to allow the rapid transmission of digital signals generated by computers. This brings a new phone line connected to a network specially developed to deal with digital signals with a much greater bandwidth to the individual subscriber prepared to pay more. An ordinary phone line allows around 1000 binary digits per second (in other words, it can cope with detecting whether a switch is open or closed 1000 times each second). This allows around 100–150 alphanumeric characters, two lines of typescript, to be received each second at maximum, and noisy lines and other problems usually reduce this maximum. This is much slower than most people read, and it would take 10 to 20 seconds to transmit a single still TV picture.

ISDN dramatically increases the information that can be sent via a phone line. The proposed ISDN home link would offer two channels of 64,000 bits per second plus a signalling channel giving a total of 144,000 bits per second over the existing copper telephone wire. One of these channels could carry the text of a 100,000 word book every minute. But it would still need to be between ten and one hundred times faster to cope with moving TV pictures. It is still therefore considered a narrow band technology.

In the next place up in the bandwidth league comes the kind of cable TV that is already available in some homes in Britain, and many more in the US and other countries. This is genuinely broad band. A copper co-ax cable, similar to the one that connects TV sets to aerials, brings a choice of TV channels into the home. But cable TV networks differ in an important respect from the telephone system as they are designed to be one-way. The essence of the telephone system is that it is two-way. Each device connected to the phone system is both a transmitter and receiver. Cable TV merely substitutes a cable for a normal aerial or a satellite dish. It uses a 'tree' architecture, that sends the originating TV signal down an ever dividing cable network until it reaches the individual subscriber. But there is no way, in a traditional cable TV set-up, that one individual subscriber can connect to another individual subscriber, although much to BT's chagrin, some cable TV networks in Britain are planning to develop telephone systems using their cables and American telephone companies have been active in taking stakes in cable TV ventures in Britain.

This is where broad band fibre optic cable comes in, as it can combine the two-way nature of the telephone system with a far higher bandwidth even than that achieved by the copper co-ax cable TV systems. Instead of sending electrical pulses over copper wire it uses lasers to send light pulses down hair-thin glass fibres. Light is part of the electro-magnetic spectrum, it is a similar form of energy to radio-waves but occupies a much higher frequency part of the spectrum. It can be encoded in a similar way to the radio-waves that bring television and radio channels into our homes, but because it occupies a higher frequency part of the electro-magnetic spectrum a single fibre optic cable can theoretically carry more information than the entire radio waveband. A simple phone line can detect electrical signals switching at a thousand times per second while light switches more than a thousand billion times faster. Although current technology has not yet reached this theoretical figure, cable already installed has a bandwidth of more than a thousand million bits per second. This is such a quantum leap in capacity that it makes sense to talk about near-infinite bandwidth in comparison with copper wires (even to the irritation of scientists to whom near-infinite is a contradictory concept.)

The uses of a broad band network

Fibre optic networks hold out the possibility of bringing together the two communications networks that have developed in Britain. They have the capacity to carry complex signals such as moving TV pictures which have traditionally been one-way but can be organized in the same way as the narrower-band, yet two-way services we associate with the phone system.

This combination makes possible a wealth of new types of services. It is probable that we can only glimpse the potential of such a communications system at present. But it is possible to list some of the new services and uses to which a broad band network would be put.

Most obviously it will allow many more TV channels. The UHF frequencies used for TV broadcasts at present only have space for five channels. Extra channels therefore need to be carried by cable or beamed down from satellite to unsightly dish aerials. A broad band network would allow Sky, British Satellite Broadcasting and other operators to reach every home without consumers having to invest in new equipment for each operator. This clearly has enormous implications for broadcasting policy which unfortunately the relevant sections of the Policy Review show that Labour has yet to take on board. Although this topic is outside the scope of this chapter, it is worth noting that Rupert Murdoch operates Sky outside the regulatory framework of British broadcasting policy as he uses non-UK frequencies. Clearly it is not possible to evade regulation if signals are carried by cable rather than direct from outer space.

More interestingly, new forms of television become possible. One cable service that is easy to operate is the video-library. Consumers dial up the library, examine on screen what titles are available and then have them relayed into their own home. Rather than relying on Rupert Murdoch or Michael Grade to choose their evening's TV, every consumer can become their own scheduler. This would open up exciting possibilities for local community groups to make their own programmes.

Cable also allows the broadcasting of the new high-definition television that gives video pictures the same quality as cinema film, which requires even more bandwidth than normal television channels. Europe has already done much of the work in developing standards for high-definition television. DMAC, which will be used by British Satellite Broadcasting, is an improvement on current standards and designed to be able to evolve into HD-MAC which is a high definition standard using 1250 lines to make up the TV picture.

But although entertainment might be the most obvious service made available over the network, there is an even greater potential for education and training uses. Some of these would be the traditional learning video of the type pioneered in schools and Open University broadcasting, with video libraries offering teachers, trainers and individual students an enormous choice at any time of day or night. But of most potential would be interactive video training packages that fully exploit the two-way nature of the cable network. These would allow students to learn at their own pace, and have access to enormous quantities of information. The desperate need to increase the skills level of the British work-force and the quality of education in schools, particularly in shortage subjects such as maths and physics is well known. Interactive distance learning could be an important part of the solution to these problems.

One fairly trivial example of an interactive package of use in the home would be a car service manual. A do-it-yourself car mechanic would be able to call up on screen, and indeed print out with the appropriate technology, the plans of the particular part of the engine he or she wishes to work on. But as well as the hard copy of the plan of the kind you can already find in books, the mechanic would be able to watch through several times a video of the operation before attempting to follow the plans in practice. This would come from a video disk kept in the video library which contained all the text, plans and still pictures found in a normal service manual, but also video sequences of various service operations that can be selected remotely by the user in his or her home.

Cable's interactive nature, and the ability to use it for small community based broadcasts – whether over a small neighbourhood or for a small but scattered community with interests in common, such as an ethnic minority – gives it the potential to be a 'democratic' technology. Not only is the individual given much more real choice over what they receive, than the more-but-worse of satellite TV, it can bind communities together and increase a sense of belonging, in contrast to the atomizing and individualizing effect of multinational TV broadcasting.

There are many other services that could function over fibre-optic cable. Not all of these would require the same bandwidth as television, and some could be delivered via ordinary phone or ISDN services, but it is likely that these would be more likely to take off with a critical mass of users on the back of the introduction of a comprehensive cable network. Remote energy control of homes could be an important contribution to conservation. Home-working can become a normal part of employment in many information based jobs. The French government has given free terminals to any subscribers who ask to hook into their text based Minitel system, operating over standard phone lines. This was initally planned to replace the need to deliver phone directories to every house, with an on-line directory enquiry service accessed by the domestic keyboard and the TV set. But it has led to many other services taking advantage of this new infrastructure, such as home shopping and banking.

Broad band cable and the economy

Two main developments have led to the emergence of the information economy. First is the increasing importance of information itself, and the capability of new technologies to collect, transmit and store it. Second is the ability of the computers and other devices involved to be integrated together into systems. The information economy is therefore characterized by the diffusion of information technology and what Gillespie and Williams have called, the commodification of information.

Gillespie and Williams identify six changes brought about by the infrastructure of the information economy with major implications for the competitiveness of firms and the regions that possess the infrastructure.

(1) *Product innovation*

This is shown by the growth of commercial on-line information services, such as data-bases for lawyers and doctors. This is the most obvious example of the commodification of information, and its most striking feature is that its availability is far less constrained geographically than for most new products. Put crudely, it's as far away as the nearest phone. As English is the most common international language for business, science and the professions, there is much export potential for on-line information services.

(2) *Distributional innovation*

New ways of delivering goods and services have now become possible. A striking example has been the success of *USA Today*, the first truly national paper for the United States, the contents of which are distributed in facsimile form from the editorial office via satellite to regional printing centres. Much financial, banking and insurance information is as perishable as news, and the ability to transmit it around the world has made possible the twenty-four hour global financial market, with the same stocks and bonds simultaneously traded throughout the world. Interaction between the the regional centres – New York, London and Tokyo – is now only limited by the constraints of time zones, not distance.

(3) *Goods production process innovation*

Although automation of various stages in the production of manufactures is not new, there are important trends towards computer integrated manufacture, where previous 'islands of automation' – such as a flexible manufacturing system – are becoming linked, either within the same factory or on a wider scale. This is not an easy process as there are formidable problems in devising and implementing communications standards in manufacturing environments, but it is a development that can only intensify. Although there has been much dispute on the left on the usefulness of 'post-fordism' as a paradigm that describes contemporary economic structures, few dispute that the moves towards shorter runs of more differentiated products that computerized manufacturing can bring are an important trend.

(4) *Information product process innovation*

Telecommunications now allows the geographical separation of workers in various ways. Most popular attention has been grabbed by the phenomenon of 'tele-commuting' where individuals work mostly or entirely at home, connecting to the office by phone links when necessary. But information networks allow more dramatic reorganizations of the production process, with information workers no longer tied to any fixed point. This can even lead to a new international division of labour with US companies, for example, using cheap Jamaican labour in 'keyboard factories' to input data into their US based computers. It also has less dramatic but important implications for job location within the UK, as it becomes easier to locate 'back-office' functions away from corporate HQs, or even to move them entirely. These possibilities lie behind the Policy Review's calls for the decentralization of many government functions to locations outside London and the South East.

(5) *Transactional innovation*

This is perhaps most evident in the retail sector, where computerized tills allow daily stock-takes that can be collected together at head office each evening. Stock can then flow from warehouses the next day to replenish the shelves or hangars, with re-orders going to suppliers for lines that have been successful. Power has passed from the supplier to the retailer, and the organization of such companies as Benetton or Marks and Spencer, show how much the efficient flow of information contributes to commercial success.

Manufacturers are also developing the same relationship with their suppliers. Companies are increasingly adopting such techniques as just-in-time production, allowing them not only to respond very quickly to market signals, but freeing them from the need to store components and other supplies. Computer to computer links between companies allow them to integrate their purchasing, delivery and supply functions, and have important implications for the relationships between firms, which now need to be based on longer-term relationships and more trust.

Complex chains of computer links between retailers, wholesalers, manufacturers and component suppliers can therefore contribute to an extremely efficient production process with a great deal of sensitivity to the market, with no particular need for the components of the chain to be that geographically close to each other. Although this has clear advantages, there is the danger that such close links between companies can make it extremely difficult for new firms to break into supplying dominant companies. Another example of an inter-firm computer network that has had a major impact is the Clearing Houses Automated Payments Scheme (CHAPS) that has automated the British banks' clearing arrangements.

(6) *Managerial innovation*

Computer networks make it easier for the headquarters of large multi-site operations to control their operations on a day-by-day basis. In many corporations this has undoubtedly led to a more centralized, authoritarian and hierarchical structure, with a real reduction in local autonomy for site managements. In others a more contradictory process has taken place, where the more widespread access to management information has led to more decentralized decision making and a more co-operative management style. This underlines the importance of rejecting 'technologically deterministic' views of the future development of industry. As the very different corporate cultures of Europe and Japan show, technology enables very different structures to develop.

These innovations are already taking place, and are not therefore dependent on a broad band system. However many would be intensified by the introduction of a genuinely national broad band network. The ability to configure extremely high data density networks from any office or home to any office or home, represents a significant step-up from the need to arrange long-term private lines with telecommunications operators, and would represent a significant step forward in the development of a telecommunications infrastructure. Broad band would also stimulate the development of services needing the higher bandwidths and/or interactive advantages of cable, such as television programmes, interactive video services and training packages. A pound earned abroad through the sale of a television programme is as important to the balance of payments as a pound earned selling a machine tool. New internationally tradable information based services that take advantage of our fluency in the international language of business, English, will also help our trade position.

There is potentially a vast international market for the technology of cable. Britain already has a world-wide reputation for optical cable in telecommunications. Careful investment in Britain would generate further innovation which could also find a ready export market. This is an area in which there is already considerable European collaboration, particularly through the EC's RACE project – one of the largest ever collaborative projects with a budget of over a billion ECU. Although British companies are playing a leading role in RACE, the UK government has been dragging its feet and other governments are much keener on the prospects for broad band. Without more enthusiasm from the British government for EC-wide progress we will be unable to take full advantage of British participation in RACE – 52 out of 192 participating companies are British and form the leaders of one third of the consortia. Our leadership in standards setting and our technological know-how is in danger of being left behind as a Community-wide market for the technology and services develops.

The right investment in infrastructure is a tried and tested way of encouraging regional development, and much recent research suggests that it may be more effective in stimulating development than the traditional subsidies we associate with British regional policy, as Peter Totterdill shows in Chapter 8. Because broad band cable in itself allows much more decentralized decision making structures it is likely that good telecommunications will help stimulate investment and recovery in Britain's less developed regions. The EC has recently given a grant to BT to introduce a network in Northern Ireland for this reason.

The Conservatives' approach

Britain is in danger of missing the broad band boat. Although there is a wide consensus that broad band cable will eventually come to Britain and that it is a 'future-proof' technology – unlikely to be supplanted by some other hightech communications system – there is no agreement on how it might be introduced. The Conservative view is given by the report of the Communications Steering Group[7] 'The Infrastructure of Tomorrow' (generally known as the Macdonald Report after the Chair of the Group, Alastair Macdonald, a senior DTI official).

Although this report is presented as a neutral survey of the possibilities and costs of optical fibre networks, its conclusions are undoubtedly shaped more by politics than economics or technology. Although it correctly stresses the potential of other forms of modern communications such as microwave video distribution systems (MVDS), it is enthusiastic about the potential of cable and the report they commissioned from PA consultants[8] concluded:

We believe that developments in the cost and performance of optical fibre transmission will tend to move all fixed communications links towards optical fibre, and that fibre will also generally tend to replace radio and satellite transmission except for broadcast and mobile communications users: the differences between scenarios are in the pace of this change, not in its direction. (p. 134)

The PA Consulting Group set out three scenarios in their report. First they consider what they call Lightly Regulated Competition, based on current government practice. Secondly, the *Laissez-Faire* scenario suggests rapid deregulation. Thirdly, they describe an interventionist National Grid scenario in which government acts to bring about a national broad band network more quickly than market forces would deliver.

Not surprisingly the Macdonald report favoured the scenario designed to be in line with government policy. In only the second paragraph of the Chairman's introduction Macdonald states:

Our Consultant's work suggested that attaining such a national goal could well require a subsidy or Government financial underwriting of some kind. We do not consider that justified. (p.iii)

But a further political consideration has stopped Macdonald recommending an early programme to cable Britain. This stems from the fact that when BT was privatized it became not only Britain's biggest private company, but one with a core business that is a natural monopoly. Because they are extremely sensitive to this charge, the government and Oftel, the regulatory authority created at the time of BT's privatization, has been extremely wary of allowing BT to gain dominance in new markets. BT has, for example, only been given a limited role in the licences for the new generation of 'telepoint' mobile phones. This is of less consequence when it is possible for other operators to run services in place of BT, but causes severe problems when no one else can sensibly replace BT. Macdonald himself identifies this dilemma for the government.

We did not see how any national goal of 'optical fibre into the home by 2000' could in practice be achieved other than by measures which would further reinforce British Telecom's existing dominance. (p.iii)

In order to prevent BT's monopoly power growing, BT are currently stopped from selling entertainment services over their network by the terms of their licence, even though cable TV operators are allowed to establish telephone services. This so-called 'asymmetry' in the licensing arrangements prevents BT installing cable networks as a speculative market-led venture, although there have been recent hints that the asymmetry may be removed in the early nineties in those areas where BT are part of the cable TV franchise and a specially licensed pilot scheme to test the technology is currently being installed in Bishop's Stortford.[9]

The present government finds itself in a Catch 22. It believes that the market should deliver advances in the telecommunications network, but it won't allow the only actor capable of making that investment to do so because it will increase its domination of the market place. The government constantly tells us that competition is the best spur to innovation and economic advance, but it seems in the case of cable that innovation and investment is being prevented in the name of competition.

The approach of the British government is markedly out of line with the approach of other EEC countries to telecommunications. Although the patterns of ownership vary widely – the BundesPost is part of the civil service while Spain's phones are privately owned – none share the British government's commitment to introducing competing infrastructures. All the others believe that it makes sense to have only one infrastructure as a natural monopoly and then regulate that through various means.

A future-proof technology?

The installation of a comprehensive fibre optic based broad band system is a long-term project, requiring considerable investment. Some critics of Labour's Policy Review have questioned whether the Party is right to put so much emphasis in this area. On the whole such critics are sympathetic to the need for investment in the telecommunications infrastructure, and do not share the dogmatic Conservative view that all such decisions should be left to the 'free market', dealt with above.

But, this line of argument proceeds, it is unwise to concentrate on one technology. Fibre optic has important applications, after all it is already used by both BT and Mercury, but there are other technologies as well, such as satellite or MVDS. In one sense this line of argument can be a useful corrective to any tendency to concentrate exclusively on the technology of fibre optics. The telecommunications and broadcasting infrastructures will always feature a mix of technologies. Cellular radio will continue to grow and as it moves forward to a third generation a Europe-wide digital system will become increasingly important. Satellite has, and will continue to have, important applications, particularly in remote areas and less developed countries, although the trend in the US has been for a move to fibre optics for long distance phone connections and away from satellites as prices have fallen. (Telephone companies there highlight their use of fibre optic cable as a selling point in their advertising due to its high reliability and good quality connections.)[10]

But these critics miss two points that rightly underlie the commitment to cable in Labour's Policy Review. First it is closely linked to an industrial strategy. As Chapter 2 makes clear, opto-electronics is identified by the report as a potential area of great industrial strength for Britain, a niche market where it makes sense to concentrate industrial resources. It is at that stage of techno-logical development where a major public purchasing programme will act as an important spur to innovation. Optical fibres are only part of a growing sector. Over a million homes in the UK possess CD players; hospitals and the military are making increasing use of lasers, and the great speed of light has led to research into optical computers – most noticeably at Heriot Watt.

Secondly a number of particular features are unique to broad band cable technology. The aim is to make cable a near universal service, thus justifying public spending on services that can be delivered via cable and that make full use of cable's two way interactive properties. Other technologies cannot make this claim. MVDS is a way of distributing TV channels and requires line of sight reception from transmitters. Indeed many of its supporters claim its main use would be to establish large audiences for new cable TV channels, before homes can be physically cabled up with the copper co-ax used for cable TV. This argument can of course be applied to fibre optic cable as well. It must be said though that satellite television, which offers the same services, seems to have beaten MVDS to the starting gate and it is unlikely that it will become a major player, without state backing, as it requires users to invest in very similar equipment – dishes and decoders – as satellite TV.

Satellite already has many other uses in business and industry. Some companies have permanent leases on satellite transponders. Other have regular bookings for particular time slots. Multinational companies use them for tele-conferencing and data exchange – General Motors have 11,000 receiving dishes for example. Satellites will retain a role for these purposes, particularly for operations that require links to areas not connected to a fibre optic network, although there is nothing to stop a mixture of technologies for the same operation.

But satellite does not have the potential for a universal service. Like MVDS, satellite requires line of sight operation. Any building in the shadow of another cannot receive satellite signals. Dishes cannot be sited in conservation areas, and tenants of multi-occupancy buildings often find it impossible to obtain access to the roof to install dishes. Although the popular image of satellite dishes are of the relatively small size required to receive the high power signals of Sky and BSB satellites, most satellites operate at much lower signal strengths and thus require larger aerials. The coverage of any satellite is therefore far from universal, and reception is worst in those areas, city centres, where the markets for (non-entertainment) services is greatest. One company investigating the sale of financial information services has informed the author that only 20% of potential customers in Manhattan could actually receive a satellite service for a mix of the reasons given above.

The suggestion that some new technology might come along that makes fibre optic redundant is impossible to disprove, although it is a criticism rarely made by technologists. Indeed experts in the field are stressing the importance of integrating services onto fibre. The 1989 EC RACE Strategic Audit, an external panel that monitors RACE, stressed 'It is important that separate development of ISDN + Cable TV services and high bit-rate data transmission services does not inhibit the future development of Integrated

Broadband Communications.' BT themselves say that their 'vision of the future UK telecommunications infrastructure comprises an all-fibre, all-digital, highly integrated, broadband network, which incorporates both the main and local networks.'[11]

Introducing a broad band network

Despite the current government's timidity, everyone seems still to be agreed that cable will come. Sir Bryan Carsberg, Director General of Oftel and a member of the Communications Steering Group has recently written in *Oftel News*:

I believe – and I think all of the [Communications] Steering Group would agree – that a broadband national network is virtually certain to be developed in the medium term.

But it seems that the lightly regulated scenario argued for by the Macdonald report is the least likely to bring it about. A government led scheme could clearly bring it about, and full deregulation would at least persuade BT to make initial investments. 'If the case for broadband were commercially attractive and "asymmetry" removed, then BT would be anxious to construct the network . . . BT would not need Government direction or financial subsidy.'[12]

There are however severe problems with the deregulated market driven approach to introducing cable. BT's technological lead and sheer size means that it is the only player likely to invest heavily in a new network. Yet if forced to follow short-term market driven priorities, it would inevitably start with the already affluent areas of the country and may well then pause to see whether this would generate significant returns for its shareholders. Such an approach would exacerbate regional imbalance in Britain, encouraging companies wishing to benefit from being on line, or to sell services over the network, to locate in those areas cabled first, almost certainly the South East. Even if successfully extended to most areas of Britain, there is still no guarantee that every home and office would be connected. The non-universal network that would result from market driven investment would prevent much public sector use of the network. For example it would be sensible for government to encourage the creation of educational and training material for use over a network that reached the vast majority of schools and colleges. This would make little sense if it only covered schools in the South East and some other connurbations.

There is another problem with a market driven approach to developing the infrastructure. A broad band cable network would require significant investment in R & D and new capacity by suppliers. The uncertainty of the market-led approach would militate against the substantial investment that would allow British suppliers to not only sell their products to BT but move into export markets as well. It is far from clear what constitutes a critical mass for cable users and how quick development and take up of new services would be. Clear government commitments to a national broad band cable network would give exactly the right kind of stimulus to investment and production by the potential suppliers of equipment by guaranteeing market demand for such products, as Paul Geroski argues in Chapter 2.

Appropriately, therefore, Labour's Policy Review has opted for a variation of the third scenario, the national grid approach:

Just as the railways and highways of the past were the product of public investment, so the development of 'information highways' cannot be left to the free market either. As countries like Japan and France have realized, the state has always had to step in to provide national infrastructure networks . . . We are clear that BT must be empowered and directed to undertake this major investment programme in the public interest. As in the case of major infrastructure investment in the past, we believe that this investment is most appropriately carried out in the public sector. We shall therefore take BT back into public ownership, so that it can invest in and exploit a new national network in conditions which guarantee that private profit-making does not take precedence over the national interest and that the consumer interest is properly protected.'

The work of the PA Consulting Group in developing their national grid scenario for the Macdonald Committee shows that this is an entirely feasible option and gives some clues to its economic effects, although many aspects of PA's work has been challenged by other experts in this field as extremely over-cautious.[13] As it still makes a convincing case for the investment, it provides a useful backdrop for analysis.

The national grid scenario would certainly cost more than the others, but the extra costs are at least partially met by increased revenue flows. PA conclude that the deficit by 2010 of National Grid's costs less revenues compared to Lightly Regulated Competition's runs at just 3% of total costs accumulated over the whole period. And although they say this could be higher with particularly pessimistic assumptions, there are many who say that they have not been imaginative enough in seeing the potential of cable, and new services which have yet to be dreamed of will generate new revenues. Lightly Regulated Competition is a scenario based on no state aid so these extra costs are some idea of what might have to be carried by the government over the next twenty years. The extra costs – estimated by PA as £2.5b – seem fairly small considering that they also conclude that more than four times as many get the benefits of inter-active cable with a National Grid than with Lightly Regulated Competition.

Cable is a technology in which costs are still falling rapidly as new research and development continues to make an impact. In the five years between 1980 and 1985 the productivity of the fibre itself increased more than a thousand fold – from $11.8 per metre for a 70 Mega bits per second (Mbps) to $0.35 for a 900Mbps cable.[14] A figure due to fall to $0.25 in 1990 and continue to fall by 5–15% per year. The costs of the fibre itself is now a marginal costs in setting up a network, which is largely governed by the cost of installing the repeaters, signal generators and input/output systems, which in turn are falling in price by 15–30% each year.

PA's key conclusion, perhaps unusual for an economic forecaster, is that:

Choices between the scenarios (and any other combinations of policy recommendations) cannot therefore be based on economic forecasting alone. (p.137)

Labour's Policy Review identifies BT as an early candidate for bringing under public control, reflecting the priority given to cable. But this is not nationalization in the old-fashioned Morrisonian sense. BT is already 49% owned by the state and the Conservatives' self-denying ordinance not to use the power that brings would not bind a Labour government. The golden share and ability to amend BT's licence also give significant powers to the government. City takeover rules consider a 30% stake to constitute a controlling interest; the government already has the means to ensure sufficient control of BT.

Bryan Gould MP, in a speech to a conference organized by the National Communications Union, made clear that a new Labour government would look to a very different relationship to BT than the kind it had before privatization:

There is nothing in our proposals which would justify the criticism that we are intent on a rigid, centralized, massively bureaucratic nationalization. We are determined to see a BT which is efficient, commercially astute, flexibly organized, sensitive to the consumer's needs and able to meet the national interest in the fullest sense. We believe that BT will welcome the freedom to exploit its current industrial and technological strengths and the glittering future which cable offers them as a commercial organization. We see every possibility of a fruitful collaboration between the company, acting in its own commercial interests, and the Government, representing the very considerable public interest in seeing this investment made.

One major difference will need to apply to the new BT. In the past most nationalized industries' borrowing requirements have featured in the Public Sector Borrowing Requirement, and governments have at times therefore been reluctant to sanction sufficient borrowing to meet investment needs. It is clearly ludicrous that borrowing for productive investment in the private sector is considered a good thing, while borrowing for productive investment in the public sector is considered bad. Labour will therefore need to exclude BT borrowing from the PSBR, in the same way that the cost of BP's Alaskan pipe-line was not included in the PSBR, even though BP was partly state-owned.

BT will also need full entrepreneurial freedom to continue to sell its products and know-how overseas, and in those areas of the domestic market where there is already substantial competition such as the supply of telephones and other peripherals for the telephone system, the public interest requires that BT should not be allowed to use unfair trading practices against its competitors. But at the same time BT would not be held back from investing in new products and services merely to assist its competitors; regulation rather than infrastructure competition is the best way of ensuring that BT does not exploit its monopoly power. Such regulation would have to insist that BT could not exclude services from its network. Although BT would be free to sell its own services, its prime duty would still be as a common carrier. Some regulation would of course be necessary, for example to stop hard porn being made available, but this should not be done by BT. The national communications network should be precisely that – free for anyone to use.

One predictable reaction to the leak of an early draft of the Policy Review was an attempt by the Conservative press to cost the cable proposals and suggest that these would all be met by the tax payer in a single year. Although this was to be expected, and will doubtless be resurrected in the run-up to the general election, the Policy Review correctly makes it clear that 'BT should be able, in its own commercial interest, to cover the cost of developing, installing and operating the broad band cable network without constituting a charge on public funds.'

But this would not mean that government would make no commitment to cable and merely leave BT to get on with the job, albeit with the full freedom to market entertainment services currently prevented by the terms of its licence. It might be thought appropriate to pump-prime particular regional investments, out of the resources to be made available for bringing Britain back into balance. Government will guarantee an important role for cable in the many activities it is involved in.

In particular there is a strong case for making education and training an important pump-primer for cable. Britain's skills gap, which will be brought into sharp relief as the 'demographic timebomb' bites, requires investment in training and retraining. The shortage of science teachers and the needs of the national curriculum pose a severe challenge to policy makers.

As we have seen, cable opens up to teachers and trainers not only a vast library of traditional distance learning material, but also the new world of interactive video. It is likely that an emphasis on the educational use of cable is likely to lead to its catching on for many other purposes.[15] Parents originally bought their children personal computers because of their educational potential, but they have also been used for games and other entertainment purposes, as well as home office applications. Cable could well catch on in the domestic market through this route as much as the marketing of different television channels. It will certainly be the way users are tempted to use the potential of the network more actively than just as a multi-channel TV, thus providing the required user mass that will make some of the more exciting services viable. Just as many home computers started off as serious statements by parents about their commitment to their children's education but have ended up primarily as game playing machines, with an associated large market for games software, home based use of cable may start off as part of homework, but move on to entertainment use as well. Indeed the creative potential for interactive games, played via cable, must be vast.

There are many potential uses for cable in improving, and making more efficient, public services. These range from the health service, where remote diganosis becomes feasible, through to open access data banks on tap in every home. The EC RACE programme is now looking at service provision and the development of new kinds of business, public and consumer services is of central importance to developing cable. And although there are important public service functions for cable, Labour should have no puritan objections to a full range of entertainment and other commercial services carried by cable as well.

A commitment to cable also raises other policy issues with which the Labour Party has yet to grapple. The need for a new approach to broadcasting policy has already been noted, and although under the circumstances of the Conservative attack on public service broadcasting, an emphasis on defending what is good about the current system is understandable, there is little indication that the Party has yet to develop an approach to multi-channel TV, which is on the way, regardless of which technology wins out at the end of the day. Interestingly the Peacock report on Broadcasting policy was enthusiastic about a broad band network.

The growth of information technology has important implications for the organization of work, and throws up some difficult policy issues for trade unions and government. 'Tele-commuting' so far has been largely confined to skilled and creative jobs such as journalism or computer programming, but more mundane keyboarding tasks can also be done at home via the telecommunications system. There is a danger of creating a new class of exploited part time home-workers, though it can also create new job opportunities, particularly for women.

Networks of communicating computers immediately conjure up images of 'big-brother'. It is important that a sophisticated telecommunications policy is matched with an equally sophisticated civil liberty and data protection policy.

A broad band cable network would be an exciting investment for the next century. It would increase the competitiveness of British business and provide a long-term investment framework for innovation, R & D and investment for the electronics supply industry. It would give Britain an important lead in a developing world market and open new export markets for hardware and cable delivered services. It would extend consumer choice, bring new services into the home and provide communications services that would enhance community life. It would make an important contribution to improving education and training, and make investment in the regions of Britain an attractive option. These are the reasons why it makes good sense for it to be given a central role in industrial strategy.

Notes

I would like to thank Geoff Mulgan for much helpful discussion on this topic, though the responsibility for the content of this chapter is mine alone.

1 P. Hall, 1987, 'The Geography of the Fifth Kondratieff' in P. Hall and A. Markusen eds. *Silicon Landscapes*, London, Allen and Unwin.

2 OECD, 1981, 'Information Activities, Electronics and Telecommunications Technologies', ICCP series No 6, Vol 1, Paris, OECD.

3 M. E. Hepworth, 'Planning for the Information City: The Challenge and Response', Newcastle Studies of the Information Economy Working Paper 6, Newcastle University Centre for Urban and Regional Development Studies. (This paper contains a useful introduction to the 'information economy').

4 Labour Party, 1989, *Meet the Challenge, Make the Change – A New Agenda for Britain. Final Report of Labour's Policy Review for the 1990s*, London, Labour Party.

5 McKinsey & Co, 1988, *Strengthening Competitiveness in UK Electronics*, NEDO, London.

6 A. Gillespie, H. Williams, 'Telecommunications and the Reconstruction of Regional Comparative Advantage', *Environment and Planning A*.

7 HMSO, 1988.

8 PA Consultants, 1988, *Evolution of the United Kingdom Communications Infrastructure*, London, HMSO.

9 For more details of BT's current capabilities and the switched star system being introduced by Westminster Cable, see Bill Ritchie and Roger Wood, 'The Information Pipeline becomes a Reality', *National Electronics Review* 1989.

10 For a discussion of these technologies see Touche Ross Management Consultants, 1988, *Report on the Potential for Microwave Video Distribution Systems in the UK*, London, HMSO and OECD, 1988, 'Satellites and Fibre Optics, Competition and Complementarity', ICCP paper 15, Paris.

11 From a speech by Dr Alan Rudge, Group Director Technology, reported in *The Network of the Future*, National Communications Union, 1989, London.

12 BT statement, 25:4:89.

13 For an industry view of this and a wide discussion of the technology see the text of the 1988 Mountbatten Memorial Lecture given at the Institute of Electrical Engineers by Sir William Barlow, Chairman of the Engineering Council and of BICC plc, who make glass fibre, published in the *National Electronics Review* 1989.

14 OECD, 1988, op cit.

15 This position was argued strongly by Dr Jeremy Bray MP in a submission to the Policy Review.

Index